D1191877

Television in Transition

PAPERS FROM THE FIRST INTERNATIONAL
TELEVISION STUDIES CONFERENCE

EDITED BY PHILLIP DRUMMOND AND RICHARD PATERSON

BFI Publishing

First published in 1985 by the British Film Institute
127 Charing Cross Road
London WC2H 0EA

Copyright © British Film Institute 1986
Individual contributions copyright © the authors, 1984, 1986

British Library Cataloguing in Publication Data
International Television Studies Conference: (1st)
  Television in transition
  1. Television broadcasting
  I. Title   II. Drummond, Phillip, *1948–*
  III. Paterson, Richard, *1947–*
  384.55'4   HE8700

ISBN 0–85170–182–5

Cover design: John Gibbs
Typeset by Type Practitioners Ltd, Sevenoaks
Printed and bound in Great Britain by
W.S. Cowell Ltd, London and Ipswich

Contents

Foreword

I

Television research has grown in a very ramshackle way. During the 1960s and 70s a whole series of academic disciplines, from political science to neurology, began to develop pockets of researchers who attempted to link their particular intellectual habits and attitudes to the massive fact of the presence of television. TV research in the 80s reveals its heterodox historical origins. So diverse are the currents of research that many, perhaps most, researchers in the field are aware of only a very small fraction of the work under way. Even in Britain, where research into the various forms of television impact is now fairly well documented, one is constantly coming across individuals and whole programmes based in unfamiliar disciplines.

The International Television Studies Conferences held in London in 1984 was an attempt to bring together as many different examples of TV research from as many different countries as could be accommodated. It was the first time the two organisations concerned, the British Film Institute and the University of London Institute of Education, had attempted anything of the kind. The first and most surprising result was that no fewer than 400 people turned up, despite the fact that available funding was scanty, to say the least. The second surprise lay in the extraordinary profusion of papers that were offered. The results certainly justified the decision to hold further International Television Studies Conferences in future years.

ANTHONY SMITH,
Director,
British Film Institute

II

The keen involvement of an Institute such as our own in a conference on television, and in the book which springs from it, is not a mere coincidence. It represents a logical extension of the involvement of education itself in popular experience and hence in popular media such as television. The children whom our teachers teach use television, in regular but complex ways, to gain images of the world long before they meet a teacher or a classroom. When they do, it is in no small measure the experience of television with which teachers are engaging in the process of their teaching. In short, the medium of television – the most powerful medium and institution for social representation in the modern era – is of key concern to educationists in every discipline, not merely to specialists in Television Studies.

Educationists should not limit their concerns, however, to the immediate short-term concerns of pedagogic practice. They must also concern themselves with the extension of the subject-field itself, with the 'knowledge' which it represents. Each of these domains – and their many points of intersection – is the appropriate concern of educational research, and we are grateful to the many visiting researchers who gladly offered their expertise to establish a powerful research basis for the Conference. *Television in Transition* is a splendid showcase for numerous examples, on an international scale, of research in action on a subject of outstanding relevance for the modern educational agenda.

Beyond this rich array of individual contributions lie the institutional structures which facilitate endeavours like a conference or the publication of proceedings. Here we were delighted to have the opportunity to join forces with the British Film Institute in hosting a major organisational initiative such as the International Television Studies Conference. The links between the institutions, already strong and numerous, were amply reinforced by an event of this ambition and complexity. We look forward to extending this support into the future, through the forum of the Conference, and through continuing liaison between members of the British Film Institute's Education Department and of our own Department of English and Media Studies.

PROFESSOR DENIS LAWTON,
Director,
University of London Institute of Education

Editors' Preface

Television is the major contemporary cultural medium in developed societies. This supremacy is in some cases due to national policies establishing the state's relationship to broadcasting as a vehicle for information and entertainment in the public interest. It is in other cases due to a convergence of consumer industry interests, on the one hand providing the hardware, the technology of television and video, and on the other hand delivering potential customers to markets through the potent force of television advertising. In the 1980s, new developments – for instance cable and satellite – promise further to revolutionise a still infant medium. Seen in this context, Television Studies is of necessity a rich and diverse field. It is a field which covers many disciplines, and which involves a range of methodologies. It is, moreover, not simply the academy which takes account of Television Studies; research in television is constantly of interest to both commerce and governments, equally aware of the importance of the medium to their various concerns.

Television in Transition reflects the growth points in this field. The essays which it brings together were presented at the first International Television Studies Conference, held in July 1984 at the University of London Institute of Education in collaboration with the British Film Institute. The collection reflects the current state of research across international frontiers, and so confirms that there is not one simple framework of culture within which television operates, but that the medium is conspicuously marked by different national experiences. Nor is television some unified essence, for as our studies show, television works at a range of levels, involving the economic and political conditions of production, distribution and consumption, as well as the formal and aesthetic operations of TV texts. These are, then, essays about a series of TV-related phenomena defined in terms of the paradigms of sociology, politics, economics, literary criticism, semiotics. The key note is diversity and openness.

Nonetheless two main emphases seem paramount. First, emphasis is placed on notions of 'political economy', whereby the political, economic and technological conditions create a world communication order which is profoundly unequal. The second emphasis is upon the procedures of 'textual analysis', whereby enquiry focuses on the unravelling of the value systems and formal characteristics that mark a particular text or cluster of cultural artefacts. In terms of content the collection covers three broad areas: political economy and cultural imperialism; the development of American television; and the relationship of television to the viewer.

These essays taken individually and as a group contain a wealth of new insights, new research procedures and provocations to further study and research. But since this collection marks the current emphases of research into television it is perhaps surprising to note the absence of any new work from the long traditions of psychological and social psychological research. The continuing concern with the effects of violence on television, and more recently the so-called video nasties, may well lead to a resurgence in this area. But more urgent is the need for work on television from the disciplines of, for instance, law and history, areas in which much work remains to be done. We need more work which integrates the all too often separated methodologies of 'textual analysis' and 'political economy'. Education, too, remains an area in need of exploration. The desire for media literacy is not a new one but becomes ever more important with the need to create an awareness of the messages of television, and of the powerful forces that organise these messages. Research into the pedagogy of television and media studies for school students is a top priority.

The ever-changing nature of the apparatus of electronic imaging must be a key focus of future work. Until now television has customarily been propagated by terrestrial broadcasting and consumed in the home; television has served the industrial establishment and presented images of the society to which there is no easy challenge. Future work must continue to adapt different paradigms for analysis of television's production, distribution and consumption. The importance of television in everyday life in the developed societies, and the growing impact of information technologies, calls for a divergent set of research concerns and methods. This collection of papers marks a point of transition in audio-visual technology. The next conference will, we hope and expect, continue to review these developments, to address the terms of the structure of knowledge and power in this domain, from within an ever wider range of research methodologies.

PHILLIP DRUMMOND
RICHARD PATERSON

viii

RICHARD COLLINS

Introduction

The dominance of American programmes in world markets and their
impact on the cultures and identities of other countries is the
dominant theme of the opening essays of this collection. Herbert
Schiller's articulation of alarm at the dominance of the American
information economy in the world communication order is echoed in
Robins's and Webster's account, which both considers the importation
of management techniques to television practices and places great
value on public service broadcasting, and in Richeri's cautionary
notes about the Italian experience. Both Connell/Curti and
Desaulniers contest the limits of this case and place a positive
evaluation on commercial television in Italy and Canada. Raboy re-
evaluates the notions of the 'public' operative in public service
broadcasting debates in Canada to set yet another context on the
continuing debate.

Schiller proposes that American media imperialism has entered a
new phase of development in which the communication sovereignty of
culturally coherent countries is under threat. But Schiller's argument
is not simply that America's comparative advantage in the production
of software and aggressive colonisation of new markets has permitted
a wider geographical extension of the movie and television majors'
reach. His further case is that a qualitatively new phenomenon is now
paramount – in which the needs of trans-national corporations
transcend those of general users and generate 'astonishing numbers
of fundamental changes in the economic, cultural and social activities
of the nation'. This is tantamount, he argues, to an irreversible loss of
alternative political and economic organisational forms to that of
trans-national corporate capitalism since 'the informational realm,
the last redoubt to total capitalist penetration, finally is breached'.

Giuseppe Richeri offers a systematisation of the tendencies
observed in different national television systems by a variety of
conference contributors, for example, Bill Bonney and Helen Wilson
on Australia and Colin Hoskins and Stuart McFadyen on Canada.
Richeri argues that three factors – the internationalisation of
television, an increase in distribution capacity, and the strength of

1

non-European software producers (for instance, Brazil, Japan and the United States) – are shaping broadcasting in Europe. As a result there is a shared international experience of reduction in the political and national coherence of the state itself, as public sector broadcasters are forced to programme not for the aggregate of 'publics' within a country but for 'the majority', thus letting other social fractions 'escape' the reach of the public service broadcaster. For Richeri, then, five consequences follow the tendency in European, particularly Italian, broadcasting to move from service to business. First, a tendency for programming to address the lowest common denominator of public taste; second, an increase in consumption of television; third, a reduction of original programmes transmitted and an increase in the transmission of repeats and foreign telefilms; fourth, a homogenisation and standardisation of programming; and fifth, news programming remaining relatively resistant to the general tendencies of internationalisation and homogenisation. The beneficiaries of these changes are commercial distributors of imported software and the leading exporters – Brazil, Japan and the United States.

Richeri asserts these tendencies to be unequivocally negative. They are, he says, 'negative results not only on a cultural but also on an economic level'. This is a judgment that is widely shared (though not by Connell and Curti in their consideration of Italian television, or by Desaulniers) but which requires further argument. Why, for instance, is the importation of a product at less than the production cost for a comparable domestic product economically damaging to the consumer? International trade is indeed based on just such a series of relationships where producers enjoying comparative advantage (e.g., that of Canada and Scandinavia in production of forest products or of Italy in wine, aluminium castings and textiles) export those products to consumers who cannot produce comparable goods at equivalent or lower prices. It has to be shown why information goods are different. There are other countries unmentioned by Richeri that are similarly powerful exporters of television programming (notably the UK) but which do not share the characteristics he identifies in Brazil, Japan and the USA. But Richeri's argument is a powerful one and his exposition not only thoroughly documents the paradigmatic Italian case but also attempts a theorisation and systematisation of the international forces currently in play in, amongst others, France, Spain, Italy and Belgium.

Kevin Robins and Frank Webster review features of the social history of capitalist organisation. Like Schiller they do not view changes in the information goods sector and the impact of this sector's development on the social whole through the optimistic perspective of a Daniel Bell (though they share his fundamental premise that

2

economic activity is becoming increasingly information-centred). For them, movement towards a 'knowledge-centred' society marks the penetration of Taylorism into sectors hitherto insulated from its baleful reach. They argue that the systematisation of the intuitive knowledge and acquired skills of workers in the information industry itself – e.g., in offices – is likely to institutionalise a modern panopticon – 'a society in which people are seen and observed but are unable to communicate one with another'. As with their other major thesis – on consumerism and television's role in putting it in place – the reader is offered powerful provocations to assent and to dissent. The essays of Schiller, Richeri and Robins/Webster mark a well-established and elaborated centre to the political-economic debate that took place at the Conference. Other essays from outside the political economy paradigm support and extend their general thesis; others from within or close to the political economy discourse – like Connell's and Curti's, Desaulniers' and Raboy's – dissent from it and offer a positive re-evaluation of commercial television and critique of the public sector and its ideology of public service.

Marc Raboy takes the Canadian experience – which has attained almost axiomatic status for communication policy analysts – and re-interprets its historical development with great originality. Raboy, instead of invoking Canada as the prime instance of a country subjugated by the media imperialism of the USA and whose communication needs could only be met by public sector institutions operating on public service principles, shows Canada as a country in which 'public enterprise' and 'public service' are particularly problematic and potentially oppressive because of the extremely differentiated nature of the Canadian public. He asks simply: what is the 'public' that 'public broadcasting' claims to serve? How does it deal with dissent from the definition of national identity and goals of the public and its interest that the federal government enjoins? The site for Raboy's analysis of this general Canadian problematic is Quebec (Alberta could also be cited) and he uses an historical survey to develop an analysis of national purpose and public service that offers potential challenges to the position elaborated by Richeri, Schiller and Robins/Webster. In the final section of his essay Raboy suggests that the new broadcasting policy of the Canadian government promulgated in 1983–4 marks an important shift away from the conception of Canada as a public enterprise economy and of television as a 'single system' led by public service goals and public sector institutions, to one in which CBC-Radio Canada will become a 'marginal if necessary element of the overall system'.

Connell and Curti review the pessimist's critique of the collapse of the potency of national public service broadcasting orders and argue that the power of the private sector to establish 'norms' has positive and revitalising effects which are usually overlooked. Their advocacy of the commercial sector is based not on the probably eccentric British instance – where a fortuitous mix of circumstances (protectionist economic regulation, a public service ethos shared by regulators and many programme makers, and the specialisation of production for the 'carriage trade' sector of the international software market) has produced programming that is arguably superior in range and depth to that of the public service broadcaster, the BBC – but on the scorned Italian commercial broadcasters. Their defence of the Italian regime is based on an inversion of the customary 'high culture' critique. Connell and Curti assert that Mike Bongiorno shows may indeed be 'the affirmation of mediocrity' but prefer his blokish disdain for the elite to the mumbo-jumbo and metaphysics of the discourse of the *cognoscenti*. They argue further that the formal characteristics of modernist aesthetic discourses offer a superior mental experience to their consumers, are not dissimilar to those present in popular culture, and that there is no reason to suppose that superior mental experience is necessarily a prerogative solely of the *couture* end of the spectrum of artistic production and consumption. Finally they propose that the impact of commercial television on southern Italy has by no means been negative.

Jean-Pierre Desaulniers offers a similar irreverent and compelling challenge to the 'good old things'. His essay, like that of Connell and Curti, contests a *bien-pensant* orthodoxy of disdain for popular taste. He argues that the impact of television in Quebec has been the reverse of making passive and depoliticising, and maintains (as does Raboy) that television had a vital role in the production of a vigorous Quebecois consciousness and collective will. But for Desaulniers the conjuring into existence of a Quebecois political self-consciousness – 'television made it possible for Quebecers to recognise themselves as a unity for the first time in their history' – is only one of the collective identifications and activations of the audience that television calls into existence.

The essays in the second section form a case study in developments in American television over time. William Boddy retraces the formation of a notion of the 'Golden Age' in American broadcasting in the 50s; Ellen Seiter reviews the work of Aaron Spelling Productions, a company with a special relationship with the ABC network, providing numerous hit programmes from *Charlie's Angels* to *Dynasty*; and Ann Kaplan reviews Music Television (MTV), the US cable provider. From a slightly different perspective Michèle Mattelart looks at the American children's television series, *Sesame Street*.

William Boddy's essay takes as its point of departure a received truth of television studies, here the myth of television's 'Golden Age'.

4

Boddy challenges the conception of American television in the 1950s as a golden age through a straightforward and enlightening historical investigation into its genesis and the forces that shaped its formative years. In particular, Boddy maps the differences between the earlier debate in radio over the social uses of broadcasting and its financing, and the influence of the powerful electronic interests in determining the commercial exploitation of television. His arguments neatly gell with those of Robins and Webster as he shows the ways the industry leaders strived to integrate television into the domestic routine. He concludes that its funding, its dominance by large corporations, its commercial ethos and its construction of an audience took by no means necessary or inevitable forms. Things could indeed have been otherwise and, had they been, a preferable broadcasting order might have been put in place.

Ellen Seiter's essay reads the fictional world of Spelling Productions, recast through the appropriation of Gramsci's category of hegemony. Describing the institutional and psychological dimensions of hegemony as a system for control, she argues that 'if *Mod Squad*, *The Rookies* and *Starsky and Hutch* dramatised coercion by force, *The Love Boat*, *Fantasy Island* and *Hotel* dramatise coercion by consent.' Her essay offers a clear description of the principal ideological motifs of mainstream American programming. Her work comes primarily from the textual analysis paradigm that constituted the other main methodological pole of the Conference, but her conclusions are very substantially congruent with those of Robins/ Webster, Richeri and Schiller.

Ann Kaplan, on the other hand, while in the same *episteme* as Seiter, reaches different conclusions in her analysis of the MTV cable channel. She maps three types of rock videos – the romantic, the modernist and the post-modernist – and, using Jameson, asserts that MTV is a post-modern phenomenon. However, she cautions against merely aesthetic analysis of the post-modern features of rock video, arguing that MTV exemplifies the capability of machines in the new technological era to produce their own narrative modalities which, though they appear to deconstruct illusionism, do not appear to do so for any political end. What MTV has done, she argues, is efface the boundary between high and low culture. The MTV phenomenon is embedded in contradictory discourses – on the one hand creating an audience based on youth culture in the USA for the Warner Amex conglomerate, but on the other addressing a need, which leads Kaplan to caution against a wholly negative evaluation of MTV.

Michèle Mattelart uses *Sesame Street* (an interesting example of an American product that is 'bespoke tailored' to specific national markets by including locally originated material) to mount a critique of 'systemism', which she regards as the kernel of technocratic thought, which in turn is an ideology that underpins the new channels of communication and is widely disseminated by them. For Mattelart *Sesame Street* is structured around the quantifiable – it is a product of positivism – that privileges the development of cognitive skills in the child (on behaviourist stimulus/response lines) and ignores his or her integral development, in particular the realisation of his or her affective and emotional potentialities. She attempts, therefore, in an analysis of one widely disseminated television programme, to elucidate the production and circulation of a dominant modern ideology.

In the third section the papers all review the relationship of television to its audience, both perceived and actual. Katz' and Liebes' essay actualises the perceptions inherent in the first section of the book by taking a number of different audiences (in Israel and the United States) and reviewing their understanding of *Dallas*, one of American television's most successful exports. Claus-Dieter Rath, from a slightly different position, engages with the new sets of identifications and cultural relations called into existence by innovations in communication technologies and practice; while both Peter Dahlgren and Justin Lewis offer new perspectives on the relationship of the viewer to news broadcasts. Finally Ien Ang attempts to take arguments about audience further, to engage with context as well as the act of viewing, using TROS, the Dutch entertainment-oriented channel, as exemplar. These essays share an interest in the cognitive activities of audiences and the imperative to, as Katz and Liebes put it, 'study the message and its incorporation into the consciousness of viewers'.

Katz and Liebes show how productive empirical research can still be. They administered open-ended questions (and stimulated subjects' résumés and interpretations of *Dallas*) to fifty small groups of viewers drawn from five ethnic communities. Their comparison of five groups' readings (Arabs, kibbutzniks and Jews of Russian and Moroccan origin in Israel and second generation Americans in Los Angeles) shows that 'groups differ significantly in their ratio of referential to poetic utterances' and that the ends of the spectrum of differentiated shared readings are bounded by the Arabs and by Jews of Russian origin. While the Arabs concentrate on statements about life, the Russians concentrate on poetic utterances. The other groups commute between both types of statement. It is clear from this essay that *Dallas* is not the same to all viewers, but rather it is understood, talked about and used in a highly differentiated fashion.

Claus-Dieter Rath's essay considers the constitution of a 'central European television reality' through the joint production and transmission of a programme engaging audiences in the solution of

6

crimes and the apprehension of criminals by television companies in Switzerland, Austria and the Federal Republic of Germany. This programme, *Aktenzeichen XY . . . . Ungelöst*, states Rath, breaks national boundaries and builds new forms of social collectivity within the television audience. This process, he argues, will increasingly be encouraged by new communication technologies which will make possible new microcosmic and macrocosmic communities. The use of video cassettes in the Federal Republic has already created a semi-autonomous video subculture for Turks and European trans-national satellite-distributed signals may foster trans-national cultural communities.

Peter Dahlgren, Justin Lewis and Ien Ang take the audience's activity of decoding the television message as one of the starting points for their essays. Lewis proposes that the limits of the dominant paradigm, studies of the TV message, have been reached and that the cognitive activity of audiences, the decoding process, should be the primary object of study. Lewis' sample of viewers were asked to describe items as they saw them. Lewis then coded the sample's responses in a five-category schedule and identified a two-stage process of decoding, from which he concluded that 'even in the case of a fairly straightforward story the channels of access available to broadcasters when making (encoding) the news may not be available to a majority of those watching it.'

Lewis argues that encoders do not characteristically understand decoders and offers concrete proposals for recoding items so that the mismatch between the encoding and decoding process may be reduced. Though the Katz and Liebes essay shows that the diversity of decoding and cognitive activities of audiences is such that the new coding procedures may not necessarily create a closer fit between encoders and decoders than the present imperfect fit shown by Lewis, the latter's analysis and proposals command serious attention and begin to open up a new research and policy problematic.

Peter Dahlgren's essay audaciously and productively reverses a number of customary research procedures, notably by turning the researcher's gaze inwards. He draws on researchers' own experience and cultural competence in order to explain the ways in which the understanding of television messages is produced. Dahlgren is concerned with the ways in which audiences make sense of the transmitted message and he reflects on the dualism of researchers' own experience of feeling involved in and satisfied by TV news programmes but without understanding, recognising or retaining much of the information offered them. A number of conclusions are drawn from this recognition of the limits of researchers' competence and the conditions in which the cognition of viewers takes place; research, Dahlgren states, has to recognise the 'very ambiguity and

7

multivalency of the images', for 'the equivocal quality of television demands methodological modesty'. Dahlgren's conception of audiences' reception and cognition is one in which the limits or conditions of existence of these activities are set by the characteristics of the message. This occurs most generally through television's 'epistemic bias'. For Dahlgren 'a shuttling back and forth between studies of the reception process and the epistemic bias will help to clarify both in a reciprocal fashion.'

Ien Ang argues that one of the two principal theoretical approaches to the study of television – the semiological – developed because of the perceived inadequacy of the other – the sociological – to deal with the *specificity* of television. She points out that recently there have been attempts – notably with the encoding/decoding heuristic model – to reconcile and integrate the two paradigms. For Ang, though, this approach is vitiated by not taking into account that decoding is embedded in a general practice of television viewing, and she argues that the way forward is to study 'the structures within which televisual discourse is produced, and in which it necessarily creates an environment in which a certain type of consumer activity is assumed and propagated'. The question, she says, is twofold. First, 'which are the arrangements constructed by the television institution for attracting viewers?' And second, 'in which ways do the position(s) of involvement as inscribed in televisual discourse relate to the audience's cultural orientations towards watching television?' Past answers to this double question have been for Ang too generalised and essentialist and have made it difficult to recognise the variety of positions constructed for audiences. Ang then develops a concrete discussion of the Dutch television system through references to TROS (a 'commercial' entertainment station) which she uses to rebut what she perceives to be inadequacies in the evaluative criteria of the critics of commercial television.

Ang's essay very interestingly reconciles and recasts the two unifying theoretical problematics of this selection of conference papers – the political/economic debate about the public interest, the market and the new distribution technologies; and the rethinking of the cognitive activity of audiences, the differentiated nature of audiences and the reciprocal shaping of the 'epistemic bias' of the television medium and the 'beholder's share' in the decoding process.

PART I

Political Economy and Cultural Imperialism

HERBERT I. SCHILLER

Electronic Information Flows: New Basis for Global Domination?

Since the end of the 1960s, the dominance of a few metropolises over the flow of international messages, especially news and TV flows, has been the basis for a wide-ranging discussion about the necessity for a new international information order. A substantial literature documents the control exercised by the US media industries and, to a lesser extent, those of Britain and Japan in the international market.[1]

This continues to be so.[2] If anything, the developments forecast fifteen years ago[3] have been exceeded by far. Not only are the poorer regions of the world blanketed with American TV, news and films; now the industrialised 'high cultures' of Western Europe are no less subject to the same cultural inundation. The case of Italy, though by no means unique, serves as a frightening model. In the last few years a country with a rich cultural heritage spanning the centuries finds that its major TV channels have become, almost exclusively, conduits for the offering of US programmes. It is estimated that 75–80 per cent of prime time on Italian TV is filled with foreign material, most of which is American, with some Japanese cartoons.[4]

There are no grounds for complacency anywhere, in either the industrialised or not-yet-industrialised world. The vision that haunts Julian Critchley, self-proclaimed 'high Tory', could just as well be a Spanish or German nightmare. Critchley confesses: 'I read to my horror that 11,000 American television programmes are stored in a Californian Fort Knox to be sold to British cable operations – a lifetime of *Starsky and Hutch*.'[5]

Yet what has been and continues to be a condition of global media domination by a powerful market economy can now be seen to represent only the initial, elementary stage of a far more comprehensive information and cultural hegemony. The latest developments foretell the creation of a still more thorough-going and all-embracing information control. A recent review detailed five trends that are

    combining in ways that have the potential to shape international communications along Orwellian lines: the treatment of

11

information as a commodity; the digitisation of all information; the emergence of a global market virtually independent of national markets; private ownership of much that was once public information; and a tendency to put more trust in market forces than in representative government.[6]

If this is an accurate appraisal of the current developments in international communications – and I believe that it is – what bearing do these trends have on the sovereignty of nations in general, and on national cultural and communication sovereignty in particular? These are the points of focus in what follows.

The Trans-National Corporate Business System
As each of the above trends finds either its source or its impetus in the phenomenal growth since the Second World War of the trans-national corporate business system, our analysis begins with an overview of the dynamics of this system, with special consideration reserved for the information connection.

In brief, for the last thirty-five years, an increasing share of the production and distribution worldwide of goods and services has been accounted for by, at best, a few thousand trans-national corporations (TNCs). These firms, two thirds of which are United States-owned and based, have plants and facilities all around the world. Their investment, production, pricing and labour policies are affected by many factors, but central and generally determining are the profitability and security of the capital investment.

The global scale of operations of the TNCs is unqualifiedly dependent on the existence of elaborate international communication networks and the capability of these connections to transmit, unimpeded and securely, tremendous volumes of data. There is no reticence about this communication dependency. Corporate and governmental figures mention it matter-of-factly and regard it as one of the vulnerable and sensitive areas requiring international negotiation and diplomacy.[7] It would be misleading, however, to view communication as merely a secondary facilitating factor in business operations. It is now a core component in the entire economic process, integral to production and distribution, as well as to marketing, public relations, advertising and all the spheres which make up the ideological conditioning of national publics, wherever the business system functions.

The world business system's reliance on information for these many uses and functions is affecting and changing the role and character of information itself. This is happening noticeably in the few most developed market economies. Its impact on the rest of the world is still to be felt. In any case, profound changes in social existence are being experienced in North America, Western Europe and Japan.

Information for Sale

One development, itself affected by and affecting all others in the information-using economy, is paramount. It is the pervasive appearance of information as a good for sale – the information commodity. By no means a phenomenon of recent origin, the extent and breadth of the process which is now transforming all kinds of information into commercial items goes well beyond pre-computer-era conditions. Actually, the new information technologies, combined with the trans-national corporations' need for a greatly expanded variety and volume of information, are the driving forces in the commoditisation of information. The consequence of this is that the informational realm, the last redoubt to total capitalist penetration, finally is breached.[8]

The latest conquest of the market is acknowledged, and is a source of elation, at the highest political levels. The Cabinet Office Information Technology Advisory Panel in Great Britain, for example, hailed the commercialisation of information in its report, *Making a Business of Information*, and noted with approval that 'there is now an expanding "tradeable information sector".'[9] A 'tradeable information sector' means that information carries a price. It is produced for and is available only to those who can afford to pay that price. From these very simple market principles, applied to the field of information, derive an astonishing number of fundamental changes in the economic, cultural and social activities of the nation.

One striking consequence is the fusion of the cultural sphere of activity with the general economy. Whatever autonomy may have existed up to this time in the creative sector is disappearing. The production techniques and marketing rules that govern industry are no less applicable to information/cultural activity. This cannot be without profound consequences for the character of the cultural outputs as well as for the creative process itself.

Private Acquisition and Ownership of What Was Once Public Information

Once information is priced and sold, a determined effort is made to acquire information stockpiles as well as to influence those institutions that have the capability to generate new information. For the Western market economies, the United States' experience may be indicative of the general pattern that will develop. What this offers, for the most part, is the calculated capture of governmentally-produced information. It extends as well to those university-based research holdings that can be converted readily into profit-making data and processes. In the United States, the government information supply is being parcelled out, hand over fist, to numerous private information industry contractors. The transfer is still in an early stage, but already deep inroads have been made in what was once a great public information holding.[10]

Coincident with gaining control of already-produced information, there are mounting efforts to ensure that information-generating institutions – universities, institutes, laboratories and the government itself – are aware of, if not enlisted in, the profit-making initiatives of the private sector. This is especially observable in the high-tech industries, electronics, space, micro-biology and artificial intelligence.

There is still another dimension to the commoditisation of information. Once information has become a source of value in the marketplace, the pressure to privatise it, at the expense of public custodianship, is unrelieved. It is no aberration that sees formerly public informational services increasingly put on a 'for sale' basis. Public libraries, willing or not, are compelled to levy charges for access to the private electronic databases in which their holdings are more and more likely to be stored. The telephone system, the public mails, and what once was proudly, if inaccurately, called 'free television' are losing their general availability and are increasingly 'costed' according to a market calculus. Prices are being set on what were once free or subsidised services, and general users find themselves progressively priced out of meaningful, and sometimes essential, information supplies.

Though not quite as visible, what is happening inside the main industrialised economies has its international counterpart. The already great differentials between the poor and the relatively well-off nations are deepened still further with the advance of private information structures employing the new information technologies and the resultant commercialisation of information.

ISDN, New Global Infrastructure for Information Control

The process of integrating the less industrialised with the already industrialised nations, to the disadvantage of the former and the enrichment of the latter, gets added impetus from an international information transmission system now in the making. Utilising the latest technological developments, and digitising all information – voice, visual and print – messages and data are reduced to common electronic impulses and hurtled around the world. The International Services Digital Network (ISDN), now being established, is the ultimate mechanism for information control.

It is expected that through this computerised global grid will pass business, military, governmental and individual messages. More to the point, it appears that the levers of control, the priority of passage, and the capability to oversee and intervene in this all-embracing system will be concentrated in a few nodal points of the world markets system, first of all in the United States.[11] In the very limited attention, outside of technical journals, that has been directed to ISDN, it is claimed that the new international transmission grid will be a great facilitator to global discourse and international development, and perhaps this is true. Yet there is a familiar ring to these assurances: they are reminiscent of what we were told were to be the benefits of earlier less powerful but still advanced systems of information transmission – the telegraph, the telephone, the international news agencies, radio, television and satellite communication. In each instance, the technology quickly was subordinated to, if it had not been created originally for, the dominating power elements in the economy. Today, in most cases, these are the trans-national corporations.

National Sovereignty and Cultural Autonomy: The Targets?
Recent actions demonstrate that, for some very influential groups and individuals, national sovereignty and international agreement of sovereign states over important economico-cultural matters are considered to be obstacles to overcome, relics of an obsolete age. The TNCs and their representatives, government officials or the business executive corps, have been insistent that democratic structures which function, for example, on a one-nation one-vote basis, a practice of most post-Second World War international bodies, are unacceptable and require modification. United States' official attacks on UNESCO, the International Telecommunications Union (ITU), the United Nations Conference on Trade and Development (UNCTAD), the World Health Organisation (WHO) and the World Court are symptomatic. These organisations are criticised because their procedural rules, and sometimes their resolutions, interfere with the operations and objectives of huge private aggregations of economic, political and cultural power.

The opposition to even partially democratically structured international organisation, openly expressed at high governmental and business levels in Washington and New York, extends to national arrangements as well. Many national structures are found no less objectionable. The PTTs of Western Europe and Japan and the Telecoms of the UK and Australia are also viewed as barriers to TNC activity. It is in this light that the commercialisation of information, the private satellite systems, ISDN and the promotion of deregulation can be understood as the instruments and processes which serve to beat down the national safeguards – such as they are – that still stand in the way of the onward march of the TNCs.

The discredited doctrine of extra-territoriality, which served European colonialism and exploitation in an earlier age, is now invoked by American leadership to batter national sovereignty in

15

Europe and elsewhere. Overseas subsidiaries of US trans-national companies have been forbidden to trade with nations that are designated as adversaries by the US Government, irrespective of whether the nation in which they are located has the same view of the trading partner in question. The doctrine of extra-territoriality basically asserts that the law of the most powerful state supersedes the law of subordinate political units. Accordingly, national efforts to exercise jurisdiction over internal information circulation, for example, can be regarded by strict American interpretation as violations of the United States Constitution – specifically, the free speech First Amendment. This interpretation has been applied to the near-unanimous expression of the international community to control the inflow, or at least to be informed in advance of, satellite-beamed transmissions. This is the so-called 'prior consent' issue in international communication.

Actually, explicit extra-territoriality demands often need not be made. 'Market forces' can be relied on to achieve the same ends. Besides, market ideology claims that individuals will make better choices than their governmental representatives; therefore, dispense with governmental responsibility wherever possible. The elevation of 'market forces' to sacrosanct status and the denigration of social action by representative government on behalf of the citizenry – 'Get the government off our backs,' is the way Ronald Reagan, the head of a fearsome governmental apparatus of coercion, puts it – now seem to be the main objectives of Western capitalism.

The powerful deregulation movement, which already has swept across the American industrial and governmental landscape, and which now moves with equal intentness across Western Europe, with particular severity in the UK, can best be understood as the structural reorganisation of the world economy, under TNC direction, assisted by the new information technologies. Commenting on the imminent retirement, in August 1984, of Walter B. Wriston, chief executive officer of Citicorp, the world's most powerful financial institution, a Wall Street analyst gave this overall assessment of Wriston's achievement:

> The whole move to deregulation is largely a result of his willingness to take an aggressive stance toward the regulators and toward Congress *and to push deregulation to the limits worldwide. . . . Every place Citicorp operates, its corporate culture pushes the limits of regulation, whether it's New York, Hong Kong, or London.*[12]

This may be attributing a bit too much to one bank's activity, though Citicorp's worldwide assets at the end of 1983 totalled $134.7 billion, it did business in 94 countries besides the United States, and half of its income came from overseas. Yet it suggests the sources and resources behind the pressure that is making deregulation the favoured policy of many Western governments.

Actually, deregulation is a code word for reducing national public accountability and for achieving a restructuring of the economy according to the interests of the largest capital accumulators in the newest industries and services. Utilising the rhetoric of 'individual rights', the newest behemoths of private power are afforded the privilege of cavorting in the world, as well as the national arena, freed of accountability. With deregulation, in effect, one protective pillar after another of the public's wellbeing is levelled or reduced to impotency. Nothing remains in the way – at least, not in the short run – of rampaging capital.

The Communication and Cultural Consequences of the Deregulated Trans-National Corporate Business System

The mechanics of unbridled growth of the TNC system under deregulation are relatively simple. The consequences in the cultural sphere are devastating. This is not the place to take up the economic and political impacts, which are no less disastrous. The fundamental point is that as the trans-national corporate order grows stronger, in large part with the assistance of deregulated private information networks, it usurps and corrupts cultural expression and information diversity globally.

The PTTs and Telecoms decline or disappear. The commercial broadcast networks and facilities expand. The main objection to the public or regulated private broadcast networks had been that they excluded or severely limited marketing. These limitations are now removed. The chief users of the deregulated system are the big businesses and the international companies. They become the sponsors, the financiers of the media and the main users of the data transmission networks. In those instances where the national (public) system continues to function, it is obliged to operate no differently from the private commercial structures. This is the observable development in those European states which once boasted of dominant public broadcast and telecommunications authorities.

In Britain, for example, the government is pressing the BBC to allow its radio stations to accept advertising.[13] It floats the idea that the BBC itself be broken up into separate functions[14] ('All the better to devour you, my dear'). The licence tax, longstanding bulwark of public service, is made to seem an intolerable imposition on individual freedom.

As private satellite systems proliferate, the big international companies will be able to *bypass* the international system, INTELSAT, and transmit their data and messages totally insulated

17

from national oversight. As the ISDN comes into operation, still more power will gravitate to the controllers of the international digitised system, whose design will strengthen further the already powerful position of the trans-national corporations. In the background, but hardly a secret, a wild race to develop a super-computer is conducted in the United States by a consortium of the largest micro-computer companies in coalition with the Pentagon and the CIA. Similar activity goes on in Japan, and Europe too is moving to 'compete'.

Wherever the research and development proceed, the initiators and likely beneficiaries have a common interest. The director of the Pentagon's Information Processing Techniques Office of the Defense Advanced Research Projects Agency (DARPA) puts it this way: 'The nation that dominates this information-processing field will possess the keys to world leadership in the 21st century.[15] Another ex-Pentagoner, Dr Ruth Davis, amplifies what 'world leadership' is about: '. . . The race we're really in is between countries, not for supercomputers, not for national security. . . . We're in a race to control the resources of the world, both natural resources and information resources.'[16]

What, If Anything, To Do?
There is now under way, spanning the North Atlantic trans-national corporate territory, and elsewhere, a vast extension in cultural control and domination, to say nothing of economic and political mastery. Here we are concerned with the effort to structure a new global system of authority on the basis of information control, of an order hitherto unimaginable. What has been a substantial influence, resting on familiar media flows – news, TV programmes, films, books, magazines – *is being extended to include the entire flow of information*, corporate data streams in particular. For this reason, customary efforts that aimed at securing some national cultural protection through subsidies to domestic media industries and similar mechanisms now are futile. The trans-national corporate order, increasingly an information-generating, -processing and -transmitting system, is now capable of bypassing national authority, where it hasn't already enveloped it.

Moreover, the TNC order is now an integral part of most of the developed capitalist world, participating in, and continually widening, its economic and social networks in individual economies. Additionally, the successful campaign to break down national broadcasting and telecommunication entities increasingly allows the trans-national combines near-total access to national information systems. They are well on the way to becoming the dominant force in each national setting, saturating the cultural space of the nation.

Given these conditions, which are made still more pervasive by the rapid spread of the new information technologies, the issue of national autonomy, if not survival, becomes a question of transcendent importance. Does the possibility exist of disengaging from the transnational system and the communication networks that undergird and make it viable? Indeed, are these even realistic and practical objectives?

The consequences of *not* attempting to dissociate and disengage may be a more useful way to consider the issue. If there is no significant break with the prevailing order, it is more than likely that existing trends will continue, possibly accelerate. This means further unemployment and under-employment as automation bites into the labour force and as the TNCs export jobs to cheaper labour sites in their international division of labour. Information and cultural services increasingly will be allocated on an ability-to-pay basis and there will be growing differentials between information 'have' and 'have nots'. Homogenised North Atlantic cultural slop will drench the population, though some 'high culture' will be available for the privileged stratum of professionals and managers in the new information society. The Welfare State, already mostly a memory, will be stripped further, while the National Security State will play a more ominous and coercive role. Nationalistic right-wing social movements will make rapid advances, recruiting members from frustrated and apathetic electorates. Note, for example, the growth of such a movement in France, as indicated in the recent European Community elections.[17]

Is accommodation to and participation in an order which produces these conditions to be regarded as realistic and practical? Could the burdens, undeniable, that would accompany disengagement from the trans-national system, be more offensive and less humane?

The practices and policies of a relatively independent economy and an autonomous culture, separated as much as possible from the present world market system, cannot be specified here. In any case, they would have to be worked out by the people desiring this course. One guideline does seem clear, however. The values, paraphernalia and practices of a marketeering society must be made the starting point of the discussion. Consumerism as a way of life, no matter how expertly promoted by the TNC apparatus and defining scores of national environments, has to be challenged. Nothing less will do, if the process of extrication and disengagement is to be begun. Undertaking a radical reconstruction of the social order on a different moral basis is a tough but a grand goal. It must gain acceptance from people and it cannot depend on advertising and public relations. It is an uncharted journey. But there is a rich historical legacy from which to select and further develop first principles for mapping the way. It is to this task that our energies and efforts can be directed.

References

1. H.I. Schiller, *Mass Communications and American Empire* (New York: Augustus M. Kelley 1969); K. Nordenstreng and T. Varis, *Television Traffic: A One-Way Street?* (Paris: UNESCO 1974); W.H. Read, *America's Mass Media Merchants* (Baltimore: Johns Hopkins University Press 1977); J. Tunstall, *The Media are American: Anglo-American Media in the World* (London: Constable 1977); A. Smith, *The Geopolitics of Information: How Western Culture Dominates the World* (London: Faber and Faber 1980).
2. T. Varis, 'The International Flow of Television Programs', *Journal of Communication*, vol. 34, No. 1, Winter 1984.
3. H.I. Schiller, op. cit.
4. G. Richeri, *Telecommunication Systems in Europe: From the State to the Market* (forthcoming).
5. J. Critchley, *Hansard*, Series 6, vol 33, 1982, col. 439.
6. S. Moore, 'Global Information Policies', *Computerworld*, 6 June 1984, pp. 49–52.
7. H.I. Schiller, *Who Knows: Information in the Age of the Fortune 500* (Norwood, New Jersey: Ablex 1981).
8. D. Schiller, *The Information Commodity* (New York: Oxford University Press, forthcoming).
9. *Making a Business of Information*, A Report by the Information Technology Advisory Panel (London: HMSO September 1983) p. 7.
10. A.R. and H.I. Schiller, 'Who Can Own What America Knows?', *The Nation*, 7 April 1982.
11. D. Schiller, 'The Emerging Global Grid: Planning for What?' *Media, Culture and Society*, vol. 7, no. 1, January 1985.
12. R.A. Bennett, 'Wriston: A Summing Up', *New York Times*, 21 June 1984. Emphasis added.
13. C. Brown, 'Ministers Aim for Radio Ads on BBC', *Guardian*, 5 June 1984.
14. P. Schlesinger, 'Privatising the BBC', *The Listener*, 31 May 1984.
15. D. Burnham, 'Debate on Pentagon Computer Plan Focuses on Military's Effect on Society', *New York Times*, 18 June 1984.
16. J. Kirchner, 'Supercomputing Seen Key to Economic Success', *Computerworld*, 3 October 1983, p. 8.
17. There are many other contradictions in the Information Society. These may produce other conditions. Some of these possibilities are examined in H.I. Schiller, *Information and the Crisis Economy* (Norwood, New Jersey: Ablex 1984).

GIUSEPPE RICHERI

Television from Service to Business: European Tendencies and the Italian Case

Throughout the whole of the 1970s most of Europe's broadcasting systems underwent more or less extensive processes of transformation. The political, economic and socio-cultural factors at the basis of these processes interacted differently in the individual countries, but also showed trends and contradictions which reveal common characteristics. The new technologies made available in the various countries, thanks to the great progress of electronics in the field of communications, also have elements in common in spite of their individual characteristics.

A comparative analysis of what has happened and is happening in the European broadcasting systems clearly shows at least two general trends: a trend towards internationalisation or, if preferred, towards denationalisation; and a contemporary trend towards decentralisation of these systems. In many cases, these two trends have been considered contradictory or even at odds with each other. But if we look at the countries in which these trends have emerged most strongly (for example, Italy, France, Spain and Belgium), internationalisation and decentralisation prove in many cases to be two organic moments of the same process. That is to say, the field of broadcasting (and many others too) demonstrates on the one hand a concentration of the control of the hardware and software market in the hands of the big trans-national holdings, while on the other an increase in the number of channels and the diversification of the means of reception.

If this design has already materialised in other sectors of the economy, for the broadcasting sector it is sufficient to note that:
(a) An increasing number of the programmes broadcast by most of the European television stations, both public and private, are acquired on the international market;
(b) The main trend in programme exchanges on the international market is from two or three non-European countries towards the rest of the world and, while there may be certain exceptions to this pattern, these have a relatively minor importance;
(c) All the European television systems show an increase in the

number of programme hours on the various channels and an increase in the number of channels and broadcasting stations.

The most obvious result of this combination of trends and elements is that of notably modifying the position of the European public broadcasting services, which on the one hand assume commercial characteristics and on the other lose, or risk losing, their national monopoly. It can, in fact, be said that European public broadcasting services are in a state of instability, of weakness and, in some cases, of actual recession.

Crisis Factors in Public Broadcasting Services

Amongst the crisis factors affecting the European public broadcasting services, some are linked to characteristics of the national conditions while others are of a more general nature. Among the latter the most important can at least be indicated.

First, the inflation spiral which, together with the restrictions on public spending (typical of all Western European countries faced with a serious economic crisis), erodes the financial basis upon which public broadcasting services traditionally operate. These cannot freely fix the means or times of increases in licence fees or advertising revenues to balance their income with the increasing production costs, the extension of broadcasting hours and the development of their services and investments.

Second, the expansion of the audio-visual market and the eruption of new media, which on the one hand stimulate increasingly stronger interests in the private sector and increase the number of distribution channels, and on the other influence the characteristics of the demand and of the forms of consumption by viewers.

Third, the loss of identity on the part of the public service owing to the difficulties in satisfying the requirements of viewers who are fragmented into an increasingly composite mosaic of interests, groups and categories, each with different tastes and political and cultural attitudes, means that while there is a mass audience which can always be reached, other types of audience tend to 'escape'. These include the revolutionary and protest movements, some of which are very strong, against the public broadcasting service which is accused of being a centralised instrument controlled by the predominant political power. Cases of this type have arisen and have been important in increasing awareness of the role of the mass media in the processes of political and social participation, in decision making and the assertion of local cultures.

Fourth, the increasingly difficult relationships with the dominant political power which, when it is no longer able to control the monopoly of broadcast information, tends to favour private initiatives through which it hopes to re-establish its margins of control.

22

An analysis of the state of public broadcasting services in different countries reveals that crisis is always determined by one of these problems or, as commonly occurs, one of their possible combinations.

Restructuring of the International Economy and the Communications Sector

The trends characterising the development phase of a capitalist economy interact with this evolution and are revealed in the field of mass communications with increasingly definite characteristics. For instance, there has been a growing international competition and the consequent entry of multi-national capital into the editorial, marketing and advertising activities of the national broadcasting service. One of the most evident signs is the increasing penetration of international products into national markets of mass communication, in particular the television networks and the cinema.

Another indication is provided by the ever more insistent attempts to increase the number of cultural products and the speed of circulation in this sector, which transforms the organisation of work and of production processes. The most evident examples are the editing and printing of daily newspapers (with the problems posed by the introduction of informatics and telematics) and, in broadcasting, the problem of the development of serial productions. The pressing need to open (or create) new markets in order to place the over-production and to invest excess capital has led to pressure throughout Europe to commercialise and make public broadcasting private, the most obvious confirmation being the Italian 'case'.

Furthermore, there have been efforts to open new markets both for technologies and for cultural products, introducing new means of transmission and reception such as videotex, cable television, diffusion satellites. With the high initial investments required, and profitability greatly deferred in time, these operations necessitate a strict alliance between the state, financial groups and private industry in an attempt to charge the infrastructure and distribution costs to public expenditure and to create the consequent development of a market for durable goods. In this case the most evident example is provided by the European projects for satellites for direct-broadcast diffusion and for cable or wide-band communication systems.

The trans-national economic system's absolute need to maximise the accessibility/feasibility of the broadcasting systems, conditioning them to their marketing and advertising requirements, induces an increasing tendency towards the commercialisation and the privatisation of European broadcasting systems which have been protected up until now, totally or in part, by the public service monopoly. In this context the function of European broadcasting is subject to a strong incentive for transformation. Its function is no

23

longer simply that of carrying out an informative, educational and entertainment activity or, if considered from another point of view, that of reproducing the dominant ideology or, again, of organising consensus and the image of power. It is, instead, a question of extending the capacity of radio and above all television to attract and entertain large sectors of the public to which the advertising messages are addressed. Television has become the main link between products and consumers in the general economic context.

The Effects of Competition on Television Networks
The increasing role which advertising revenue plays in the economy of the main European television networks and the general competition which is growing stronger among them offer a particularly clear indication of the state of the relationship between public and private television. In many European countries it can be observed that when one single public can receive programmes transmitted simultaneously by several stations operating independently (whether they are from networks or from single stations) and when all or part of these stations rely on advertising as a determining or exclusive source of finance, a competitive process is set in motion based on the maximisation of the viewing figures and therefore on programming; an effect which normally produces several unambiguous results.

This occurs where competition is found exclusively within the sphere of the public broadcasting service, as in the case of the two French national networks, now mainly financed by advertising; where competition is between public and private networks, as in England where the public network (BBC) is financed exclusively by the licence fee paid by viewers and the private network (ITV) is financed exclusively by advertising; where competition occurs between a public network and a private foreign station, as in the case of Belgium, where the public network is financed exclusively by the licence fee, and the majority of viewers can receive, via cable, more than ten foreign channels including the private Luxembourg television (Radio-Télé-Luxembourg) financed exclusively by advertising (aimed mainly at Belgian viewers!); where competition occurs between hundreds of local channels and public national and regional networks, as in Italy where the public broadcasting network transmits advertising on the two national networks and obtains in this way a financial income which it cannot do without, and hundreds of local channels (in some cases organised in national and inter-regional networks) are financed exclusively by advertising.

All these cases present very similar results. The quality of programmes tends to move towards the minimum common denominator of public taste, especially during the hours in which

24

viewing is potentially high; while the programmes with a cultural, informative or educational content, where they exist, or the programmes which deviate from the average taste, are diverted towards secondary viewing hours. Further, the objective of obtaining the maximum overall share of viewers imposed by advertising leads to an expansion in the number of daily programme hours. In turn, the necessity, on the one hand, of resorting to programmes which correspond to average taste and, on the other, of increasing the daily transmission hours as much as possible has the effect of reducing the percentage of original programmes transmitted; of increasing repeats of programmes already transmitted; and of favouring the purchase of standard programmes (telefilms, TV serials, musicals, cartoons, etc.) on the international market where only the United States (and for a few sectors, the Japanese and recently the Brazilian) TV-film industry is able to offer merchandise which is absolutely competitive both in quantity and quality. The combination of these factors leads to a general homogenisation of programming (both public and private) and a tendency for national television production to move towards standardisation to increase its selling possibilities on the international market. The only kind of programme which is not subject to these mechanisms is, for the moment, that concerning information in the strict sense. This sector, however, is still the most resistant to the pluralism of ideas and opinions and, above all, most separated from the dialectics with which the real processes reveal themselves.

In the words of Jacques Thibau, ex-assistant director of French television and a sharp critic of the French broadcasting reform of 1974:

> We can see today's opponent clearly taking shape. This is not the bureaucracy of yesterday, it is the system which has come from across the Atlantic which penetrates the European networks and imposes upon them the concept of a commercialised advertising and, preferably, standardised audio-visual 'product' which leaves no space for creation or for the expression of classes, groups, individuals or nations. . . . Installing a few small, weak and rival companies in the place of the ORTF the Giscardian reform has facilitated the ideological and cultural invasion from across the Atlantic. . . . As if the universe in the field of televisions consisted of small, kind and pluralistic organisms which throw themselves into the competition for quality, and may the best one win. How puerile and what rubbish![1]

In the 80s Europe has entered an era of generalised competition in the television field. What cable TV has produced in Belgium, the private channels in Italy and all the rest in France and Finland, the

25

direct diffusion satellites might achieve in a few years in all the European countries. There is no shortage of examples. The risks that the public broadcasting system of the German Federal Republic is running in this regard are emblematic. Albrecht Muller, responsible for the Federal Government's planning, has declared that the planned use of direct diffusion satellites by Radio-Télé-Luxembourg and by a private Anglo-Swiss consortium (Lux-Sat and Tel-Sat) has nothing to do with the exchange of information and of opinions but that their objectives, among others, are to cover a large part of the territory of the German Federal Republic in order to widen their own advertising market. Towards the end of 1980 Muller noted:

> The commercial programmes would compete with the public system and the struggle over the viewing figures would result in a decline in the quality of the programmes. This would lead to a greater number of television serials and quizzes, fewer information and social criticism programmes and a reduced pluralism. In my opinion the foreign commercial television programmes specifically produced for transmission in the German Federal Republic:
> – would represent a means of destroying the still-acceptable liberal and pluralist structure of the mass media;
> – would result, together with cable TV, in an immense increase in programmes; this would have extremely negative consequences on the level of interpersonal communications;
> – both these aspects would reflect on the political situation in the German Federal Republic in that the country would become less democratic, not in a formal sense but as regards the actual participation of the citizens.

It is interesting to see the ideas on this subject of the advertising and marketing executives operating in Europe. A former director of Lintas London, Rein Rijkens, stated:

> In my view, the arrival of commercially exploited satellites will have many advantages; first and foremost it will be another big step forward towards Europe becoming a really united continent, instead of the individual countries continuing their political quibbles and exaggerating beyond measure their own importance, at the expense of being accepted by the great powers as equal partners. As far as our business is concerned, it should force international advertisers to sharpen their skills in planning their marketing and advertising operations on a pan-European, rather than a country-by-country basis.[2]

Who Produces and Who Watches Television Programmes? The Move Towards an International Market
Faced with the rapid increase in the overall number of programme

hours which impose a parallel increase in television production capacity, and faced with competitive mechanisms which impose a different quality of programme and a different programming logic, the European television networks interested in these changes were unable to meet the demands with their own production capacity. Up to the mid-70s, most European television networks operated in a completely protected position: the public monopoly. Both television production and diffusion were regulated by the same centre. The quality and quantity of the programmes were easily adapted to the financial resources available – which depended only marginally on advertising, where this was permitted. Television productivity was calculated in cultural, social and political terms. Now, however, it is mainly calculated in strictly economic terms or on the basis of viewing figures.

This logic, which produced its first effects during the 70s in England (where the first commercial television network began in 1955) and, afterwards, in Belgium, France and Italy, is now penetrating almost all the other European television networks. These, on the whole, are unprepared for the logic of the market-place and the mechanisms of competition, above all because the conditions and the logic of public monopoly have tried to favour a 'creative' and 'quality' television network, based on the production of original works and therefore of workshop-type productions: a diversified television with strong national characteristics.

Meanwhile the new conditions in which many networks have found themselves in recent years have brought about the need for an industrial production of programmes capable of creating many hours of transmission at high speed and a lower average cost than original productions, together with a commercial organisation capable of selling these programmes in a wider market than the national one. It is this inability to respond with their own production means to the demand for a different type of television imposed by the logic of competition which resulted in the definitive internationalisation of many European television systems. What we are witnessing is reliance on the international market for programme-purchase, leading to the presence of programmes of the same origin and the same type in the programming of the different European networks; by the same token, there is the affirmation of the commercial television model.

In Europe the most intense and varied experience of the systematic shift to the world market to feed domestic television demand is certainly the Italian one. Among the disruptive effects brought about by the mushrooming of approximately 450 private commercial television stations between 1976 and 1979 was the rapid drying-up of all the warehouse stocks – mainly old films. These private stations, on the other hand, had neither the financial resources nor the production capacity to make their own programmes directly. It was also impossible to think of having them produced by a non-existent national television industry. In fact, RAI, the only body capable of producing on an industrial level and in possession of an enormous quantity of television programmes which could have been put back into circulation by sale to private television, has refused to have any contact with these competitors.

In 1981 Italy became the greatest importer of television programmes from both Japan and the United States, while it soon discovered another supplier on the international market, Brazil (little known in Europe up until then). Among these producers today there is a clear-cut division of the work, neither imposed nor agreed upon, which makes Japan the main supplier of children's programmes in the form of cartoons. Brazil supplies the *telenovelas*, which are television serials considered in Europe to be of lower quality than those produced in the United States and which are bought to fill up the transmission hours during the morning and early afternoon. The United States supplies the top-quality serials, those which are shown during peak viewing time, and successful film classics.

The leading position of these countries is explained by the fact that the United States and Japan (the first in the mid-50s and the second at the beginning of the 60s) were able to integrate their television and cinema industries and make the latter a production structure of the television system. Moreover, in the case of Japan, there was a rapid application of the most sophisticated technologies for the production of certain types of programmes – for example, the use of computers in the production of cartoon films.

In Brazil, it was the cinema and the theatre which provided the structure upon which the industrial production of soap operas could be developed. In fact, the main authors, screen-writers, directors and actors for the *telenovelas* come from the theatre and the cinema. The virtual monopoly enjoyed by TV Globo, the fourth most important television network in the world, has produced the financial resources to set up industrial structures for the production of *telenovela* serials. TV Globo has a specialised *telenovela* for each viewing time and, therefore, for each type of viewer.

Another characteristic common to the three countries is that their commercial television system consists of networks and their affiliates and is based on competitive logic, to which must be added a population of television viewers which is much higher than that of the individual European countries. This means higher advertising revenues and the possibility of defraying the production costs of the programmes on the home market before selling these programmes on the international market at prices much lower than the real costs. It must also be remembered that in all three cases there is a strong commercial structure for foreign sales.

The Italian Case

The Italian experience in recent years provides a particularly useful lesson. It is certainly not one to be followed by anyone who is studying the possibility of developing a system of private networks alongside the public system. In France, Belgium, the Federal German Republic and Spain, as in the past in Italy, the reasons being put forward in support of the private stations are the need for decentralisation, pluralism, freedom of information and expression, things that it is essential to fight for.

The Italian experience clearly shows that the development of local radio and television initiatives outside the sphere of the public service might play a part in satisfying these requirements, but on condition that the logic relative to the market, the profits, and therefore the competition, is not the prevalent or exclusive logic. In Italy, this logic has prevailed among the private stations with the result, by now obvious to everyone, that the truly local initiatives inspired by the need for pluralism, freedom of information and expression, have been eliminated from the market or have been reduced to a marginal level. The leading position is now held by the stations (in some cases organised in networks or chains) whose only function is that of being distribution points for standard programmes, mainly bought from abroad and lacking in any informative, educational or original cultural value and without any relationship to true local requirements. What is more, the existence of these stations has certainly not helped to change the organisational and production model of public television, but has set in motion a process of denaturalising the very functions which public television should, by definition, guarantee.

Private Television Programming What conditions and determines the composition and structure of the private televisions' programme-grid is the fact that advertising revenues are their only source of income. This imposes the iron rule of maximising viewing figures together with extending the daily transmission periods to reach fringe audiences, thus increasing the total quantity of viewers.

Private television activity consists mainly of the distribution of programmes bought on the market, since actual origination of shows, films, serials and information programmes involves extensive financing and amortisation time, and there is always the risk of not reaching the viewing figures necessary to obtain sufficient advertising revenue. For this reason, the stations first resorted to domestic cinema stocks, which were rapidly exhausted, and then to the international market, either directly or through importers. Here were programmes whose appeal had already been tried and tested and which were offered at much lower prices, having already been partly or completely amortised on other markets. These types of programme, consisting mainly of films, TV-films and serials designed for the peak viewing hours, and of cartoon films, sport and documentaries for other viewing times, account in all for 70–75 per cent of the transmissions.

If to this percentage we add the 15 per cent of time taken up by advertising, the space for original programming is extremely limited (it has fallen progressively over the years) and is normally accounted for by the presentation of programmes, horoscopes, auctions, a few information programmes taken straight from the press and the odd sports or local folklore programme (in dialect). It should be noted that the better-quality programmes bought are disputed on the market between RAI and the big private networks, while the independent and fringe stations normally have second- or third-class films, serials, shows, etc. In 1979/80 Italy became the greatest world importer of Japanese cartoon films and, according to RAI estimates made between 1979 and 1981, used up about fifteen years of Japanese production of this kind. In 1982, Italy also became the leading world importer of television programmes from the United States.

After 1982 the two main private channels began to develop a policy of original television productions and co-productions with foreign countries. In that year the two main private networks reached co-operation agreements regarding programmes and management, planning policies, relationships with affiliates, etc., with two of the largest United States networks (Rete 4 with ABC and Canale 5 with CBS), while RAI signed a co-operation agreement with NBC.

The Relationship between RAI and Private TV RAI has progressively suffered the competition of private television in various ways. On the international market there has been a heavy increase in buying prices (up to 1000 per cent), while in Italy the transfer of some of the best professionals at management level from RAI to the private networks and the transfer of some of the most popular presenters, showmen, and stars from the public to private TV was accompanied by a marked increase in fees. There has also been a reduction in the viewing figures of the public networks. In 1982 the Italian television audience was divided as follows: considering the yearly average of transmission hours (12.30 to 23.30), RAI accounted for 53.9 per cent of viewers and the private stations 46.1 per cent.

The most important and obvious effect of the competition between private and public services is shown at the level of RAI's production and programming activities. On the basis of the competition, the programme schedule was modified. In an attempt to limit the loss of audience in favour of the private stations, the programming and quality of RAI's output have tended to move towards the minimum common denominator of public taste, especially during peak viewing hours, while the cultural, educational and quality programmes or those which differ from the average taste have slipped to secondary or fringe viewing hours. The programming of the two national networks has tended to become increasingly more homogeneous instead of developing a calculated complementary nature, which would have been logical in the case of a public service, while the objective of capturing the greatest overall share of viewers has tended to expand the daily programming hours to correspond with the hours already fairly well filled by the private stations which, in many cases, transmit 24 hours a day.

Films, TV-films and serials have been deployed in the programming of both public national networks in order to utilise the budget allocated to programming to fill the greatest number of daily transmisson hours. It has become imperative to reach bigger audiences at a lower programme unit cost. Peak viewing hours are normally excluded from this rule, since this period involves the most competition. The necessity, on the one hand, of resorting to programmes corresponding to the average taste and, on the other, of increasing the transmission hours as much as possible (with the difficulty of proportionally increasing the expenditure for the programmes) has the effect of favouring the increase in standard programmes and, in part, of increasing the repeats of programmes already transmitted. Moreover, and most important, it necessitates an increased recourse to programmes bought on the international market which unite two features: standard format and lower costs than those of original programmes. Lastly there is a tendency for many of the self-produced programmes to become standardised to increase the possibility of their international circulation.

From the production point of view, and on the basis of the current competition from private television, RAI has been forced to change policy and to resort with increasing frequency to productions made by outside companies or aimed towards the broader programme market. The concrete effects on the activity of the public television networks, which after the reform operated independently from one another, were identical. They abandoned or notably reduced the direct production of 'quality' programmes (TV films, plays, variety shows, etc.), a sector in which each production structure of RAI was able to produce not more than twenty instalments a year, and changed to a 'lighter' and more repetitive type of production (quizzes, chat shows, mini-variety shows, children's programmes, and so on) in which the same production structures can turn out some 150 instalments a year. Priority was given to in-house productions with costs as close as possible to the value of the fixed costs alone (i.e. those of RAI's permanent personnel) to keep the financial budget at the disposal of the networks to use for external purposes.

The Structure of Private TV and the Networks   About 150 of the 450 private stations which operate regularly in Italy are affiliated to a netwɔrk. Some of the networks operate on an inter-regional scale, others throughout the whole of the country, the latter being the protagonists in the private field. The disappearance of the network owned by the publisher Rizzoli, owing to the legal problems encountered by the group, left three major networks in 1982: Canale 5, owned by Berlusconi (the property and newspaper magnate); Italia 1, formerly owned by Rusconi (the book and magazine publisher) and bought by Berlusconi; and Rete 4, owned by Mondadori (the most important Italian publishing group, operating on an international scale, printing daily newspapers, periodicals and books).[3] These networks have dominated the private television sector, both in terms of advertising and the purchase of programmes on the international market.

Advertising   A comparison of the advertising expenditure for 1977, the year in which private television began to make its presence felt in advertising, with those for 1982 reveals a great increase in the role of television as an outlet (from an 18 per cent to a 35 per cent share) and a marked reduction for both newspapers and periodicals (from 62.2 to 52.5 per cent). Data for 1983 shows a further marked increase in the television share, to 52 per cent. Television has thus become the dominant advertising medium in the Italian market.

The total amount spent on television advertising in 1982 was 700 billion (thousand million) lire. Of this RAI received 285 billion (40.7 per cent) and private TV stations 415 billion (59.3 per cent). The division of advertising among the private TV stations indicates a very high degree of concentration: almost 80 per cent of the revenue went to the three main networks (Canale 5 – 200 billion lire; Italia 1 – 70 billion lire; Rete 4 – 53 billion lire), while the remaining 20 per cent (93 billion lire) was divided between a few hundred other private stations, some of which are organised in inter-regional circuits. As far as the private sector is concerned, the figures tally perfectly, according to commercial logic: in 1982 the three main networks had both 80 per cent of the private television viewers and 80 per cent of the advertising which went to the private television stations.

The only protagonists of the buying policies, the competition with RAI, the co-production initiatives, co-operation with foreign companies and self-productions are therefore a very small group of stations which, besides the three most important networks, include a few inter-regional networks such as STP, GRT and Euro-TV.

The State of the Italian Broadcasting Industry In 1982, the public and private television stations spent a total of 136 million dollars or 200 billion lire (double that of 1981 and four times that of 1980) to buy about 21,000 films, TV-films and plays from abroad. The Italian broadcasting industry has been unable to meet the great increase in demand from the television networks, which are obliged to resort above all to the United States (80 per cent), Japan and Brazil.

The inability of Italy's broadcasting industry to cope with the current state of affairs has many causes, including the lack of integration between the cinema and television industries and the fact that, for many years, the public broadcasting service had the monopoly, making it possible to maintain a steady balance between the demand and supply of programmes since the decisions were taken internally by a single body, RAI.

Since RAI refused to sell its own stock of programmes to the private stations, these were obliged to resort to the foreign market once the stock of Italian films had been exhausted, as the cost of domestic origination was too high for a direct recoup of the initial outlay and the risk of awaiting their sale on the market was also too high. There was also no managerial preparation to deal with such productions.

The proportion of the programmes bought out of those transmitted from a significant sample of private TV companies rose from 68 per cent in 1979 to 87.4 per cent in 1981.

The Problem of Resources Only in 1981 did RAI manage to re-establish the 1974 level of revenue from the licence fee, in real money terms. In fact, between 1974 and 1980 the licence fee, which remained the same, was progressively reduced, in real value, by high inflation rates. With this same fixed revenue, RAI transmission hours increased from 5,000 in 1974 to 12,000 in 1981. The overall revenue derived from the licence fee and advertising did not, therefore, grow in proportion to the increase in transmission hours.

In the cinema, box-office returns and advertising revenue registered a steady fall. In monetary terms they decreased from 800 billion lire in 1975 to 381 billion lire in 1981.

Private television was the only sector which registered a marked net increase. By 1981 the advertising revenue of the private television stations had risen to 185 billion lire – i.e. nearly half the total revenue (box office and advertising together) of the cinema. During the same period RAI's advertising revenues also increased, but less sharply.

In short, the revenues for production and distribution in the Italian audio-visual system fell during the same period (1974–81) in which RAI's transmission hours more than doubled, and those of private television reached a level of hundreds of thousands of hours every year. To give a comparative figure, in 1981 the advertising revenue of

33

the only English commercial network, ITV, was about the same as the total financial resources of the Italian audio-visual system in the same year: cinema, public and private television. On the one hand, the only solid television production structure, RAI, was not even able to cope with its own consumption needs and in 1980 was obliged to cover 57 per cent of its transmission hours with bought programmes (28.6 per cent) or repeats (28.9 per cent); on the other, the film industry, in a state of progressive crisis, saw a drastic reduction in its returns: the loss in cinema box-office takings in 1980, compared to 1974 in real value, was 64 per cent, while the annual number of films produced fell by 24 per cent (from 170 to 128).

Only from the beginning of 1983 when competition between the main Italian television networks on the international market had greatly increased the prices of foreign programmes did the private stations begin both to plan the setting up of an important number of self-productions and to make international agreements for co-productions. Additionally, RAI worked out a national production strategy to enable it to reduce its dependence on imports.

An important fact must, however, be underlined. The Italian economic system is certainly not able to supply the national audio-visual system with sufficient resources to balance the relationship between the supply and demand for audio-visual products. This means that either the number of overall television transmission hours must be reduced or Italy will still be obliged to rely heavily on the international market to satisfy its audio-visual demand.

Conclusion The Italian case illustrates the problems and contradictions which arise in a television system run for many years on a public monopoly basis when the number of 'private' television stations multiplies following only the rules of the market and the conditions of competition. The main effect of this multiplication has been a marked increase in television viewing which, in the absence of a corresponding increase in domestic production, has greatly increased the import of programmes. This has had negative results not only on a cultural but also on an economic level.

Another equally important effect which is not always considered, however, is the progressive sliding of the RAI from public service towards a 'commercial' logic in programme planning and thus in buying and production. The situation has deteriorated so much that the problem of the 'quality' offered by television has taken second place. The major objective is production of Italian products to replace the imported programmes. But here too an opportunity is being lost since the ideal answer is thought to be the creation of a domestic television industry capable of mass production, while this represents only a partial solution to the problem. Alongside mass production, it is necessary to be able to develop local productions (regional or provincial) which are 'low cost' and which can circulate throughout the country. The multiplication of the television stations could provide the chance of modifying the traditional image of television. If each television station, as well as being a programme diffusion and viewing point, also became a production centre of programmes which could then circulate to other stations, this would mean a true multiplication of the sources and a widening of the production base of the different kinds of programme (information, entertainment, fiction, etc.). This is also the only way definitively to consolidate the decentralisation of the television system and to take the necessary step towards making television a democratic instrument.

References
1. J. Thibau, 'Pour un service public de l'audio-visuel', *Télécine*, no. 218, May 1977, pp. 7 and 8.
2. R. Rijkens, 'Satellites Present Industry Challenge: Ad Potential Lacks Self-Regulation', *Advertising Age*, 22 October 1979, section 2, pp. 5-7.
3. Editors' Note: Berlusconi purchased Rete 4 in autumn 1984.

KEVIN ROBINS AND FRANK WEBSTER

'The Revolution of the Fixed Wheel': Information, Technology and Social Taylorism

> In the end, it is the static nature of the society that stares us in the face, in spite of all the upheavals. All the talk of change turns out to be changing people so that they fit the modified needs of cold economic processes; and the only revolution turns out to be the revolution of the fixed wheel.
>
> Jeremy Seabrook, *Working-Class Childhood*

Introduction

The lengthy opening section of our conference paper, not reprinted here for reasons of space, reviews salient features of the history of capitalism which are seen as important contexts for the rise of television and the new information technologies. It sketches four elements:

– The extension of corporate capital throughout and between societies, indicating the rise and spread of the large modern corporation domestically and internationally, involving at once a spatial expansion and a deeper penetration into the social fabric.

– The growth of the state and its increased involvement in manifold economic and social activities.

– The post-war boom, leading to the era of consumer capitalism and then recession that has led to a search for escape by means of traditional policies of the 'free market' in union with the imposition of the 'strong state' to see these through.

– Underlying these trends, the spread of what is called, for want of a better term, the rationalisation of control, by which is meant that spheres of life have become more consciously and systematically regulated, more distinctly managed than in the past (when hunger, oppression and the tyranny of nature were major means of control), the better to predict, guide, act upon, and take advantage of people's desires, wants, motives and actions. Our view is that control is more integrated into social relations than previously and that, though this may not take a harsh or even an unpleasant form, it is more extensive than before, such that even 'escape attempts' from the routine and predictable arena of work into hobbies, holidays, fantasies etc. are usually packaged and scripted.

This spread of calculative, methodical and deliberate means of conducting social affairs has been undertaken largely by capital seeking how best to further its interests and an interventionist state usually, if not always, supporting it. Our claim is that, both by market strategy and state plan, the management of life has qualitatively and quantitatively extended far beyond work organisations where it began and is most refined. Information technologies, television included, and the more general issue of information generation, analysis and dissemination, require situating within this development since they are responsive to it as well as essential to the perpetuation of control.

We go on to describe some of the strategies devised in service of these ends: Taylorism, the method of 'scientific management', with its corollaries of work-fragmentation, specialisation, precise measurement of labour, and insistence on the separation of the mental and the practical, with knowledge and planning becoming the prerogative of management; Fordism, applying Taylorism in the direction of bureaucratisation and mechanisation; and Sloanism, applying Taylorism to the customer with its refinement of techniques for selling and advertising and deeper penetration of capital into the domestic sphere. Aided and abetted by the 'visible hand' of managerial capitalism, these strategies, which co-ordinate manufacture, distribution and marketing, together represent major moves towards the systematisation of relations throughout society, towards the extension of Taylorism to Social Taylorism. They contributed to the rise of consumer capitalism which brought with it the increased 'primacy of the private' alongside an increasingly oligopolistic and enriched corporate sector, and paved the way for the arrival of television, a medium significantly influenced by principles of commercial operation and the informational requirements of consumer capitalism.[1]

Television and the Extension of the Market
It is in the context of an extending and encroaching corporate activity which required the best possible regularisation of sales achievable that television should be placed since it was both shaped by and responded to these trends. The spread of Social Taylorism – more monitoring of sales, greater efforts to plan marketing strategies, the intrusion of market values into more social relations – was an important variable influencing television.

In the United States of America in the pre-war years broadcasting was tailored to corporate and especially advertisers' requirements. For the broadcast agencies sponsorship and advertising were the means of survival, while for the corporations they were an important means of disseminating information about their goods. From the start in the USA, first with radio, then with television, broadcasting was designed as an adjunct of corporate capitalism, as a means of further controlling markets by both advertising goods and services and generally extolling the virtues of the market, and these purposes found expression in overall programming and advertising spots themselves.[2]

The history of broadcasting in the USA cannot of course be reduced to a ready formula and it is marked by many programming achievements, but these highlights should not divert us from the fact that from the outset television was developed at once as reliant on corporate capital and as a means of best serving its interests.[3] In America these have not always been entirely synonymous and one must pay homage to the documentary makers, dramatists and journalists who have tried to create openings in the medium. Against this, however, must be set the insistent pressure of corporate capital trying to reach more effectively the populace both to sell its wares and lifestyles appropriate to capitalism. As Martin Meyer puts it, 'Television is undoubtedly the greatest selling medium ever devised,'[4] and at the least this has meant that television has attempted to maximise audiences for programmes the better to appeal to advertisers (which has had serious consequences for content in terms of pandering to escapist, attention-grabbing, action entertainment) while advertising agencies have endeavoured to use television to influence potential customers. To this extent television has to be regarded as a means of extending the reach of capital, as another aspect of its search for control.

Its audiences were from the earliest days scrutinised to test the efficacy of the new communications medium. As early as the 1930s in America the Nielsen National Television Index was adopted as a measure of the TV audience, and so complex was this surveillance that Nielsen was told by IBM that the data gathered by his Audimeter recording equipment was 'the most complicated process using IBM equipment in private industry anywhere in the world'.[5] From the television companies' point of view this careful measurement of programme preferences was a way of maximising business standing (the bigger the audience, the higher was advertising revenue), but it signified much more than an economic process. By the time television had arrived the advertising industry in the USA had markedly advanced. In particular it had caught up with the need for 'systematised information',[6] for more precise feedback from its campaigns and more exact data on those with whom it intended to 'communicate', and it was this that the Nielsen ratings began to supply. Advertising wanted television not simply as a means of disseminating information, but also as an efficient and effective way of transmitting messages to targeted audiences. This called for monitoring who watched what and when so that copywriters' materials could be more carefully honed. As a complement to the arrival of this greater precision, advertising was refining its methods of 'motivation research' to enable them better to persuade consumers of the virtues of their products.

In recent decades corporate users of television have become much more sophisticated. In the early days televised advertising could only adopt a scatter-gun approach and Nielsen could supply only general information, scarcely touching upon factors such as conditions of viewing, location and class of audiences. Modern advertising, with its array of researchers and step-by-step campaigns, has moved way ahead of its forerunners. Television has nicely complemented the advertisers' advances in precision. In Britain today BARB (Broadcasters' Audience Research Board) issues every week two substantial books crammed with statistical data about time and duration of TV viewing, number and characteristics of people watching and responses to programming. It is this sort of precision that allowed London Weekend Television to take a half-page advertisement in the *Observer* newspaper on 5 September 1982 to recommend the new Channel 4 to potential buyers of time. The copy commended Channel 4 as 'the most cost-effective way to advertise to the most highly specific audiences with by far the most exciting and persuasive selling medium'. The new channel could offer this because its 'programmes will tend towards very specific audiences' (careful dissemination of information) and because 'we closely monitor 12 sub-demographic groups of viewers' and 'can guarantee to reach at least 65 per cent of any sub-demographic group you request' (careful monitoring of information).

Private versus Public Television
If this thesis is accepted – television is as it is not just because it is arranged on commercial lines but also because it grew at a time and as a means of furthering the consolidation of corporate control throughout society – current debates about television now and in the future take on a rather different complexion. What needs now to be examined is not simply the potential of new technologies for this, that or the other 'new' use, but the weight of the historical legacy of Social Taylorism for continuing *established* modes.

As a bulwark against the intrusion of market priorities, public service television has real achievements to its name (set against the 'cultural wasteland'[7] of American network television, the BBC has much to be proud of), though these are too readily seen simply as results of its independence from market funding. This autonomy is important and the recurrent financial crises of the BBC, which mean it is compelled to use considerable amounts of imported programming that are cheap while producing soaps, quizzes and the like that gain large enough audiences to justify licence fee submissions,[8] highlight difficulties of organising television on alternative principles in a society otherwise thoroughly defined in market terms. But public service television has also be be formulated at a distance from the impulse of capital to control, to create in customers desires for goods and the lifestyle of consumerism. In our view the fact that the BBC has remained independent of this effort to control market outlets has meant that opportunities for alternative programming (for education, for minorities, for serious drama, etc.) have been retained.

Similarly commercial television, launched in Britain in the mid-50s on American lines following an intensive lobby, has from the outset been influenced by this public service ethos which has instilled in it values, reflected in its charter and its programming, somewhat at variance with the goals of capital.[9]

The thing British commercial television has most in common with the American system and from which its programming and financial arrangements stem is its role as a means of extending the mechanisms by which corporate capital operates. At a minimal level this has meant that to date its main purpose has been delivery of large audiences to advertisers. More generally, commercial television was formed and has developed in accord with consumer capitalism, aiding in the perpetuation of attitudes appropriate to a market system which requires an insatiable appetite for goods and services that are for personal consumption. This was recognised by some supporters of commercial television from the outset:

> Many of its advocates were perceptive enough to understand that the subtle and long-term impact of commercial television would reinforce the political results of the vast expansion of hire-purchase, government subsidised loans for home ownership, the drive to get low income groups to purchase shares of corporate stocks, and the pervasive growth of advertising inspired by motivational research. They had observed and benefited from American experience in selling 'people's capitalism' in a welfare state.[10]

The introduction of commercial television into Britain in the mid-50s can be seen as at one with numerous changes (occupational changes, sectoral shifts, patterns of home ownership, the availability of credit facilities, new forms of leisure, etc.) which, taken together, marked an important shift in the way of life. Richard Hoggart's remarkable *The Uses of Literacy*, published in 1957, detailed ways in which working-class attitudes and beliefs – their 'stock of moral capital'[11] – that he had known as a boy in the 30s were coming up against the values of an encroaching consumer society. What he described was not the world of work which had long since begun rationalisation on lines appropriate to capital, but the extension of market practices and values into spheres beyond work. It was here, in what he termed the 'progressivism of things', in the ideology that it was up to each individual to seize as much for himself as possible, and in the raucous celebration of novelty, escape and excitement, that Hoggart delineated changes in society. The innovations of the time, the new gadgets and modes of leisure, were responding to felt needs of hitherto deprived people and the 'popular publicists' in magazines and newspapers knowingly appealed to these sentiments. However, these appeals were also and primarily a means of furthering the requirements of capital by extending market principles into everyday life. These involved 'the turning over of so many areas of human experience to the marketplace. . . . Intangible moral, spiritual, human qualities . . . transformed into commodities that can be bought and sold'.[12]

Television was in part an expression of this change and, when commercial television appeared, an important means of mediating consumerist ethics between corporate producers and the public. Because it signified the development of a consumer capitalism which required greater control over the public – more 'communication' with them, more 'education' of them about 'modern' ways of living – we ought not to be surprised at the content of commercial television. It is surely only to be expected that it would present dramas that would parade the lifestyles of the West and, being exciting and entertaining, seek the widespread appeal that would appease the advertisers intent on projecting more specific messages into the living rooms of the masses. Indeed, what is surprising, given that consumer capitalism was then enjoying a long boom and making marked inroads into social life, is the survival of a public service ethic in any broadcasting system, not least its shadowy presence in British commercial television itself.

The BBC
We take public service broadcasting to be a type institutionally set apart from outside pressures of political, business and even audience demands in day-to-day functioning, not pressed by the imperatives of commercial operation and made available to and produced for the benefit of the community at large rather than for those who can afford to pay either for subscription or sponsorship. It is committed to providing high-quality and comprehensive services to viewers regarded as composed of diverse minorities which are to be catered for without endangering the provision of programming – news, current affairs, drama, documentary – aimed at the whole audience. This is of

course an ideal type, though the BBC, while it has interpreted 'public service' with particular emphases over the years, has approximated to it.

Given our argument that television should be understood as part of the history of a twentieth-century capitalism which has moved through Taylorism at work to Social Taylorism as it has evolved from productive to consumer capitalism, then the prospects for public service television must be poor. Capital has always sought to control its activities and consumer capitalism represents a stage of development in which market values and practices are more pervasive than hitherto. Television in this system is a privileged means of reaching consumers and, as such, unlikely to be allowed to operate on non-market principles.

But if this is so, how does one account for the survival of the BBC? How is such an important exemption to be explained? We shall argue that the ethics of consumer capitalism do endanger many public service features of our society, broadcasting included, but first we review the origins of the BBC that we might better comprehend its contemporary position. This takes us to another major feature of the 20th century, the extension of the state.

To account for the continuity of public service broadcasting in Britain one has to appreciate that the BBC was formed in the early 20s in particular circumstances. Above all, there was a peculiar unity of radicals and conservatives which allowed ready acceptance that the BBC be formed as a state institution aloof from the interests of private capital. As A. J. P. Taylor has observed, 'Conservatives liked authority; Labour disliked private enterprise,'[13] and this combination on the one hand led to a revolt against the indiscipline and tawdriness of an American system, and on the other to a willingness to endorse the Crawford Committee's recommendation that 'the broadcasting service should be conducted by a public corporation acting as Trustee for the national interest, and that its status and duties should correspond with those of a public service'.[14]

In this way the BBC was 'born in Britain as an instrument of parliament, as a kind of embassy of the national culture within the nation',[15] granted a monopoly over broadcasting and funded from a tax on wireless – later television – receivers (the licence fee). The formation of the BBC by parliament and its aloofness from commercial interests had important consequences. It allowed an emphasis, explicitly called for by the legislators, on broadcasting as a means of education as well as entertainment, and over the years this has been consolidated and expressed in much BBC output from current affairs and news through to minority programmes of music, drama and hobbies. The BBC, as a parliamentary creation, has been influenced in its practices and assumptions by the parliamentary model.[16] This has found expression in a presentation of political issues that on the whole has limited itself to the bounds of established party politics[17] with occasional extensions in drama and documentary, but at the least it aided the treatment of politics in a serious and considered manner (in contrast to commercial systems where politics has been relegated in favour of non-controversial entertainment) while differences between political parties have provided some space within which the BBC could function.[18]

The Reithian legacy, the credibility achieved during the Second World War and its uncontested monopoly for some 30 years, were important factors in rooting the public service ethic. Moreover, there was the additional factor that the BBC, withstanding government interference, notably in 1926, has remained genuinely distanced from politics, being state-linked in contrast to state-directed systems where broadcasting has commonly been regarded as an instrument of government.[19]

Krishan Kumar has described the BBC's separation from commercial and political controls as 'holding the middle ground'. It has undoubtedly contributed to the 'quite unusual cultural importance that attaches to the BBC in Britain', which has in turn stimulated the entry into broadcasting of many talented persons instilled with a public service outlook and sceptical of the 'moving wallpaper' mode dominant in the USA: 'State and commerce: around one or other of these poles are gathered the vast majority of the broadcasting systems of the world,' but the 'BBC has, in certain important ways, been able to resist these two forms of identification'[20] and has managed to create a distinct *raison d'être*, institutional flavour and pattern of behaviour.[21]

If the BBC's public service role was to set it apart from commercial impulses it was not aloof from outside pressures. It could not be so since it was part of a society in which commercial interests were and are a powerful lobby, at the same time as it was an institution created by the state and therefore susceptible to pressures that could be brought to bear by and on the state. Further, the recruitment of BBC personnel has been from a certain social type (Oxbridge, arts graduates) which has brought with it values and orientations that are scarcely representative of the public at large. The BBC's evolution has been accordingly influenced by these pressures and their priorities which, while varying in effect, have led the BBC from the outset to function generally as a vehicle for orthodoxy.

However, this is not to say that the BBC is some sort of conduit for the powerful. It has a distinctive autonomy from business and politics which has been established over the years,[22] though features of its independence have changed. In its early days under Reith it was separate from government officials but it was an autocratically run organisation with firmly elitist orientations. Public service then was interpreted as transmitting materials that were considered worthwhile by custodians of an outdated moralism. In the 60s circumstances allowed public service to be interpreted in quite a daring and even at times radical and irreverent manner while the ideals of institutional independence and education remained. Under Sir Hugh Greene as Director General, at a time when the economy was booming, TV ownership increasing and providing the BBC with an annual increment from licence fees, when the political climate was tolerant and relaxed, and when commercial television had been admonished by the Pilkington committee, public service was liable to be perceived as including challenging, innovative programming that could awake audiences to disturbing experiences.[23]

The autonomy that Greene fought for has steadily lost ground to two forces that have gained in significance and ambition: corporate capital with eyes on the BBC as a means of at least projecting business in favourable terms and even allowing the entry of commercial enterprises, and the state itself which, led by a determined government, has come in recent years aggressively to support capital. Together these forces threaten the public service ethos of the BBC.

The State in Capitalist Society

We have reviewed the growth of consumer capitalism and its search for avenues of control and additional markets as one aspect of this threat to public service television. The state's role is altogether more complex and ambiguous because it responds to, functions for and was developed by numerous, often contentious, forces.[24] But if we draw attention to the uneven record of the state we would emphasise that, originating and operating in an unequal society, it has never been the case that the state has been an 'honest broker' between conflicting partners. It has persistently favoured the more powerful and this is evidenced in the bulk of practical policies and suggested in the social backgrounds and connections of leading state personnel.

Moreover, an overriding aim of the state has been to achieve order and this even to the extent that change itself has had to be managed in an orderly fashion. Whether it has been state intervention to rationalise chaotic economic performance by, for example, encouraging mergers between companies unnecessarily competing, or to take over industries with unattractive prospects for return on equity, most state activity can be regarded as seeking stability. A requisite of this is that the populace is better known and informed as the state deems appropriate. It is a major feature of the modern state that it accumulates information about people (social security records, residency, educational performance, criminal records, car licences, etc.), supervises a great deal of everyday life (in schools, health

44

services and much economic organisation) and disseminates large amounts of information to and about the public that social relations might be more effectively managed.[25] This extension of surveillance and information provision can be regarded as another expression of the rationalisation, the systematisation, of social control we earlier described as Social Taylorism: it is an example of the observation and recording of the citizenry's activities and habits so that they might be better managed materially (for example, in housing, in transport schemes) and ideologically (the control of information by the state has assumed more importance in recent years).

These developments are not all negative. Undoubtedly the growth of the state has meant that areas of people's autonomous activity have been restricted, but the process of more systematic gathering of data about social life has its positive dimensions (for example, information on social deprivation can lead to awareness of and thereby help remedy suffering that might otherwise remain unknown). Nonetheless, we refuse to endorse the view that this state surveillance is a neutral activity for two reasons. The first is that, as we have argued, the state has developed in an unequal society and to this extent the surveillance it practises is influenced by the realities of power; where information is gathered, on whom and in what circumstances, depends very much on whose interests its agencies pursue and who has greatest influence on these agencies. The second is that the history of the 20th century has been one in which state expansion has paralleled the rise of corporate capitalism which has in turn exercised influence on the state's efforts to regularise life. In recent years this has attained a heightened degree through interest groups, lobbyists, parliamentary representation and party political funding,[26] but the pressures of corporate capital on the state need not be so direct as to have, for example, company chairmen sitting on cabinet committees, still less instructing civil servants whom to observe. It is rather that the state endorses the world view of capital because, without a healthy market economy, the state itself is in crisis, and because leading actors on both sides have similar family and educational backgrounds that socialise them into orthodox opinions.

The state's supervision and monitoring of social relations – which itself has been an important stimulant for the development of information technologies such as computer networks – has entailed at once an intrusion into the everyday lives of people (one can scarcely escape the tax system, health services, educational records) and a centralisation of power in that the fruits of surveillance are gathered in by integrated, and increasingly integrating, state agencies. Here are found roots of the modern *panopticon* – a society in which people are seen and observed but are unable to communicate one with another – a useful metaphor for comprehending social relations in the late 20th century where state agencies and corporate capital are primary powers.

This claim accords with our earlier characterisation of consumer capitalism as heightening the privatisation of life alongside assisting the centralisation of corporate organisations. However, we would distinguish these two dimensions of Social Taylorism. Consumer capitalism has extended its reach into personal life to control more effectively in order that the marketing of its goods and services might be facilitated. The state, however, has been more ambiguous in effect and, lacking the single-mindedness of capital, has functioned chiefly as its complement rather than as a spearhead for consumerism. The state's responsibilities in policing, education, etc., while they require the gathering-in of information on people so that they might be better controlled, put the goal of stability of social arrangements before that of encouraging the sale of products. To this extent the state's Social Taylorism is real but separable from capital's practices.

Crisis
The past decade has brought the relationships between the state and capital closer. In response to depression, capital has tried to find better means of selling that it might escape the doldrums, while the state has come more aggressively to implement policies that would assist in the recuperation of a market economy. A result has been that the state has developed plans and practices that more effectively control the populace so that capital accumulation might be invigorated. The policies are encapsulated in the slogan 'strong state, free market' and illustrated in the state's operationalisation of Social Taylorism at a quite intense level so that the market is better able to function.

This is the context in which to place any discussion of contemporary television and information technologies. Nowadays, when 'strong state, free market' principles form the backcloth to a host of new technologies, their introduction to further the Social Taylorism sought by consumer capitalism and the state's efforts to assist this by itself vigorously practising Social Taylorism should be acknowledged. It is a context within which public service institutions are threatened since they may hinder attempts to control the populace for capital's purposes and are in themselves an anathema to market organisation.

Information Technologies and Recession
The fact that numerous forms of information technology (IT) have appeared recently is pertinent because Social Taylorism cannot be effected without sophisticated technologies that allow information to be amassed, analysed and acted upon. The attempted resolution to the crises of recent years has been an intensification of Social Taylorism and to this end a spate of new information technologies has

found application in corporations and the state. Part of this process has been the provision of information and information technologies that are marketable and both practices – use of IT to further Social Taylorism and production of IT on market criteria – are complementary. Let us consider some of these developments.

Neo-Fordism

Recently it has become possible to discern an important innovation in corporate structuring, a shift from mass production located in a centralised plant towards production, often by batch, in decentralised factories and offices which remain closely monitored from headquarters where a few employees oversee advanced information technologies. This is a stage beyond the Fordist variant of Taylorised work whereby machinery is designed to replace the skills/knowledge of workers; the neo-Fordist factory is a continuation of Taylorism in that it uses technologies as repositories of knowledge of production, but it allows the large, usually trans-national corporation to locate production in small units in geographically diverse sites. It moves beyond Taylorism of the labour process in that it also requires management's gathering-in of a great deal more information (proximity to markets, transport facilities and costs, labour characteristics, relations between separate plants, etc.) that location and relocation may most carefully be appraised. E. Bradley Jones, president of Republic Steel, drew attention to this phenomenon in 1981 when he described the emergence of 'geo-economics' as 'a way of saying that the trading nations of the world are stepping up their intermingling of resources, manpower, technology and capital', continuing to observe that, with the blurring of national boundaries, two elements in particular, capital and information, have been criss-crossing the globe 'with growing ease and speed'. As an example of this, which without IT would be unthinkable, he cited Ford's Escort car which is assembled in three countries from parts made in nine.[27]

Complementing these developments is the provision of information services, mostly financial but including geological, social and political, to serve corporate goals. Always supplied on the market basis of ability to pay, these services from the likes of Datastream and Reuters are beyond the pocket of ordinary citizens though indispensable to the wealthy corporations whose operations traverse the globe.[28]

Large corporations, adopting high technology, are shifting their plants to disparate locations at the same time as they establish smaller units of production, and this is not merely a strategy for efficiency. It is also a strategy of control, since employees are isolated from similar groups and often in regions (Scotland, the Far East, Southern Ireland) only too glad to find work.

47

Recent Corporate Strategies to Improve Control

A cognate aspect of this Taylorist work organisation that has recently enjoyed a rapid expansion due to the availability of technologies has been a management emphasis on 'better communications' with employees. Constantly presented as 'information', the array of video programmes from the boardroom are in truth instances of efforts to better control by persuading workers of the propriety of management decisions. While some companies have in-house facilities for video production, many others employ specialist companies to do the job for them, thus ensuring professional productions, expert presentation and technique which enhances the credibility of a medium already well in advance of other forms. These shows – which present new managerial staff, provide a monthly report on company performance or instruct workers on production targets, and which often use full-time actors and expert script writers – are an instance of a more sustained attempt by managements to increase their effectiveness. They seek to tighten their control over workforces for whom special messages are designed to meet, and where necessary overcome, any apprehensions that might present obstacles to management priorities. Behind them lie specialist communications agencies whose expertise may be drawn upon to present capital's arguments in the best possible way both within – and increasingly without – the company.

Company uses of new technologies and techniques of 'communication' go further than this, reaching into that most pervasive of all media, the television. We have already stressed television's close connection with the development of consumer capitalism as advertising outlet and general educator in modern ways of living, but this has been thought to be inadequate and recently managements have moved to use the visual media to present their case more effectively.

Michael Barratt, one-time television anchor-man and now a consultant specialising in sponsored film, commends video as an effective means of transmitting corporate images. Pointing out the use of video for 'keeping workforces up to date about new developments', Barratt also identifies schools as outlets for corporate propaganda: 'The majority of schools now use videotape machines and offer a potential captive audience of millions of impressionable young children, many of whom will soon have considerable spending power and who already influence their parents' spending.' He goes on to suggest that, with 25 per cent of homes now having videocassette recorders, corporations might consider special promotions (for instance, 'watch and wipe' offers) of sponsored films within which products are packaged.

48

Identifying the 'more or less unrecognised opportunities offered by broadcast TV and the cinema', Barratt sees no reason why sponsored films in general should fail to achieve television exposure:

> The main requirements would seem to be a very high standard of work, a suitable subject, a small amount of product 'sell' and fulfilment of union requirements regarding payment of crew and artists. The same criteria are applicable to the cinema, which is desperately short of good films to support the main feature. The extra exposure gained on either TV or in the cinema makes even the most expensive sponsored film relatively cheap. . . . Demand for broadcast-standard material will clearly accelerate with the establishment of cable and satellite TV, and this demand will be multiplied by television developments abroad.[29]

Barratt's final sentence reminds us that, if his strategy is to be successful, television services will need to be either set up on commercial principles and therefore eager to adopt materials that contribute to revenue or, if 'public services', so starved of funds that they will be willing to turn to sponsors for assistance in programme provision. This is by no means unlikely to come about in Britain, and indeed in the USA we have a portent for the future where 'public service' broadcasting is dependent on the largesse of large-scale corporate capital.[30]

Public relations in Britain is booming in spite of the recession. Corporations pay the requisite fees because public-relations firms can 'offer a very sophisticated service based on analysis, research and planning which can be compared with that of the best management and chartered accountancy consultancies'.[31] They provide speaker training, lobbying, media relations, advertising advice, publicity-seeking extravaganzas – a battery of ways of better presenting the corporation's ideology and image. It is a means of more effectively plotting capital's future by assuring that information and avenues for transmission of information are carefully managed, rehearsed and massaged to the advantage of business.[32]

Sir Michael Edwardes, one-time head of British Leyland and chairman of ICL, is well aware of the need for 'good communications'. BL uses video for in-house communications with the workforce, but Sir Michael long since foresaw a need for effective management to go further, to reach out to the wider society that opinion might be mustered in favour of boards of directors. Convinced that 'communications are becoming more complex and more efficient, for their technology is becoming unlimited in its scope', he believes that 'in ten years' time perhaps most major companies will be taking the battle outside.' Professional managers cannot leave this to chance;

their spokespeople cannot be left in the hands of the broadcasters without preparation. The media must be used so that management can present to the wider public their messages at their most persuasive. To this end BL 'arranged for some fifty executives to have television and radio training'.[33] It is indeed common for senior management of large corporations to undergo media training since it is increasingly part of their responsibilities for furthering company interests to handle information dissemination.

The grooming of management representatives is by no means the only way in which capital can present itself on television. More assured access, if less credible, is by the established practice of buying time. In the UK in 1982 total advertising revenue was £3.1 billion of which 30 per cent went on television, a gain of 15 per cent on 1981.[34] Most of this went on orthodox commercials for consumer products which are illustrative of the Social Taylorism we described earlier, but corporations now buy time on television (and media generally) to sell directly themselves (corporate advertising) and to recommend policies of which they approve (advocacy advertising). These forms of puffery are only a small part of total expenditure, but it need scarcely be said that they are way beyond the purse of most other groups in society. Always they convey an image of social responsibility, patriotism, cool-headedness, warmth and sensibility combined with tough reasoning.[35]

Another means of 'communicating' with the public used by corporations is sponsorship. As Texaco, an active sponsor of sports and the arts in Britain, recently put it: 'We want to associate ourselves with things British . . . and we're burrowing down into the social infrastructure because we'll be here a long time.'[36] Of course, sponsorship that receives extensive media coverage (especially television) is what companies are most after since it is important that they are in the public eye, so we are becoming increasingly familiar with the indirect advertising that comes from events paid for by the likes of Rothmans, Sun Alliance, Sony, Embassy and Benson and Hedges.[37] Sponsorship is a part of modern management's judgment of how best to secure their company's future. Significantly many feel that traditional advertising is insufficient, that the corporation's title and logo ought to be 'burrowed down' into the society by association with exhibitions in art galleries and museums, athletics meetings and charitable events. In these ways 'scientific management' plans to reach beyond the individual consumer into the wide arena of culture, leisure and even education.

Saatchi and Saatchi
In the light of the aforesaid the genesis of Saatchi and Saatchi deserves particular comment. This company is the largest advertising

50

agency in Britain and the eighth largest in the world with 65 offices in 38 countries. It is youthful, aggressive and far-sighted, its success relying heavily on the abilities of its directors to pioneer the selling strategies required by contemporary capitalism.

Saatchi and Saatchi relies on most thorough research before undertaking a 'campaign' (military metaphors litter its 'review of operations'): it 'is continually examining results of research to bring us closer to the heart of what makes consumers tick – their wants, needs, desires, aspirations'. When 'probed deeply', people are found to buy goods for 'a complex mixture of rational and emotional factors'[38] though the latter outweigh reason and cover those specialities of copywriters – ideas of worth, status, fashion and security.

There is nothing special about Saatchi and Saatchi carefully surveying the public that it might better persuade them to purchase a client's goods. What is different, however, is the agency's recognition that trans-national capital, the leading edge of advanced capitalism, requires special techniques of Social Taylorism since it is the force of the future and a 'need for pan-regional and world marketing is emerging at the heart of business strategy'. Saatchi and Saatchi accordingly lists among its clients in three or more countries a roll call of leading multi-national corporations which include Avis, Johnson and Johnson, Procter and Gamble, Timex, Kodak, Max Factor, IBM, Nestlé and Pepsico.

Saatchi and Saatchi concludes that 'research will be conducted to look for market similarities between countries, not to seek out differences', that *world marketing* will require advertisers to find a formula for commercials 'so deep in its appeal that it can transcend national borders previously thought inviolate'. Though global, this operation demands more exact surveying of consumers, a capacity to recognise that 'there are probably more social differences between Midtown Manhattan and the Bronx, two sectors of the same city, than between Midtown Manhattan and the 7th *Arrondissement* of Paris'. What will be required is 'analysis of all these demographic, cultural and media trends' so as to allow 'manufacturers to define market expansion timetables. Essentially, marketers will be tracking trends which indicate when a region is ready for attack'. 'Armed with this information, the most modern marketers are achieving a new perspective on world markets. From the high ground, they can survey the world battlefield for their brands, observe the deployment of their forces, and plan their international advertising and marketing in a coherent and logical way'.

Television is axiomatic to Saatchi and Saatchi's examination of 'world marketing'. On the one hand it helps create the 'cultural convergence' which provides for universal recognition of products: 'The worldwide proliferation of the Marlboro brand would not have

51

been possible without TV and motion-picture education about the virile rugged character of the American West and the American cowboy – helped by increasing colour TV penetration in all countries'. On the other hand a spate of new television technologies both consolidates and extends the potential of the medium by allowing more carefully directed imaging: '"Media fragmentation" has become a byword for commentators describing the new structure of the media world. This will intensify the rifle rather than the shot-gun approach to planning advertising campaigns. Advertisers will face difficult dilemmas in determining how to effectively deliver their messages, and advertising agencies will need every ounce of their specialised knowledge and expertise to capitalise on the rapid expansion of media delivery methods'. It might be a challenge, but Saatchi and Saatchi sees a great deal of promise in cable as an advertising medium which can 'attract audiences through selective programming aimed at more clearly defined groups than the mass audiences of the major networks. Multi-national advertisers with a specific target audience in each country will be able to reach their target segment through a cable channel concentrating on their specific interest'.

Saatchi and Saatchi's emphasis on the trans-national corporation as its favoured target (the 'major multi-nationals' that spend $125 billion per annum on advertising[39]) is in line with ongoing trends: the world economy is dominated by mega-corporations and the advertising agencies (themselves large corporations) will increasingly be called upon to help assure their markets by better analysis of potential outlets and designing and implementing campaigns aimed at convincing people to purchase their goods and services. But Saatchi and Saatchi is of itself an indicator of an important social trend in that it is an updated version of Taylorism. Advertisers' strategies and actions would have been appreciated by the founder of scientific management, and would have been applauded as efforts to better control by systematic scrutiny and supervision of a company's operations. At the core of this task is information, its gathering-in, analysis and careful dissemination; Saatchi and Saatchi knows that 'knowledge has value, and there is greater "value-added" during periods of turmoil and change (as now) in the business world',[40] and it proclaims its function as use of this knowledge to control potential customers in ways advantageous to capital.

Advertising and Politics
Prior to discussing the further implications that these developments have for television and associated information technologies, there is another feature of the Saatchi and Saatchi operation which signifies both a general decline of the 'public sphere' in our society and its replacement by the values of the market, and reveals much about

political relations in recent years. We refer to the advertising agency's forays into the political arena during the last two elections in Britain.

While it is the case that many managers are taking steps to project a favourable image and even advocating particular policies in the media, on the whole they have steered clear of overt political activity. This is not to say that they have not been intensely interested in political decisions, have not lobbied to achieve appropriate legislation, and systematically supported the Conservative Party in Britain. Nevertheless, corporations have usually been keen to distinguish politics from economics. What Saatchi and Saatchi have been doing is bridging that gap in an important respect by applying expertise gained in selling products to selling politicians. This signifies something important about the conduct of political life in contemporary Britain: Saatchi and Saatchi is an index of the way in which politics has been changing to become a matter of 'selling' ideas and 'delivering up' votes; a sign that 'scientific management' has entered into politics as market values have permeated deeper into social relations.

Saatchi and Saatchi's handling of the Conservative Party campaigns in 1979 and 1983 is well known – the careful calculation of people's attitudes, the targeting of posters, TV slots and press advertisements to best exploit them, advice on party political broadcasts, slick, professionally produced messages – as is its complement in the form of Gordon Reece who entered Conservative Central Office after a successful career in journalism and commercial television to package Margaret Thatcher. Notable results were a toned-down, huskier voice, a 'softer' face and a new hairstyle and, above all, a shift towards manipulating the media to best transmit a favourable image rather than to engage in serious political debate.

Television is a central constituent of this packaging of politics and the entry of advertising experts into elections has meant that its role has been defined increasingly as a means of projecting a party, policy or spokesperson in terms of image rather than one which is a locus of debate, information and analysis that could enlighten the viewer. Though Barry Day of McCann-Ericson has dated 1970 as the origin of the use in British politics of 'established techniques of commercial marketing',[41] 1979 marked a heightened intensity of the advertising mentality which used television as a conduit for carefully arranged 'events', for 'photo-opportunities' such as factory visits, shopping-mall tours and civic receptions that assured plenty of pictures, plenty of 'exposure', but little in the way of informed political debate. We regard this as the management of political life by people who find little difficulty in transferring their expertise to politics. They take with them an attitude of mind which is concerned not with issues, principles and argumentation, but with image projection, avoidance of serious, sustained and unsettling discussion, an enthusiasm for winning votes on slogans, imagery and catch-phrases.

Consequences for Television

What does this growth of 'scientific management' mean for television? One could conclude that these examples of managers searching for greater control within their organisations and in the wider society are merely instances of the medium being used in particular ways and that a vigilant service could guard against their becoming a tool for fulfilling corporate plans. Similarly, one could argue that advertising agencies acting on behalf of manufacturers or political parties merely misuse television. The problem with this view is that it underestimates the intimacy of the connections that television has with these developments. For instance, television is often established on market principles and generally is dependent on corporations for financial survival. As such it is likely that television companies will be predisposed to look favourably on people or institutions on whom they rely for revenue and with whom they share the same mode of organisation. If for some reason – professional ethics or parliamentary legislation – they do not accord with such views, the dependency can be of decisive significance. We are, of course, referring to the limits placed upon television by its establishment on commercial principles and/or dependency upon corporate sponsorship.

Kenneth Gill, Saatchi and Saatchi chairman, observed in his annual statement of 1983 that 'UK advertising industry prospects generally are enhanced by the development of new media in the form of Channel 4, TV-am, as well as cable, satellite, video, etc.', and in so doing suggested restrictions that will be placed on television dependent on revenue from this source.[42] We note that Mr Gill's future has no role for public service television since by definition this has little or no role for advertisers. For services that are to be reliant on advertising and/or sponsorship, the restrictions will be either an insistence on audiences large enough to command adequate advertising payments (size varying with the quality of market prospects) and/or programming which is generally favourable to free enterprise.

These are not, of course, uniform pressures and some space can be found for independent programming. In addition, as in the case of Channel 4, the legacy of public service is still of significance in the evolution of a service which, in the words of the then Home Secretary William Whitelaw, was to have 'a distinctive character of its own'.[43] Nevertheless, that Channel 4, on the eve of its first anniversary, was making desperate attempts to increase audience ratings by offering more entertainment in order to draw in advertising revenue is evidence of the limits imposed on television operating on commercial principles. Almost from the outset Channel 4 has been under pressure from the major commercial television companies to make itself more popular so that they would not have to subsidise its operation.[44]

Much the same story has been repeated during TV-am's short history where a dream of an 'electronic newspaper' woke to the reality that audiences of several hundred thousand were inadequate to satiate the advertisers who were to fund the new station. TV-am has lurched from crisis to crisis, but the drift and outcome are unmistakable: more programming that is 'young and popular', the sort that is undemanding 'junk-food' information, which can attract audiences in excess of a million. Roland Rat and associated gimmicks from TV-am are indicative of the type of 'information' to be expected from television whose primary purpose is the delivery of audiences to marketers.

Commercial television is not only something that has been established to assist Social Taylorism by creating opportunities for advertisers nor just a medium being used increasingly for public relations. It is necessary to appreciate that the panoply of new technologies which has appeared is an expression of values and priorities. Cable, video, satellite television, etc. are being pioneered for the home on market principles and as such the technologies have been shaped by these criteria. It is not to ask for much effort of imagination that we recognise that existent technologies are social products, that there was no immanent logic which led to the manufacture of videodiscs and the like, but rather that commercial principles were the guiding light. It is significant that all the new technologies for the domestic market are enhancements of the television which has been an outstanding commercial success. These information technologies are manifestations of a process which has examined characteristics of television purchase and viewing and decided that a sound commercial bet is more of the same, hence TV games, videocassettes and the rest. Market outlooks are present in their planning, production and sales and a consequence is the consolidation of the trend towards privatisation of life, the retreat into the home, that television has done much to encourage. As this occurs the isolated consumer is further subject to the panopticon of centralised, corporate capital which monitors patterns of behaviour and puts out saleable information and more of the same technologies.

Recent years have been ones of boom in the sale of consumer durables since most people fortunate enough to remain in employment have enjoyed wage increases above the rate of inflation simultaneous with a 40 per cent decline in the relative price of household goods over the past two decades.[45] Programmers have built on this boom in hardware to offer a familiar type of content: sex, sport and movies constitute the bulk of shows for video and cable and will, no doubt, in the case of satellite television, and all are results of diligent research on customer desires and susceptibilities so that they can be assured commercial success.

It is for these reasons – that numerous new television services are being founded on principles which make them subservient to the needs of advertisers and sponsors; that information technologies for the home have been manufactured as forms of enhanced television on market criteria which consolidate a privatised way of life; that the programming for these services is produced as a commodity to achieve maximum return – that the growth in intensity of 'scientific management' cannot be dismissed as merely an abuse of media. While it is the case that corporate groups have improved their capabilities when using the means of communications, these too have developed as part of capital itself, as part of the Social Taylorism that corporations have long been practising and whether it is as deliverers of audiences to advertisers, provision of more television-type durables or still more entertainment programming, it is more difficult than might first appear to separate television from the general trend of increasing corporate control of social relations.

Thatcherism
With this, thoughts return to the BBC since it is so evidently organised on different lines from commercial systems. It may be that corporations try to present themselves effectively on the BBC by grooming, public relations and various forms of sponsorship, but the institution does not lend itself to the dependency of other media (though, because of public service clauses, the ITN and commercial television's current affairs and some drama programmes are similar to those of the BBC).

However, in recent years circumstances have weakened the role of public service broadcasting. One of these has been the steady march of consumer capitalism itself and its provision of goods and services that undermine the BBC. As video, cable and more commercial programming comes available, there is the challenge to the BBC from loss of audiences which makes it harder to justify the revenue from the licence fee for a national service. Another challenge has come from the polity where forces have marshalled with a vehement commitment to restoring the health of capital by reducing public expenditures and extending market principles to as many public services as is feasible.

We are referring here to the advent and effects of Thatcherism and its practices of 'strong state, free market'.[46] We have argued that the state has long been involved in Social Taylorism in that observation, analysis and planning of social life has been a major feature of its extension. The reasons for this were diverse, though the results – a more monitored populace watched over by more centralised state agencies – were similar. More recently this Social Taylorism has taken on a special ferocity and has been impelled by government's enthusiasm to bolster corporate interests.

Information and information technologies have been at the core of these policies – as long ago as 1979 the Conservative Party announced that 'information is the commanding height of tomorrow's economy'[47] – which include:

(a) Increased monitoring of the public, notably via police forces equipped with computer networks;[48]

(b) The privatisation of public services, which means that information will be generated and made available only if commercially justified. British Telecom is the axis of this policy, and widely predicted consequences of its privatisation are that some areas – the countryside, poorer parts of towns – are likely to receive inferior services. Similar expectations are held about the provision of cable on commercial principles;[49]

(c) Reductions in public expenditure ranging from health and education to government information services such that not only do standards decline, but services are reshaped to suit the more politically approved (for example, in education the shift of resources to science, technology and vocational courses at the behest of 'industry' to the detriment of arts and social sciences is well known). In these circumstances some information is less regularly supplied to the public (for instance, the Central Statistical Office provides information on take-up of means-tested benefits less frequently than formerly), some areas of investigation are reduced in scope (for example, social science research has both been cut and redirected to favour 'industry'), public libraries have been subject to massive expenditure constraints,[50] and charges for information from public sources are set at rates that the market can command which inevitably reduces access;

(d) Increased manipulation of information and of media organisations evidenced in various examples of restrictions of access to information held by the state, dissemination of what can only be described as disinformation and the 'Saatchi and Saatchi approach' to image handling, a startling illustration of which has been the management of media over defence before and after the Falklands War.[51]

Though it has been camouflaged by rhetoric, there is little secret about the government strategy which has precipitated these policies. Since the mid-70s there has been a remarkably coherent policy by which British industry would restructure and re-equip with new technology and market forces would be given free rein. To facilitate this, it has been necessary to adopt a policy of 'cuts with control' whereby public funding in key areas was reduced while being expanded in disciplinary spheres such as the police.

Consequences of this 'drift toward authoritarianism' [52] that corporate capital might emerge from recession include two of special importance. The first is that the state's surveillance capabilities are significantly increased – and we can see this in a host of cases from police information networks through to legislation for stronger police powers which specifically allow them access to information on computer systems such as social security, medical records, and vehicle ownership while exempting information on police computers from parliamentary scrutiny. Another dimension of this Social Taylorism – monitoring processing, plotting to control people that industry might thrive,[53] pushing determinedly towards 'a managed society, whose managing director is money and whose production manager is the police' [54] – is, as we have noted, more diligent control of information within and from government.

A second aspect is the reduction of what has been called the 'public sphere'[55] under assault from shortages of monies and insistence that commercial practices are more efficient. This comes as no surprise since the purpose of the state's Social Taylorism is to substitute market organisation for public services so that corporations can, wherever possible, enjoy further avenues for sales. That is so that capital can enter where hitherto it has been excluded in order to introduce its criteria of control.

Under these pressures the 'public sphere' (quintessentially information sources such as libraries, the Central Statistical Office, education, the Arts Council) has often reduced its standards and sought out sponsors from private capital and other ways of increasing revenue (for example, by charging for some library services). In our view this assault on the public sphere has consolidated social arrangements best understood in terms of a panopticon. It is increasingly evident that as public sector institutions decline so also diminish the areas that are, however inadequately, accountable and committed to presentation of information about issues in as comprehensive a way as is possible to the whole population. What is replacing them, if they are at all replaced, is corporate capital, increasingly centralised, able to examine and inveigle the consumer at home while being bolstered by a state apparatus that is not as publicly answerable as it might be and which watches over the populace to ensure order so that capital might thrive.

The BBC is a part of this public sphere and it has felt the effects of government policies in recent years. Kept short of funds to which it has responded in part by aping commercial practices (in proposals to operate satellite transmission on a subscription basis, through numerous joint productions with US corporations), and pressured by government on political presentations (from Falklands reportage to the more recent outcry over *Panorama*'s exposé of right-wing infiltration of the Conservative Party), it has not to date been threatened with privatisation. This is of course not easily done since revenue from a licence fee is not so readily changed as funds from the exchequer, but that it has not yet been openly mooted by market ideologues is testament to the respect enjoyed in the UK by public service broadcasting. Nonetheless, the spate of new communications technologies in combine with straitened finances suggests that the BBC might be undermined in other ways, overtaken by market organisations and left stranded as a vulnerable minority force.

Conclusion

Michel Foucault described a 'great carceral continuum' which extends from prisons through society.[56] The 'carceral texture of society' that Foucault delineated has noticeably thickened, coarsened and strengthened. This is what we foresee: a society in which capital mediates more social relationships than ever, in which it intrudes further into our everyday lives in the name of 'choice' and 'freedom' with subtle advertising and high-tech products for the consumer whom it observes, analyses and schemes about, that any changes might be perceived as favourable and desirable for those able and willing to pay. Behind and often in front of this centralised corporate capital is arrayed a disciplinary state, equipped with the latest surveillance technologies, able and willing to contain dissent from those unwilling to accede to capital's controls or unable, through unemployment or poverty, to participate in its technologies of abundance. In this more intensively market and individualistic society, public service institutions have little or no place (other than perhaps as charities) and we cannot say with any optimism that they can withstand capital's intrusion or assaults from government. Already they have a tarnished image, somehow out of place when set beside the dynamism and progressivism of the 'magic of the marketplace'. Today public service institutions, television included, are a remnant from a past age. Public service broadcasting will surely have to fall into line with the bulk of television products and attend to the market.

> Cuchulain stirred,
> Stared on the horses of the sea, and heard
> The cars of battle and his own name cried;
> And fought with the invulnerable tide.

> W.B. Yeats, 'Cuchulain's Fight with the Sea'

References

1. Our theoretical and historical approach draws on the work of M. Foucault, *Discipline and Punish: The Birth of the Prison* (Harmondsworth: Penguin 1979); M. Weber, *Economy and Society* (New York: Bedminster 1968); D.F. Noble, *America by Design: Science, Technology and the Rise of Corporate Capitalism* (New York: Oxford University Press 1977); A.D. Chandler, *The Visible Hand: The Managerial Revolution in American Business* (Cambridge, Mass: Harvard University Press 1977); D. Pope, *The Making of Modern Advertising* (New York: Basic Books 1983); S. Ewen, *Captains of Consciousness* (New York: McGraw-Hill 1976); J. Seabrook, *Working-Class Childhood* (London: Gollancz 1982). Our argument here is elaborated in our book *Information Technology: A Luddite Analysis* (Norwood, New Jersey: Ablex 1985).

2. See E. Barnouw, *A History of Broadcasting in the United States*, vols. II and III (New York: Oxford University Press 1968 and 1970).

3 See R. Bunce, *Television in the Corporate Interest* (New York: Praeger 1976). For the Pilkington Report's eloquent formulation of the key dilemma facing commercial television in its attempt to satisfy the needs of, on the one hand, advertisers, and, on the other, 'a service of television broadcasting which will realise as fully as possible the purposes of broadcasting', see *Report of the Committee on Broadcasting, 1960*. Cmnd 1753 (London: HMSO June 1962) pp. 166–7.

4. M. Meyer, *Madison Avenue U.S.A.: the Inside Story Of American Advertising* (London: Bodley Head 1958) p. 198.

5. Ibid. p. 188.

6. Ibid. p. 206.

7. R. Hoggart. 'Must We Be Casualties in the TV Explosion?' *Guardian*, 13 September 1982, p. 7.

8. J.Tunstall, *The Media in Britain* (London: Constable 1983), ch. 4.

9. 'Because politicians as well as businessmen were involved from the start in determining the shape of broadcasting, there were bound to be "controls" and "compromises". The language of "service" and "responsibility" was always as relevant in the debate – and the legislation – as the language of "liberty" and "enterprise".' Thus comments Asa Briggs, *The History of Broadcasting in the UK*, vol. 4: *Sound and Vision* (Oxford: Oxford University Press 1979) p. 429.

10. H.H. Wilson, *Pressure Group: The Campaign for Commercial Television in England* (New Jersey: Rutgers University Press 1961) pp. 16–17.

11. R. Hoggart, *The Uses of Literacy: Aspects of Working-Class Life With Special Reference to Publications and Entertainments* (1957. Harmondsworth: Penguin 1968) p. 325.

12. J. Seabrook, 'Have We Reached the End of the Working Class Epic?' *New Society*, 21 January 1981, pp. 135–7; cf. J. Seabrook, 'Richard Hoggart and the Waning of the Working Classes', *New Society*, 9 December 1982, pp. 415–17.

13. A.J.P. Taylor, *English History 1914–1945* (Oxford: Oxford University Press 1965) p. 233.

14. Quoted in A. Smith (ed.), *British Broadcasting* (Newton Abbot: David and Charles 1974).

15. A. Smith, *The Shadow in the Cave: A Study of the Relationship between the Broadcaster, his Audience and the State* (1973. London: Quartet 1976) p. 54.

16. For a statement by a recent Director-General of the BBC on the Corporation's ideology of 'liberal democracy', see C. Curran, *A Seamless Robe: Broadcasting Philosophy and Practice* (London: Collins 1979) p. 106.

17. See M. Tracey, *The Production of Political Television* (London: Routledge and Kegan Paul 1977).

18. A. Smith, 'Britain: The Mysteries of a Modus Vivendi' in A. Smith (ed.), *Television and Political Life: Studies in Six European Countries* (London: Macmillan 1979) ch. 1.

19. A. Briggs, *The History of Broadcasting in the UK*, four volumes (Oxford: Oxford University Press 1961–1979).

20. K. Kumar, 'Holding the Middle Ground: the BBC, the Public and the Professional Broadcaster', in J. Curran, M. Gurevitch and J. Woollacott (eds.), *Mass Communication and Society*, (London: Edward Arnold/Open University Press 1977), pp. 231–48. Quotations from p. 234.

21. See T. Burns, *The BBC: Public Institution and Private World* (London: Macmillan 1977); E.G. Wedell, *Broadcasting and Public Policy* (London: Michael Joseph 1968).

22. See S. Hall, *The External-Internal Dialectic in Broadcasting: Television's Double-Bind*, University of Birmingham Centre of Contemporary Cultural Studies, Stencilled Occasional Papers, February 1972.

23. On the BBC's quality of public leadership under Greene, see M. Tracey, *A Variety of Lives: A Biography of Sir Hugh Greene* (London: Bodley Head 1983), p. 229.

24. C. Crouch, 'The State, Capital and Liberal Democracy', in C. Crouch (ed.), *State and Economy in Contemporary Capitalism* (London: Croom Helm 1979) pp. 13–54.

25. See A Giddens, *A Contemporary Critique of Historical Materialism* (London: Macmillan 1981) pp. 169–81.

26. See D. Marsh and G. Locksley, 'Capital in Britain: Its Structural Power and Influence over Policy', *West European Politics*, vol. 6, no. 2, 1983, pp. 36–60; M. Useem, *The Inner Circle: Large Corporations and the Rise of Business Political Activity in the US and UK* (New York: Oxford University Press 1983); M. Useem, 'Business and Politics in the United States and United Kingdom; The Origins of Heightened Political Activity of Large Corporations During the 1970s and Early 1980s', *Theory and Society*, vol. 12, no. 3, 1983, pp. 281–308.

27. *New York Times*, 11 October 1981.

28. See K. Robins and F. Webster, 'The Mis-information Society', *Universities Quarterly*, vol. 37, no. 4, 1983, pp. 344–55; H.I. Schiller, *Who Knows: Information in the Age of the Fortune 500* (Norwood, New Jersey: Ablex 1981) especially chs. 5–6.

29. M. Barratt, 'Too Negative on Film', *Marketing*, 5 October 1983, pp. 31–5.

30. cf. E. Barnouw *The Sponsor: Notes on a Modern Potentate* (New York: Oxford University Press 1978).

31. Marie Jennings, 'Time Trap: Pitfalls In the Search for Profit', *Campaign*, 10 February 1984, p. 48.

32. cf. N. McLaughlin 'Solving PR's Problems', *Management Today*, November 1983, pp. 94–7, 170, 173. See British Petroleum's 1983 *Annual Report* for a statement of the company's extensive use of communications media.

33. M. Edwardes, *Back from the Brink: An Apocalyptic Experience* (London: Pan 1984), pp. 292–3.

34. *Financial Times*, 13 October 1983.

35. See J. Lee, 'Corporate Puffery', *New Society*, 23 November 1978, pp. 464–5: R. Meadow, 'The Political Dimensions of Nonproduct Advertising', *Journal of Communication*, vol. 31, no. 3, summer 1981, pp. 69–82.

36. Quoted in N. Rosen, 'The Trade Marks That Spell Culture', *Guardian*, 26 January 1984.

37. cf. H.I. Schiller, *The Disappearing Public Sphere*. Minneapolis: Walker Art Center, mimeo, 1982, P. Taylor, 'How to Light up a Concert Hall', *Guardian*, 26 March 1984, p. 13.

38. Saatchi and Saatchi Compton Worldwide, *Review of Operations*, 1983.
39. The figure is from a Saatchi and Saatchi advertisement in the *Observer*, 29 January 1984. The cost of the two-page advertisement – over £30,000 – is itself an index of the corporate resources necessary for modern campaigns.
40. Saatchi and Saatchi Compton Worldwide, *Review of Operations*, cit.
41. In M. Worcester and M. Harrop (eds.), *Political Communications: the General Election of 1979* (London: Allen and Unwin 1982) p. 5.
42. Saatchi and Saatchi Plc, *Shareholders' Report and Accounts*, 1983, p. 3.
43. *Hansard*, Series 5, vol. 979, 1980, col. 55.
44. For example, Thames Television complained of the 'intolerable' burden of Channel 4 in April 1983; John Freeman, head of London Weekend Television, in November 1983 thought that 'the present bleeding of ITV through Channel 4 cannot be allowed to flow unstaunched for very long' (*Guardian*, 24 November 1983); and Harlech Television complained of a net loss due to Channel 4 on 20 October 1983 (*Guardian*, 21 October 1983).
45. T. Jones, 'Consumers' Expenditure', *Economic Trends*, September 1983, pp. 96–107; 'Relative Prices Over Twenty Years', *Economic Progress Report*, no. 161, October 1983.
46. cf. A. Gamble, 'The Free Economy and the Strong State', in R. Miliband and J. Saville (eds.), *Socialist Register 1979*, (London: Merlin 1979) pp. 1–25.
47. Conservative Party, *Proposals for a Conservative Information Technology Policy*, Provisional Draft Report, 1979, mimeo, p. 6.
48. See S. Manwaring-White, *The Policing Revolution: Police Technology, Democracy and Liberty in Britain* (Brighton: Harvester Press 1983); I. Will, *The Big Brother Society* (London: Harrap 1983); D. Leigh, *The Frontiers of Secrecy: Closed Government in Britain* (London: Junction Books 1980); J. Michael, *The Politics of Secrecy* (Harmondsworth: Penguin 1982); C. Aubrey, *Who's Watching You? Britain's Security Services and the Official Secrets Act* (Harmondsworth: Penguin 1981); D. Burnham, *The Rise of the Computer State* (London: Weidenfeld and Nicolson 1983).
49. cf. P. Golding and G. Murdock, 'Privatising Pleasure', *Marxism Today*, October 1983, pp. 32–6, CIS Report, *Private Line: The Future of British Telecom*, no. 32, 1983; POEU, *The American Experience. . . . A Report on the Dilemma of Telecommunications in the USA*, October 1983; S. Hastings and H. Levie (eds.), *Privatisation?* (Nottingham: Spokesman Books 1983).
50. National Book Committee, *Public Library Spending in England and Wales* (London: National Book League, 1983).
51. R. Harris, *Gotcha! The Media, the Government and the Falklands Crisis* (London: Faber and Faber 1983); House of Commons, *First Report from the Defence Committee, Session 1982–3: The Handling of the Press and Public Information during the Falklands Conflict*, 2 vols, (London: HMSO December 1982); Ministry of Defence, *The Protection of Military Information*, (London: HMSO, December 1983).
52. Burnham, op. cit. p. 234.
53. The 1984 national miners' strike has involved new levels of intelligence-gathering by the police and the complex mobilisation of 20,000 officers from all over the country. For a demonstration that this is much more than a response to a short-term contingency and that it has been instigated at high levels of government, see K. Jeffery and P. Hennessy, *States of Emergency: British Governments and Strikebreaking Since 1919* (London: Routledge and Kegan Paul 1983) pp. 222–61.
54. E.P. Thompson, *Writing by Candlelight* (London: Merlin 1980) p. 211.
55. See P. Elliott, 'Intellectuals, the "Information" Society and the Disappearance of the Public Sphere', *Media, Culture and Society* vol. 4, no. 3, 1982, pp. 243–53;

N. Garnham, 'Public Service versus the Market', *Screen* vol. 24, no. 1, 1983, pp. 6–27.

56. M. Foucault, op. cit. p. 297.

MARC RABOY

Public Television, the National Question and the Preservation of the Canadian State

The history of public broadcasting in Canada can be read as a struggle between opposing conceptions of the public, and opposing conceptions of the Canadian nation. In the course of this struggle – in which the Canadian state has played the leading role – the actions of a succession of federal governments have caused one conception of the public, and one conception of the nation, to emerge as dominant. In the discourse on broadcasting in Canada, 'nation' and 'public' have been used interchangeably to refer, in effect, to what is a single Canadian market. I would suggest that in this simple fact resides the 'problem' of public broadcasting in Canada – or state broadcasting, to call it by its proper name.

The Canadian state appeared on the scene in the second half of the 19th century as a rearguard action by British North American entrepreneurs to establish an autonomous market north of the 49th parallel. At the same time as the idea of 'the public' was beginning to emerge as a political principle among Western states in general, the Canadian state was beginning its career as builder of the Canadian nation. In Canada, the 'national' and the 'public' would be virtually interchangeable. What Herschel Hardin calls 'the public enterprise culture'[1] would become the mainstay of the Canadian nation, and in the 20th century the key terrain of struggle over the public sphere and the definition of the Canadian nation, the point at which the two would overlap most perfectly, was the broadcasting system.

Before television, there was radio. The appearance of this unimagined new medium in the 1920s, at a time when the industrial state was undergoing unprecedented expansion, irrevocably changed the context in which institutions like the press and ideas like democracy had to be discussed. In all the industrial societies, the bourgeoisie was split on the question of the state and, since it was a new domain, broadcasting became the focus of the split in many countries. Free-enterprisers fought to keep broadcasting in the commercial 'private' sector, while more enlightened elements argued for major state support for 'public' systems. Liberals and progressives naturally allied with the statists, whose 'public service' rhetoric they shared. The leading social questions of the era – involving the relative weight to be given public and private ownership in the future expansion of capitalism, the distribution of social resources, the mechanisms of democracy – were all dramatically present in the broadcasting issue. Nowhere was this truer than in Canada.[2]

In analysing the Canadian context, one must take care to avoid the erroneous and dangerous assumption that the public meant the same thing to each of the architects of the Canadian broadcasting system. Historically, the *raison d'être* of public broadcasting in Canada was to promote and support the Canadian difference vis-à-vis the United States. But in the process of dealing with the 'external contradiction', it also became more and more involved with the 'internal contradiction': promoting and supporting Canadian national unity against pressures for regional autonomy and threats of fragmentation, especially the threat posed by French-Canadian nationalism concentrated in Quebec. 'Public' broadcasting in Canada has historically meant 'national' broadcasting, and since Canadians do not agree on the national question, we have tended to be confused in our expectations from the public service. As soon as we recognise that there are different notions of the Canadian nation, we can separate the idea of the public from its connotation as the protagonist of one particular view of the nation, and begin to look critically at what it really means in the Canadian context and at its political potential.

Canadians like to remember the early history of broadcasting in Canada as one of a struggle between the promoters of a nationalist public sector and frontierless private-enterprisers, and so it was. But it was also a struggle involving different conceptions of Canada.

The First World War had been the occasion of a major confrontation between Canada's two nationalisms, as the French-speaking population of Quebec massively opposed what it saw as Canadian participation on the shirt-tails of the British imperial parent. The nationalism of French-Canadian leaders like Henri Bourassa, who sought independence from British policy, was often perceived by patriotic English-Canadians as narrow provincialism. The thrust towards provincial autonomy most strongly pursued by successive governments in Quebec was seen as petty, chauvinistic, and especially counter-productive in the struggle to build a pan-Canadian alternative to the US cultural model. This attitude contained an unfortunate blindspot: it prevented its holders from seeing that the French-Canadians were engaged in an even more difficult struggle for cultural and political autonomy, in which the dominant majority was English Canada, politically represented by the federal (then dominion) government in Ottawa.

When the Liberal government of Mackenzie King created the Royal Commission on Radio Broadcasting in 1928, it was looking for a solution to the emerging crisis of US domination of the Canadian air-waves – a crisis felt especially by English-Canadian nationalism. This nationalism contained its own internal contradiction. On the one hand, it was another way of saying 'one market coast-to-coast' for the flourishing of Canadian capital. But it was also the cohesive element in an idea of Canada as a federation of local and regional communities, particularly popular among voluntary associations of workers, farmers and women, and in peripheral regions like the west. While the first conception would enable the Conservative prime minister, R.B. Bennett, to justify creating the Canadian Radio Broadcasting Commission in 1932, the second was fostered by many (but not all) of the organisations and individuals who supported the public broadcasting lobby known as the Canadian Radio League. This grassroots progressive nationalism could not be ignored by the Canadian political élite. But in seeking a 'typically Canadian solution' to the broadcasting question in which business would eventually prosper, the federal authorities had to suppress the strong sentiment in the provinces that radio, *as a means of education*, should not be centralised under federal jurisdiction, where, in spite of rhetorical claims to the contrary, common sense said the medium would inevitably be turned to commercial or partisan purposes, or both.

'Canadian radio listeners want Canadian broadcasting,' the Aird Commission concluded in 1929, and the only way to serve their interests was through 'some form of public ownership, operation and control behind which is the national power and prestige of the whole public of the Dominion of Canada'.[3] So it recommended creation of a national company, which would own all stations and operate them on a basis of public service, with a minimum of indirect advertising.

However, the Aird Commission dealt not only with the issue of public versus private broadcasting; it also had to face the question of central or regional control. The province of Manitoba was already operating Canada's first 'public' radio stations, even before the commission was set up. New Brunswick indicated it was not willing to abdicate responsibility for broadcasting to Ottawa. In Quebec, the government of Louis-Alexandre Taschereau welcomed the commission's initiative, but underlined that it considered the province constitutionally competent to legislate in the field of radio communication.

Pressure from Quebec against a federally controlled public system was especially strong. The French-Canadian representative on the three-member royal commission, Dr Augustin Frigon, insisted on a major role for the provinces in the system, and in order to gain his support, Sir John Aird and Charles Bowman, the other two commissioners, conceded the notion of provincial control over broadcasting *content*. The commission recommended a mechanism to give provincial authorities full control over the programmes of the station or stations in their respective areas. This was not only a concession to Frigon, it was also a concession to the BNA Act, which gave jurisdiction over educational matters to the provinces, and the Aird Commission did consider broadcasting as an educational resource, as well as a nation-building one. However, this was the one area of the commission's recommendations which would never even get to the drawing-board. If it had, it would have drastically changed the course of Canadian communications and, probably, of Canadian political history as well.

The report of the Aird Commission confirmed what most thoughtful English-Canadians apparently felt: that the only viable alternative to US domination of the Canadian airwaves was a national public enterprise. But the powerful lobby mounted by the private broadcasters and their supporters was a force to be reckoned with. Even before they could be dealt with, however, the constitutional question had to be resolved.

The Quebec government responded to the tabling of the Aird Commission report by introducing a Radio Act in the provincial legislature, giving the province the right to set up its own radio stations. This short-circuited the anticipated federal action even before the central government had decided on a political course to follow. Ottawa asked the Canadian Supreme Court for advice and in June 1931 the court ruled that it had sole jurisdiction over radio communication. Quebec (supported by New Brunswick and Ontario) appealed to the Judicial Committee of the Privy Council in London, and in January 1932 London upheld Ottawa's position. This decision was seen as a historic judicial shift in favour of Ottawa after half a century of creeping provincialism and, flushed with success, the federal government moved quickly to introduce legislation creating a national public broadcasting service.

The constitutional crisis stemmed from the absence of any reference to culture and communication in the British North America Act of 1867. The provinces, particularly Quebec, claimed competence on the basis of their jurisdiction over matters concerning education. The dominion argument was based on the view that radio communication involved transmission of signals across provincial boundaries. The provinces were thus fostering a cultural view of communication, the dominion a technological one. The legal decision was based on the federal parliament's constitutional right to legislate for 'peace, order and good government'. While it appeared to resolve things, the judicial decision of 1932 placed communications at the centre of controversy over the nature of Canadian dualism, where it remains to this day.

The role of the Radio League in the constitutional debate is interesting. The founders of the League had realised at the outset that they needed the support of French Canada. Their contacts there, however, tended to be among the federalist sector of Quebec opinion rather than among provincial autonomists, and so when the constitutional question arose, the League was advised that it would be prudent to support the dominion position, which it then proceeded to do. But the Radio League itself reflected the tensions and ambiguities of the two conceptions of the Canadian public – the democratic and the technocratic – and while a democratic socialist like Graham Spry was torn on the question of alienating Quebec, future Liberal cabinet minister Brooke Claxton, then a young lawyer, leapt on the case with gusto. According to Margaret Prang:

> Many of the moving spirits in the League were interested in this appeal to the courts on jurisdiction over broadcasting for reasons broader than the fate of radio itself. . . . They were dismayed by the general trend of judicial interpretation of the BNA Act during the 'twenties and wished to see an end to the steady growth of provincial powers. The radio case presented a chance to argue for Dominion power. . . .[4]

In this important episode, which gave broadcasting jurisdiction in Canada to the central government, we see the conflicting and competing conceptions of the Canadian public and the Canadian nation at play.

The constitutional question out of the way, the Conservative government of R.B. Bennett proceeded to introduce the Canadian Radio Broadcasting Act, creating the Canadian Radio Broadcasting Commission. To the lobbyists, it was a victory of public service over private profit. But the official discourse was one of 'national purpose', not public service. Graham Spry said R.B. Bennett, the champion of private enterprise, 'had a conflict within his soul'. But, in fact, Bennett recognised the need for state intervention on this typically 'Canadian' problem, and did not shy away from it. 'As in earlier Canadian enterprises,' writes Prang, 'there was not commitment to public ownership in principles. . . . The decisive force was national feeling.'[5] As the idea of the public was equated with the dominant conception of the Canadian nation in the minds of Canadians as different as R.B. Bennett and Graham Spry, a new type of problem began to emerge as the Canadian broadcasting system began to operate.

Having created a system on the basis of nationalist feeling, the architects of Canadian public broadcasting found themselves unable to reconcile competing and conflicting concepts of the Canadian nation. For Canadian broadcasting there would soon be two audiences, two markets, two publics . . . but one policy, one mandate, and one corporation.[6]

As Frank Peers points out, a major unresolved question hampered the CRBC:

> . . . The disagreement on the meaning of Canadian nationhood, and in particular, whether French language rights should be recognized outside the province of Quebec. . . .
>
> National radio was one of the most direct ways of reminding English-Canadians that they shared their country with French-speaking citizens, and the reminder was not always welcome.[7]

E.A. Corbett, who was an outspoken advocate of educational public broadcasting in the 1930s, remembered the early days of the CRBC this way:

> During the summer of 1933, a particularly bitter wave of feeling against the Commission occurred as a result of the preponderance of programs in French, originating in Montreal and broadcast over the Canadian network. A great many people in Ontario and in Western Canada awoke to the fact that Canada is a bilingual country; and led by certain Dominion-wide organizations, vigorous protest was made against what was considered to be an infringement of majority rights.[8]

Some thirty years later, in its submission to the Royal Commission on Bilingualism and Biculturalism (convened when the national question threatened to blow the country apart), the Canadian Broadcasting Corporation reflected on this aspect of its pre-history:

> . . . From the outset the national broadcasting agency has had to come to grips with the realities of bilingualism and biculturalism. . . .
>
> The very nature of broadcasting brought [the CBC] from the start into contact with [bilingualism and biculturalism] and, in coming to grips with them, the Corporation's decision was that the national broadcasting service should be equally available to the English and French communities and that it should function in both languages.[9]

The Corporation had two choices: either provide a single service using both languages, so that both English and French audiences would hear the same programme, or provide 'parallel services', one in each language:

> The first alternative was tried in the mid-thirties as being the simpler in practice and more feasible in view of the limited human,

69

technical and financial resources then available. Obviously, such an alternative was only workable as long as the program needs of both groups could be met by a single network. With the passage of time and the development of broadcasting techniques and resources, the demands of each group for a more complete service continued to grow, presenting the Corporation with a situation which could only be met adequately by duplicate networks, English and French. These the Corporation proceeded to establish and the pattern then adopted has prevailed to the present.

Needless to say, the transition was not as simple and orderly as the foregoing would suggest. The point, however, is that, over the years between 1932 and 1941, the Corporation moved from one service using two languages to two services each using one language. This is not meant to suggest that after 1941 no English was heard on the French network or French on the English network, since indeed they were. It merely emphasizes the cardinal fact that, as far as the overriding obligation to provide 'a national broadcasting service' was concerned, the Corporation found itself compelled by circumstances to use separate English and French networks for the purpose.[10]

The CBC discreetly neglects to elaborate on these 'circumstances', which were nothing less than the refusal of anglo-chauvinists in Ontario and western Canada to recognise francophone equality as the *sine qua non* of the Canadian compromise. Be that as it may, the result was the splitting of the public broadcasting system into two parallel services.

Paradoxically, the creation of a separate French service was welcomed by cultural nationalists in Quebec, who had feared inevitable marginalisation as the 'minority' part of a single, bilingual service. Reflecting on this in 1960, Gérard Lamarche, head of the French network, said the existence of Radio-Canada was 'a political miracle'.[11] The French network achieved full autonomy between 1939 and 1945 because of 'the need for national unity raised by the war'. But no sooner was the French service in place than it became the focus of a national crisis.

It may be argued that French-Canadian pacifism emerged as a self-interested form of resistance to British rule following the Conquest of 1759. Nevertheless, the fact is that it has been over 200 years since French-Canadians voluntarily went to war. As of 1 September 1939, street demonstrations in Montreal and parliamentary intervention by MPs in Ottawa made it clear that French-Canadians would not easily be convinced to participate in a Canadian military expedition in Europe. The government for its part, even in declaring war on Germany, imposing censorship and introducing emergency war measures, making opposition to the war effort illegal, made a solemn commitment that no Canadians would be sent to fight against their will.

The CBC/Radio-Canada quickly became a major propaganda vehicle for the Canadian war effort. By 1940, it was beginning to get people used to the idea of an expeditionary force. Its pioneering live coverage from the front – in both French and English – captured the imagination of hearth-front listeners at home. In January 1942 the government announced that it would hold a plebiscite asking the people to free it of its obligation to respect an earlier engagement restricting the methods of mobilisation for military service – in other words, clearing the way for conscription.

In the ensuing campaign, the Ligue pour la défense du Canada (League for the Defence of Canada), a broad common front of political and social leaders opposed to actual Canadian military participation, sought the right to use the public air to urge citizens to vote 'No'.

CBC policy restricted political election broadcasts to parties represented in the House of Commons. But the plebiscite was a different type of political consultation. It was known that all parties in the house supported the 'Yes' side, and the Ligue argued that as Canadian citizens they had a right to use the public air to try to convince their compatriots of the validity of voting 'No' – an option, they pointed out, that the government must consider legitimate and not a threat to the Canadian war effort, since it was itself organising the plebiscite.

The Ligue wrote to the CBC deputy director Augustin Frigon (the former Aird commissioner) asking for equal time for both sides. Frigon replied to Ligue chairman André Laurendeau:

> Your League may use the unaffiliated private stations if it wishes and if they consent; but it may not use our corporation, which, because of its national character, must remain neutral in all political matters.[12]

Laurendeau wrote back pointing out the inconsistency of this policy: since the CBC proposed to allow political parties to go on the air, and since all of these favoured the 'Yes', the CBC would thus find itself in the untenable position of exercising great political pressure on the people – far from the neutrality it was mandated to maintain. The 'No' side in the conscription plebiscite was thus restricted to the use of paid advertising – which the private stations were only too glad to accept – but only on a one-at-a-time basis, with each intervention subject to approval by the government censor. Frigon's correspondence with Laurendeau also revealed that this policy was dictated by the government: the CBC's participation in the plebiscite campaign, on both English and French networks, was to consist of addresses by party leaders from Ottawa.

On 27 April 1942, the people of Canada voted 63.7 per cent in favour of the government's proposal to lift restrictions on the manner of mobilising a military force, and conscription soon followed. But in Quebec, 71.2 per cent of the people had said 'No', and they would not soon forget the sordid role played in the affair by the national broadcasting service.

During this period, conflict between Quebec and Ottawa was manifested at the government level as well. In the Quebec provincial election of October 1939, outgoing premier Maurice Duplessis was denied access to the public airwaves when he refused to submit texts of his speeches to the government censor. Duplessis, a conservative nationalist and provincial autonomist, lost the election and held a lifelong grudge against Radio-Canada. When he was returned to office in 1944, he proceeded to adopt legislation creating a provincial educational broadcasting network. The law was never put into effect, and would surely have been contested by Ottawa and probably overturned. More than twenty years later, a subsequent Quebec government would resurrect this statute and use it to create Radio-Québec, successfully reclaiming this small sphere of jurisdiction from federal control.[13]

After the war, both private and state-owned radio flourished. With the new technology of television in the offing, the federal government created a Royal Commission on National Development in the Arts, Letters and Sciences (the Massey Commission), and asked it, among other things, to recommend 'principles upon which the policy of Canada should be based, in the fields of radio and television broadcasting'.[14]

The Massey Commission reaffirmed the principles first stated by the Aird Commission and somewhat implemented by the legislation of the 1930s, providing for a (public) 'national broadcasting service'. It detected some hitherto neglected problem areas with the CBC, like over-centralisation, excessive influence of advertisers and unequal coverage – while the English service had reached from coast to coast since 1938, this was not the case with the French. French-speaking groups outside Quebec complained to the Massey Commission that they were poorly served and wanted a nationwide network:

> It has been pointed out to us repeatedly in different parts of Canada that the French-speaking Canadian listener does not receive a broadcasting service equal to that intended for his English-speaking neighbor.[15]

Yet another Royal Commission on Broadcasting, the Fowler

Commission, reported in 1957 that there were still many parts of Canada unserved by the French system. There had been a significant evolution of public sentiment in Canada since the early days of radio, it said:

> It remains a moot question, however, whether Canada has yet reached the stage of complete national maturity where the introduction of French on the airwaves of Ontario . . . would not be regarded by a substantial majority as an intolerable intrusion rather than the cultural complement that in truth it would be.[16]

The Fowler Commission seemed to feel the reluctance to share channel time was understandable, if somewhat regrettable, and took solace in the fact that French-Canadians appeared to be satisfied with their service:

> The general tenor of the briefs submitted by organisations representative of French-speaking Canadians is one of contentment with both the public and private operations of the Canadian system in the French language.[17]

That this was so is a reflection of the powerful place occupied by an indigenous French-Canadian television which developed during the 1950s and came to play an important role in the reshaping of French-Canadian society and its transformation in the 1960s into a modern Quebec.

In the 1950s, television in Quebec became an active focus of opposition to the Duplessis government and to clerico-nationalist conservatism in general.[18] Radio-Canada's public affairs television played a leading role in airing ideas which could be discussed nowhere else, save in a few tiny-circulation intellectual journals. It may be difficult to grasp for people unfamiliar with the extent of the intellectual repression of the period; suffice it to say that television brought political and social debate on to the public stage for the first time. In the context of institutionalised opposition between the provincial government in Quebec and the federal government in Ottawa, an independent spirit emerged in the public affairs programming of Radio-Canada, which became the rallying point of the extra-parliamentary opposition in Quebec. While Ottawa had no complaint with this, it still felt that the tendency to concentrate on *provincial* affairs was an abuse of the service's mandate. Thus, Duplessis' virulent attacks on Radio-Canada and Ottawa's sensitivity to controversy combined with a climate marked by taboo and self-censorship to limit the expressive instinct of the times.

Television not only played a key role in crystallising opposition to the conservative provincial power structure, it also created a new type of political star, the prototype of which was René Lévesque, who went from being French Canada's most popular television personality to being Quebec's most dynamic politician in the elections of 1960 which swept Duplessis's Union Nationale out of office and ushered in the 'Quiet Revolution'.

The Quiet Revolution is seen as the birth of modern Quebec nationalism, and in the political events leading up to 1960 one event stands out: the strike by television producers at Radio-Canada in the winter of 1958–9. Radio-Canada's television producers went out on strike a few days before Christmas 1958 to support their demand for the right to unionise. This was the first instance in Canadian labour history of middle-level manager-employees seeking to form a union. The producers' move was in harmony with the spirit of promotion of collective rights which would characterise Quebec's Quiet Revolution and come to distinguish the province from the rest of Canada. But it was totally out of sync with English-Canadian labour values of the period and, as such, not only was the move met with bemusement (if not hostility) on the part of management, it did not elicit significant support from the workers of the English-language service either. What made things most difficult, of course, was the fact that the employer was an agency of the federal government.

Gérard Pelletier has pointed out that a major problem that emerged early on in the dispute was that the French network executives lacked the authority to negotiate the issue of unionisation with the producers. Only head office in Ottawa could move on it, and as the head office was slow to treat the matter seriously, things soon deteriorated. Radio-Canada quickly came to be seen as an institution which was betraying its promise. The strike lasted 68 days, during which time the French service was paralysed, nurturing the idea that Ottawa really didn't consider Radio-Canada an indispensable service, and accepting the historic inequality of French and English Canada. As René Lévesque put it in his first public espousal of the nationalist ideology which would propel him to the head of the Quebec independence movement, a similar strike by the English network would have been settled in half an hour. In the case of the French network it lasted 68 days.[19]

The apparent indifference of English Canada and the federal government to the crisis of what had become a major cultural institution in Quebec provoked a quantum leap in *québécois* nationalist consciousness. Yet, as late as 1960, the chairman of the Board of Broadcast Governors, Dr Andrew Stewart, could still say:

> It appears to me that Canadians now take the political unity of the country for granted. We no longer consider it possible that any part of the country might move to secede.[20]

The Massey Commission (1951) had examined the new technology of television and recommended a policy course analogous to the one that had been tried and proven successful (according to it) in radio. The Fowler Commission (1957) had been more sympathetic to the private broadcasting lobby, and had recommended separating the regulatory function from the CBC's other functions while reiterating that the Canadian broadcasting system is 'a single system embracing public and private elements subject to supervision and control by an agency of the state'. Neither of these royal commissions questioned the wisdom of the dual-network system.

As budgets and annual grants from parliament began to soar, so did the bureaucratic impulse and political grumbling. Wholesale privatisation of the Canadian broadcasting system began with the Broadcasting Act of 1958, creating the Board of Broadcast Governors as recommended by Fowler. While this created more space for the private sector, it did nothing to reduce public cost. In 1963, yet another royal commission, this one on government organisation (the Glassco Commission), devoted a chapter to the Canadian Broadcasting Corporation which it considered a 'special area of administration':

> The interplay of national, regional and local activities gives rise to a degree of organizational complexity which, in the case of the Corporation, is compounded by the need to operate not one but two television broadcasting services – one in English and one in French. In addition two distinct radio operations, one in each language, are conducted.[21]

The CBC's submission to the Bilingualism and Biculturalism Commission, cited earlier, explained the political necessity of this situation, regardless of the bureaucratic or economic implications:

> There are of course, some features of the Canadian outlook and attitude which tend to make the Corporation's task more difficult. Canadians are divided by their political history and although that history is full of colour and romance and enterprise and imagination, French- and English-speaking Canadians do not view it with the same eyes or the same hearts. They honour different heroes; they subscribe to different and often conflicting interpretations of our past. Even among Canadians of one language, French or English, there is no consensus about those events in our past which we should take pride in or condemn.[22]

During the 1960s, while private enterprise occupied more and more space in the profitable commercial sector of the overall system, the national/public broadcasting service continued to be, theoretically at least, a crucial link in the federal strategy for maintaining national unity. It was during this period that Radio-Canada's news and public affairs programming policy was adapted to deal with the growing threat of radical Quebec nationalism and the new independence movement. Officially, Radio-Canada's news and public affairs policy called for discouraging 'separatism'. Many journalists, producers and other programming staff – perhaps the majority – were sympathetic to the goals of the movement, however, and Radio-Canada's newsroom was soon the site of informational guerrilla warfare.[23] Beginning around 1968, the Radio-Canada branch of the Syndicat général du cinéma et de la télévision (SGCT) began to consider it had a role to defend 'the public's right to know' against an information policy which expressly denied the legitimacy of the national question as a newsworthy issue.

At the same time, parliament introduced a new Broadcasting Act restating the mandate of the 'national broadcasting service' and spelling out for the first time the 'national unity' role of the CBC. Among its other functions:

> The national broadcasting service should ... contribute to the development of national unity and provide for a continuing expression of Canadian identity.[24]

The standard approach of Radio-Canada's top news executives – who tended to be political appointees – was to interpret the Broadcasting Act's 'national unity' clause to mean 'Give no solace to the enemy,' underscoring the federal government's one-dimensional view of Canada. Thus, when a police riot broke out at a nationalist demonstration during Quebec's traditional Saint-Jean-Baptiste Day festivities in 1968, Radio-Canada's cameras were ordered to remain trained on the traditional floats and parade, and the one enterprising journalist who managed to circumvent the blackout was summarily suspended for his efforts. As social tensions in Quebec rose during 1969 and 1970, the climate in Radio-Canada's newsroom deteriorated. Three unionised journalists who wrote occasional freelance articles for a nationalist review were formally ordered to cease or face dismissal. Two complied and the third was fired.

Matters came to a head during Quebec's 'October Crisis' of 1970, when the federal cabinet closely supervised what was and was not broadcast by Radio-Canada. Again, as at the time of the conscription plebiscite, the Quebec public had to turn to private media for a more objective coverage of events. Again, the commercial vocation of these media overcame their sense of patriotism, this time as they scrambled over one another to be first off the wire with the latest communiqué from the outlawed Front de libération du Québec. The government, meanwhile, found itself in the absurd situation of controlling the national service but being unable to thereby control the flow of news. When the journalists' union held a press conference to denounce the muzzling of their service, their two principal leaders were dismissed

76

on the spot for insubordination.

This hard-line approach continued apace through the 1970s, coming to a climax in 1976 with the election of the pro-independence Parti Québécois to form the provincial government in Quebec. Instead of taking this as a sign of public sentiment, the federal government actually seemed to feel that CBC/Radio-Canada was to blame.

On 4 March 1977, Canadian prime minister Pierre Trudeau wrote to the chairman of the Canadian Radio-Television and Telecommunications Commission (CRTC – the regulatory agency which replaced the Board of Broadcast Governors in 1968 and was modified to include the telecommunications function in 1976) as follows:

> Doubts have been expressed as to whether the English and French television networks of [the CBC] generally, and in particular their public affairs, information and news programming, are fulfilling the mandate of the Corporation. . . . Accordingly I am writing to invite [the CRTC] to establish an inquiry into the matter.[25]

The CRTC enquired, and concluded that the CBC had, in its view, failed in its very important responsibility to 'contribute to the development of national unity' – but not in the sense the prime minister had suspected. The problem was not separatists in the newsroom, it said, but deficiency in representing each of Canada's 'two solitudes' to the other. In fact, the studies done for the inquiry showed that the Canadian public (or publics) were much more in touch with each other than was the CBC, which was over-centralised, over-bureaucratised, and tended to over-dramatise as it contributed to the communication gap between Canada's two principal linguistic communities:

> The CBC represents one of a series of innovative policies that Canada has developed during the century of Confederation to preserve its identity as a distinctive presence in North America along with its gigantic and friendly neighbor. . . .
>
> The effort needed to keep Canada together is at least as great as it was in 1867, and the communications media have a grave responsibility to keep Canadians fully informed on subjects on which they will have to make fateful decisions.[26]

The *operational* solution proposed by the CBC only became evident two years later, when the CBC's licence came up for renewal. Referring to the French network's tendency to behave as a Quebec network as 'unidimensional regionalism', the CRTC said:

> The CBC French television network should broadcast to all francophones, wherever they may be, and to all others who want

more information about events that illustrate the cultural, economic and political life of French-speaking Canada.[27]

In other words, Radio-Canada should cease to behave as a Quebec network and adopt a pan-Canadian approach. In the context of Canada's two nationalisms, this was akin to telling the English service of CBC that it was not paying enough attention to the United States!

As we have seen, there has been a consistent alternative to 'national' broadcasting policy in Canada in the demands and actions of government and non-government actors in Quebec since the 1920s. Beginning in 1968, when Ottawa and the provinces began looking seriously at constitutional reform, every Quebec government, regardless of party, has demanded control over communication policy, claiming it essential to the protection and development of the *québécois* language and culture. In Quebec today, as Dallas Smythe points out, we find communications agencies

> deeply engaged in the struggle for national survival of the *Québécois* while in anglophone Canada these agencies reflect and produce indifference to, and even aggression against, the *québécois* movement.[28]

The Broadcasting Act of 1968, in creating the CRTC, reaffirmed centralised federal control over the broadcasting system. At a constitutional conference in Ottawa only weeks before its adoption, Quebec premier Daniel Johnson reasserted Quebec's claim for competence over radio and television, defining these as instruments of education and culture. When he returned home, Johnson had his government implement Duplessis's 1945 law establishing Radio-Québec as an 'educational' television network. This was a direct challenge to Ottawa, whose new broadcasting legislation contained provision for federal intervention in educational television. As provincial jurisdiction over education is one of the clearest provisions of the Canadian constitution, Ottawa was forced to recognise Quebec's move – but provincial educational networks, like all broadcasting enterprises in Canada, would still be subject to CRTC regulation.

There would be further challenges. When Ottawa created a Department of Communications in 1969, Quebec followed suit, and was soon imitated by the other provinces. In the 1970s, as communications became a major area of federal-provincial dispute, Quebec's position could not be more clear. In a 1971 policy statement, communications minister Jean-Paul L'Allier stated that 'it is first of all up to Quebec to elaborate an overall communications policy'.[29] On the basis of this position, Quebec moved to intervene in the new area of cable distribution, thus entering into another protracted jurisdictional conflict with Ottawa. Quebec claimed that the 1932 Privy Council decision gave Ottawa jurisdiction over 'carriage' but not 'content', and recalled the Aird Commission recommendations for a provincial authority. Thus, during the 1970s, both Quebec's Régie des services publics (Public Service Board) and Ottawa's CRTC claimed jurisdiction to regulate the cable companies.

In 1973, on the occasion of a federal-provincial conference on communications, Quebec published a definitive policy statement in which it distinguished between national 'unity' and 'uniformity', and more important, distinguished the federal government from the Canadian nation. Objecting to Ottawa's unilateral formulation of policy, it said:

> It's normal for the federal government to publish a document on 'federal' communications policy, but to present this unilaterally as 'national' or 'Canadian' policy is inadmissible.[30]

This position of Quebec's is all the more remarkable insofar as it was developed by a (provincial) Liberal government with impeccable federalist credentials. Needless to say, the pro-sovereignty Parti Québécois has reiterated Quebec's claim for jurisdiction in communications[31], and needless to say it has got no further than its predecessors. Herein lies not only the problem of communications in Canada, but the very problem of the country itself. Historically, the federal government has appropriated to itself the right to speak for all Canadians, for the Canadian 'nation' as a collectivity. But the Canadian nation is not the only national collectivity with which Canadians identify.

Of course, Ottawa never recognised Quebec's claim, and the cable question dragged through the courts until 1977, when the Supreme Court of Canada ruled in favour of Ottawa. Curiously, the judges split neatly along national lines, the three judges from Quebec dissenting from the majority opinion. As a leading constitutional scholar, Gil Rémillard, put it:

> On the strictly legal level, both options were defensible. The decision was based on the judges' different conceptions of Canadian federalism. . . .
> The example is interesting insofar as communications illustrate in a particularly eloquent fashion the problem of Canadian dualism. . . . To some people [Canadian dualism] signifies that Canada is made up of two nations or peoples, the French Canadians and the English Canadians. To others [it] signifies that Canadian federalism includes the national phenomenon of Quebec. In this latter case, the dualism is between Quebec and Canada.[32]

Canada's constitutional and political crisis of the past fifteen years is based on the conflict between these two interpretations.

The Parti Québécois government of Quebec elected in 1976 had promised to hold a referendum to seek a mandate to negotiate 'sovereignty-association', a proposed new constitutional arrangement with Ottawa and the other provinces. As Canada and Quebec prepared for the referendum, which was scheduled for May 1980, CBC president Al Johnson indicated the corporation's attitude towards the country's national crisis. Johnson's statement to the federal Task Force on Canadian Unity is worth quoting at length, as it reflects the low-key, soft-pedal approach the CBC adopted at this crucial juncture of Canada's political history:

> The CBC's current affairs programs, in short, must fully reflect the debate about Canada's future. They must reflect the case for Canada as a nation, whatever its form of federalism – the social and economic, the cultural and political benefits of nationhood to individual Canadians. We must not make the mistake, in reporting on the current difficulties in our society, and the pressing debates about alternative options for Canada's future, of forgetting to reflect the contributions which Canada has made to individual Canadians over the years. At the same time, our current affairs programming must reflect, too, the tensions of Canadian society, and the arguments for changes in the political and constitutional arrangements designed to reduce those tensions. They must explore as well the costs and the consequences of the changes being proposed. The CBC's current affairs programs must examine, too, the arguments against nationhood as we know it – the arguments, for example, in favour of the independence of Quebec, with or without economic association with the rest of Canada. And they must explore the costs and the consequences for Canadians across the country of such a course of action – and whether indeed such a course would be acceptable to them.
>
> For Canada's public broadcasting system even to air such arguments against nationhood is distasteful to some Canadians. But if we are to exemplify and to respect the freedom of speech and discussion upon which Canada is founded, we must accord 'freedom for the thought you hate', as an internationally renowned jurist once put it. To give expression to this freedom is not in any way to tolerate a bias against nationhood; any such bias would be quite unacceptable to the CBC. Rather, it is a matter of respecting, as we say, the basic tenet of freedom of expression and debate. The very credibility of the CBC as a service to the people of Canada depends upon taking this posture. Put another way, it is not for the CBC to suppress any particular point of view: only the community of Canada, through its Parliament, has the power to do so, to declare

subversive, and thus to suppress, any particular point of view.

What is critical for the CBC is to ensure that the choices being put to the Canadian people be reported fully, fairly, and responsibly, and in a balanced manner, taking into account the weight of opinions which support the several choices. It is critical, too, to ensure that the choices are explored with equal fairness, thoroughness, and responsible balance.[33]

'Full', 'fair', 'responsible' and 'balanced' reporting, in a context of 'freedom for the thought you hate' . . . let's overlook the apparent contradiction in terms. The point is, an important shift in the function of public television was taking place in Canada at the dawning of the 1980s.

The 1980 Quebec referendum on sovereignty-association was perhaps the first Canadian political campaign since the arrival of television in which politicians sought to address the population directly, rather than by influencing news programmes. The goals of the campaign were to mobilise constituencies, rather than convince people. One constituency was perceived as people whose country was threatened with being split apart; the other as those seeking a better deal within the existing political framework. Television advertisements addressed to both 'Yes' and 'No' groups' perceptions of their respective constituency formed the main substance of the media campaign; actual programming was only incidental.

One researcher involved in studying the referendum from a 'news-analysis' perspective had this to say:

The referendum, or rather the questions raised by the referendum, had been part of the *québécois* political discourse for several years. They had been discussed and debated at length. There had been leaflets, pamphlets, books, editorials, debates, conversations among friends, interventions by activists, and so on. The referendum had thus already been constituted as a socio-political phenomenon, within certain limits.[34]

In short, in 1980 it was no longer a question of using the public media as an organ of state power. The liberal rationale for this in fact merely covered up the new reality: the media were no longer perceived to be the crucial agents of influencing public opinion.

This new understanding of the politics of media would be reflected in subsequent policy modifications and a new economic thrust. It is not specific to Canada, but is general to Western society, and is to be seen, for example, in the dismantling of the European state media monopolies in the 1980s. The result is a new constellation of relationships between public and privately owned media. Governments retain public service media as a kind of emergency political

81

reserve, for rudimentary political communication, and as a last bastion of cultural sovereignty. Private enterprise, meanwhile, is seeing its wildest fantasies come true.

With the defeat of the Quebec government's referendum on sovereignty-association in 1980, the national question seems to have receded into the background of Canada's media politics. The 1982 Federal Cultural Policy Review Committee was not too concerned about it, but pointed out the problems with respect to the CBC's national unity mandate:

> It is not easy to determine the extent to which the objectives . . . have been achieved. The task is difficult partly because the objectives are vague and largely unmeasurable, and partly because they are inconsistent.[35]

The minister of communications responded to this criticism in a recent policy document, attempting to clarify the CBC's 'national unity' function:

> The phrase in the CBC mandate, 'contribute to the development of national unity,' is deemed to mean being 'consciously partial to the success of Canada as a united country with its own national objectives, independent from those of other countries,' while maintaining the highest standards of professional journalism.[36]

The phrase in quotation marks actually comes from the 1974 CRTC decision renewing the CBC's licences, so Francis Fox hastens to add:

> Only with such high standards and complete autonomy with respect to content will the CBC be able to fulfil its essential role in contributing to the development of national unity – that of reflecting and interpreting as fully, fairly and accurately as possible Canada's cultural, social, political, economic, linguistic and regional reality.[37]

This is a curious accolade to the importance of journalism from a minister who in 1980–1 sat back with benign indifference while a bitter labour conflict kept the news services of Radio-Canada off the air for eight months.[38] Indeed, it underscores the new reality of Canadian communications, which is decidedly *economic*, even while nation-boosting remains the major political function of the public service. In the new scheme of things the CBC is seen increasingly as a marginal, if necessary, element of the overall system, as a source of *alternative* programming to the private/commercial mainstream. All lip-service aside, the present government has taken a step further the remaking of the Canadian broadcasting system begun when the Conservatives first recognised the equal status of the private sector in 1958.

The main purpose of the Department of Communication's 1983 broadcasting strategy for Canada is 'to provide Canadians with greater programme choice and make the Canadian broadcasting industry more competitive'. In both respects, the main thrust is towards an increased role for the private sector. In announcing the strategy, the department candidly confessed that it did not know quite what to do with the CBC:

> The CBC will continue to play a central role in the Canadian broadcasting system. Because the CBC is such a profoundly important national institution, the federal government is now consulting with the general public, the CBC itself and Parliament. . . . This debate on the role of the CBC has already begun and will continue over the coming months. . . .[39]

Six months later the minister issued a new statement, this time dealing exclusively with the CBC.[40] The statement situates the public service in the new broadcasting environment of 'electronic abundance' augured by the evolving new technologies. The main thing the CBC has going for it, Francis Fox makes clear, is that it has been around for 50 years as a 'national institution'! Where it was once the core of the system, the CBC's main purpose today is to ensure 'a clear-cut Canadian broadcasting alternative to private broadcasters' in the new 'multi-channel' environment. It is further made clear that increased efficiency and accountability will henceforth be expected for the considerable amount of public funds consumed annually for this evidently marginal service.

Conclusions
The Canadian political system was established to create, support and maintain a single market from coast to coast. In the course of its development, and faced with the threat of absorption into the more powerful US market, it has used the idea of 'Canada' as a vehicle of mobilisation. For some 50 years, the most powerful instrument of mobilisation at its disposal was the national/public broadcasting system. From the beginning, this political system has been threatened, harassed, undermined, subverted and continually resisted by adherents of an alternative vision of Canada. These adherents, too, have claimed the right to use broadcasting in support of their own nationalism. Today, broadcasting – and more generally, communications – has been given a new economic vocation. The grand design of the federal Department of Communications depends on a strong and centralised federalism. Again, this design is coming under strong attack from Quebec.

In 1983 the government of Quebec held an 'economic summit on communications', bringing together concerned parties from private enterprise, unions and community groups, and the public sector. The working document for the conference[41] recognised the paradox of such an initiative in a field where virtually all the powers are held by another level of government. But Quebec would take advantage of its adversary's weak spots – for example, pressure towards 'deregulation' – which by undermining Ottawa's power appears to enhance its own position.

Quebec, too, is shifting away from a cultural and political concern with communication and towards an economic and technological approach:

> The economic turning . . . is relatively new in our approach, which is traditionally structured around social and cultural dimensions. These are not being abandoned, far from it, but have taken on a new partner, the industrial and financial community.[42]

Like the federal government, Quebec is seeking to use communications to establish a strong economic position in both the domestic and foreign marketplace, and is giving this objective priority over traditional cultural goals. Paradoxically, this shift is being overseen by a government committed to the cultural/political goal of Quebec sovereignty . . . but paradox would appear to be the leading characteristic of the broadcasting environment in Canada and Quebec.

This essay has dealt with *one* of the contradictory aspects of Canada's broadcasting history, namely that aspect which has brought together the Canadian state, Canada's two nationalisms and the public broadcasting system. In the course of this attempt to demystify the political role of the public broadcaster, I may have given the impression of advocating the substitution of the Quebec state for the Canadian one as a solution. This was not my intention. I set up the Quebec 'alternative' in order to deconstruct the mythology of Canadian nationalism and the glorious role of public broadcasting therein. In fact, rather than suggest that the solution is a more benevolent state, I believe that the Canadian experience points to the inevitable limitations of the national principle as a basis for an emancipatory approach to communications media: every nation, every state, just as it organises solidarity against the enemy without, simultaneously and contiguously mobilises and legitimates the repression of dissidence within.

The Canadian broadcasting experience shows how the modern nation-state, while acting in the name of such notions as self-determination, cultural sovereignty and public service, can skilfully maintain a set of internal power relations based on the most fundamental social inequality. It shows how an idea – in this case, the idea of the public – can be mobilised in support of a particular political project and how, under the guidance of the state, communications media – in this case, the media of public broadcasting – can become a legitimating force for alignments of power which have nothing to do with the public in any democratic sense of the term.

In spite of the use to which it has been put as an ideological mechanism of repression, I should like to think that the idea of 'the public' has not been utterly drained of its potential as a focal point for emancipatory media practice. However, the renewal of this idea depends on its being divorced from the companion notions of 'nation' and 'state', and re-appropriated from those who insist that the public, the nation, and the state are merely different labels for the same thing.

References

1. H. Hardin, *A Nation Unaware: the Canadian Economic Culture* (North Vancouver, British Columbia: J.J. Douglas Ltd 1974) pp. 92–3, 136, 140.
2. See E.A. Weir, *The Struggle for National Broadcasting in Canada* (Toronto: McClelland and Stewart 1965) and Frank W. Peers, *The Politics of Canadian Broadcasting, 1920–51* (Toronto: University of Toronto Press 1969).
3. *Report of the Royal Commission on Radio Broadcasting* (Aird Commission) (Ottawa: Government of Canada 1929) p. 6.
4. M. Prang, 'The Origins of Public Broadcasting in Canada', *Canadian Historical Review*, vol. 46, no. 1, 1965, p. 22.
5. Ibid. p. 31.
6. The Canadian Broadcasting Corporation was actually set up in 1936 after the Liberals returned to power and decided to reform the system. The details of the differences between the CRBC and the CBC are not our main concern here, but it should be pointed out that the reform was generally seen as beneficial and corrected a number of structural faults that were built into the system.
7. Peers, op. cit. pp. 136, 159.
8. E.A. Corbett, 'Planned Broadcasting for Canada', in Josephine H. Maclatchy (ed.), *Education on the Air* (Columbus, Ohio: Ohio State University Press 1934) p. 22.
9. *Submission to Royal Commission on Bilingualism and Biculturalism* (Ottawa: Canadian Broadcasting Corporation 1964) pp. 2, 5.
10. Ibid. pp. 5–6.
11. G. Lamarche, 'Radio-Canada et sa mission française', *Canadian Communication*, vol. 1, no. 1, 1960, p. 7.
12. In A. Laurendeau, *La Crise de la Conscription* (Montreal: Editions du Jour 1962) p. 105.
13. Alberta and Saskatchewan also tried to get into provincial broadcasting after the war. Interestingly, Alberta, Saskatchewan, and Quebec were each governed at this time by populist regional parties at odds with Ottawa's centralising tendencies.
14. *Report of the Royal Commission on National Development in the Arts, Letters and Sciences* (Massey Commission) (Ottawa: Government of Canada 1951) p. xvii.
15. Ibid. p. 297.
16. *Report of the Royal Commission on Broadcasting* (Fowler Commission) (Ottawa: Government of Canada 1957) p. 242.
17. Ibid. p. 239.

18. See G. Laurence, 'Le début des affaires publiques à la télévision Québécoise 1952–1957', *Revue d'Histoire de l'Amérique Française*, vol. 36, no. 2, 1982.
19. See G. Pelletier, *Les années d'impatience (1950–1960)* (Montreal: Stanké 1983).
20. A. Stewart, 'Broadcasting in Canada', *Canadian Communication*, vol. 1, no. 3, 1960, p. 36.
21. *Report of the Royal Commission on Government Organisation* (Glassco Commission) (Ottawa: Government of Canada 1963) p. 34.
22. *Submission to Royal Commission on Bilingualism and Biculturalism*, cit., p. 29.
23. See M. Raboy, 'La tour infernale: la petite histoire de l'information à Radio-Canada', *Le Temps Fou*, no. 14, 1981.
24. *Broadcasting Act, 1968*, Revised Statutes of Canada, 1970, ch. B–11, Art. 2(g), iv.
25. *Report of the Committee of Inquiry into the National Broadcasting Service* (Ottawa: Canadian Radio-Television and Telecommunications Commission 1977) p.v.
26. Ibid. pp. 7, 9.
27. *Decision: Renewal of the CBC's Television and Radio Network Licenses* (Ottawa: Canadian Radio-Television and Telecommunications Commission 1979) p. 18.
28. D. Smythe, *Dependency Road: Communications, Capitalism, Consciousness and Canada* (Norwood: Ablex 1981) p. 291.
29. *Pour une politique Québécoise des communications* (Québec City: Ministère des Communications du Québec 1971) p. 2.
30. *Le Québec, maître d'oeuvre de la politique des communications sur sa Territoire* (Quebec City: Ministère des Communications du Québec 1973) p. 20.
31. See *La politique Québécoise du développement culturel* (Québec City: Ministère des Affaires Culturelles 1978).
32. G. Rémillard, *Le fédéralisme Canadien: eléments constitutionnels de formation et d'evolution* (Montreal: Québec-Amérique 1980) pp. 349, 350.
33. In *The CBC: A Perspective* (Ottawa: Canadian Broadcasting Corporation 1979) pp. 371–2.
34. P. Attalah, 'Axes d'une recherche sur le référendum', *Communication Information*, vol. 5, nos. 2–3, 1983, pp. 66–7.
35. *Report of the Federal Cultural Policy Review Committee* (Ottawa: Government of Canada 1982) p. 275.
36. *Building for the Future: Towards a Distinctive CBC* (Ottawa: Department of Communication 1983) p. 16.
37. Ibid.
38. See Raboy, op. cit.
39. *Towards a New National Broadcasting Policy* (Ottawa: Department of Communication 1983) p. 200.
40. *Building for the Future: Towards a Distinctive CBC*, cit.
41. *Le Québec et les communications: un futur simple?*, Québec City: Ministère des Communications du Québec, 1983.
42. Ibid. p. 6.

IAN CONNELL AND LIDIA CURTI

Popular Broadcasting in Italy and Britain: Some Issues and Problems

This essay is motivated principally by the issue that has been made of the impending privatisation of broadcasting and of other means of communicating. In the UK, we are now regularly told that we are on the verge of some fairly substantial changes – of a 'communications revolution'. To provide a measure of just how substantial these changes will be, it has been suggested that before too long the transmission of fixed and similar schedules of programmes from a (very) few centralised sources will have become but one relatively minor part of a considerably 'freer' system of communication in which consumers will have much greater choice. What is now the norm will soon be surpassed and marginalised by a number of alternatives based on the exploitation of satellite, cable, video and computer technology. Indeed in the UK there are already signs that this norm has been passed, given the rapid expansion in the use of video recorders to play back material rented from video libraries, as well as the equally impressive expansion in the use of 'home computers' for a variety of purposes, not least for games of one sort or another. Increasingly, the television set is being used as a VDU as much as, if not more than, a receiver of programmes.

While some are fairly optimistic about the prospect of terminating the 'tyranny of the schedules', others are found to be profoundly pessimistic and concerned. What all the glossy promotionals mask, these pessimists argue, is the fact that from this exploitation of the technology will emerge a system of communication thoroughly dominated and shaped by market forces, their philosophies and rules. There will be a wholesale privatisation of communication with various, more or less calamitous consequences. Consumers will be no freer than at present – if anything, less so. Video recorders and home computers are already used in the main for pre-packaged materials, thus reproducing users as consumers. The pessimists suggest that privatisation has already led to standardisation and that this will spread to every aspect and process involved. There will be a loss of accountability coupled with increased opportunities for supervision and control from above (the '*1984* syndrome'). Never as before, access to the system at any point will depend upon an ability to pay and, in time, this will construct new social divisions between those rich and those poor in information. And, moreover, it is predicted that 'national' cultures will be steadily eroded and disintegrated by the products of a very few 'deep pocket' capitalist enterprises whose influence will be global.

So, if this is to be the state of things to come, the tide of privatisation has to be turned. It has been argued that this can only be done by defending public sector broadcasting, which in the UK would mean having to 'defend the BBC's role as the major public service presence in television'.[1] For some of the critics of privatisation this is a somewhat uncomfortable position to be in, having in the past been critical also of the BBC's haughty refusal to break from safe, established views of its own role as a broadcasting organisation and, more generally, of the character of British society. Defending public sector broadcasting for them also involves, therefore, reform in the hope (perhaps a vain one) of making the BBC rather more accountable and responsive than it has been willing to be in the past. However, there are certain factors that seem to render this attempt to turn the tide a little like Canute's.

Calls to defend and reform public sector institutions like the BBC come at a time when these institutions are under increasing pressure from the private sector. Moreover, this is not at all just a local difficulty, but rather one experienced wherever mixed systems occur. Tunstall has observed that certain long-term weaknesses of public service systems can no longer be hidden, so intense is the pressure being exerted. Despite appearances to the contrary, 'commercial media systems . . . almost invariably win in terms of market success if and when allowed to compete with public service systems'.[2]

A win for the commercial sector certainly seems to be on in the UK. During the last couple of years there has been a steady decline in the BBC's share of the audience and, in the same period of time, the number of top ten positions in peak viewing time that it has secured has sharply decreased. The clearest signs of a win, however, are perhaps found in the BBC's attempts to counter the situation in which it finds itself. When, of late, it has achieved success in the ratings, it has been with material that has all the properties of having been designed for 'market success'. The transmission of *The Thorn Birds* has been the most publicised example of this increasingly commercialised approach, an approach which, of course, has been cultivated inside the BBC for many years now. The novel factor at present is the erosion of much of the opposition to it, both within and without the BBC.

As the critical response to the transmission of *The Thorn Birds* demonstrated, there are those who still support an orthodox public service role for the BBC. Though regretted and criticised by some educators and representatives of political and civil interests, this commercialisation under pressure appears to have, at least, the passive support of those usually lumped together as 'the audience'. Ordinary viewers, those who have till now been interested in broadcasting principally as a resource for entertainment or relaxation, have clearly been drifting away, although not just from the BBC. Sufficient numbers have turned to electronic alternatives to promote a certain amount of concern in the advertising industry about just how many remain and about what sort of attention they give to network TV. There also seems to be little enthusiasm for an orthodox public service among those intellectuals and political forces with the power to influence policy. The present government in the UK has made it clear that in the area of communication enterprises, as elsewhere, it is committed to a policy of privatisation. The Adam Smith Institute, with its recently published communications policy,[3] has indicated that within Conservative spheres of influence there are those who would willingly embark on the manifest privatisation of the BBC. The prospect of commercial success has, for them, overpowered any sense of value they might once have seen in a BBC given over to cultural leadership.

Another factor which contributed to this scaling down of opposition to such developments lies precisely in the manner in which the BBC opted, more often than not, to play the role of cultural leader. Too often the BBC has behaved as an irreproachable purveyor of quality cultural fare above and beyond the doubts, reservations, or criticisms of its users. Too often it has acted as if it did indeed know best what viewers *really* wanted. It has therefore been far from accountable and considerably less than responsive to views of its activities different from those internally canonised. It has never really cast off that arrogant conviction that its chosen editorial paths are the correct ones and just possibly the only ones worthy of consideration. If challenged or even questioned, the BBC has characteristically responded dismissively and not infrequently in an insulting manner. The tone of the replies remains much as that adopted by a previous director-general advising the troops, who said, 'We must not allow ourselves to slip into the despairing attitude of seeing ourselves as casting pearls before swine. . . . The course of wisdom is for us to see ourselves as casting pearls before people who have been taught by us to appreciate their values.'[4] Following this advice has done much to encourage the swine to look for other troughs, sometimes because what was cast were not pearls at all, or were pearls upon which consumers put a quite different value from that intended.

So whether we look to those who have been consumers of BBC programmes or to those who are also consumers in positions that enable them to formulate policies which can shape the organisation's future, there seems to be little enthusiasm to support it, let alone to preserve it or expand it with increased public funds. It would not be unreasonable to suppose that the balance has tipped decisively in favour of the private sector and that within the term of the present government there will be at least a further deterioration in the BBC's financial position, making the privatisation of some of its activities an even more attractive proposition than at present.

What is true in the UK now appears to be true with regard to most public services in mixed broadcasting systems. In Italy (which will be considered in some detail below), since the legislation of the mid-1970s the private companies have gone from strength to strength and now dictate the terms to which RAI must respond. RAI-1 and RAI-2 are now both motivated by the same commercial aspirations as the private networks, and to realise them now employ much the same spectacular offerings. As a consequence, RAI has succeeded in pulling back some of the viewers lost during the initial period of enthusiasm for the liveliness and vigour which the private operations introduced into broadcasting. RAI's success in the ratings has been most notable during the daytime. It has gone on the offensive by buying out successful presenters from one or other of the private companies, in much the same way as the BBC when it was staffing Radio One. Sometimes the fees paid have been astronomical, as in the case of Raffaella Carra, who now hosts the lunchtime show *Pronto . . . Raffaella* – a mixture of family games, music, chatting with special guests and a telephone quiz. The 1,860 million lire contract that RAI offered Carra to keep her quickly became the centrepoint of a controversy, a scandal indeed in a country trying out an austerity programme under the Socialist-led coalition. With news of the contract breaking in the press, Craxi summoned Zavoli, president of the board of RAI directors and fellow member of the Socialist Party, to convey his displeasure at the offer and his view that it betrayed the policy of sacrifice. Legally, after the legislation of 1975, Craxi has no rights whatsoever to interfere. The fact that he did, and that he almost succeeded in reversing the board of directors' decision, indicates just how fragile RAI's position still is in comparison with the private networks whose commercial dealings run none of these kinds of risks.

Given the measure of commercialisation that has already been accomplished, then, the privatisation of broadcasting and its incorporation within privatised systems of communication seem like a certain, ineluctable formality. There seems to be little evidence to suggest that some kind of 'save our public service' campaign would secure the necessary popular support to maintain public service operations. Furthermore, it seems unlikely that public service operations are open to the sorts of reforms that have been recommended to make them more accountable and more integrated with particular, local communities. We would recommend, then, that the shadow-boxing with the private sector, in which critical commentators are currently engaged, be brought to an end. Despite all sorts of fancy footwork there is no real opposition to privatisation, and so the contest should be stopped before any severe and permanent damage is inflicted. What we need now are new tactics, to learn how to live with the private sector, and how to deal with the opportunities that it presents. But, is there any such thing as 'opportunities' in a privatised future and, if so, just what are they?

To suggest that there are any opportunities at all is, we acknowledge, to be quite heterodox. It could be argued that to look for opportunities within the private sector is to ignore or to misunderstand what has already been accomplished away from or outside of the mainstream sector entirely. Perhaps various grassroots initiatives could be cited, or the local or national attempts to develop domestic production and community-based alternatives. The existence of S4C demonstrates palpably that such initiatives can be successful if pursued in a sufficiently determined way. What sense is there in suggesting that the mainstream presents opportunities when so many of the hopes for experimental innovation have been frustrated by the actions of the editorial executive at Channel 4? We do not wish to deny everything that has been claimed for extra-mural ventures, though we would dispute whether they can be seen as the main plank in a strategy to overthrow all that follows from the commercialisation of the intra-mural. Where there is already a highly developed private sector which has established a complex web of international and trans-global relations, and where about 95 per cent of nations have little effective choice but to be media importers, local initiatives need not present any threat at all. Apart from anything else, they simply do not have the economic resources to sustain much more than one-off productions. There can also be relatively peaceful co-existence between the two. Small-time outfits on the ideological fringes can run the sort of risks which the big-time outfits will not, and when acceptably successful can be used to refurbish the mainstream operations. National or local operations can also be the means by which trans-nationals obtain access to particular domestic markets, as the state of affairs in Italy illustrates.

Small-scale or fringe activities do not, then, have the resources to challenge the mainstream, and may even depend upon the handouts given by the mainstream, as has been the case with a number of independent initiatives associated with Channel 4. Moreover, there is nothing intrinsically or essentially better about an operation simply because it functions on a different scale, or collectively, or in organic communion with its users. At best such an operation might enable

91

what Eco once called 'semiotic guerrilla warfare', but it is difficult indeed to see how this can become the basis for reconstruction.

Almost all commentators now agree that the private sector exercises a leading role in the affairs of broadcasting. That sector has, in other words, the power to establish the norms. We want to suggest that the exercise of this power *can* have positive and revitalising effects which are usually overlooked in focusing upon the limitations and constraints which unquestionably exist. In the course of this attempt to specify where these can be located and what they might be, we do not want to lapse back into one-sidedness of the sort that can too easily be found in the existing literature on commercialism and media or cultural imperialism. We do not want simply to argue that the private sectors are enabling where others have argued that they are constraining, though we will suggest that what have been taken as constraints are not necessarily so. As with any other practice, commercial ones in broadcasting can never be said to be just this or that. Exactly what they are and what they can achieve will depend upon the conditions established in particular contexts. Commercial operations can indeed be limiting and regressive. That we know they can be depends, however, not just on the peripheral activities of an avant-garde, but also upon the renovative activities undertaken at the commercial centre.

The commercial centre is capable of producing material that is *excessive*, that extends and may undermine the limits which previously produced material had helped to maintain. It is certainly capable of sounding 'depths of taste' as yet unknown to those who will readily pass judgment upon the most recent sitcom or formulaic *telenovela* for all sorts of inadequacies. The commercial centre frequently articulates a universe of taste and sentiment which is obviously quite different from that of its critics. However, this difference is not sufficient to license the conclusion that the commercially articulated universe merely reproduces things as they are or that it is inevitably ideological, while at the non-commercial periphery there can be found material which defamiliarises and deconstructs things as they are and then anticipates things as they might become. This simple opposition does little justice to the situation.

In what follows we want to suggest that the commercial sector has promoted a certain standardised set of offers to consumers; what is on offer in the UK is much the same as that in Italy. A certain view of these offers has been taken by those who have done much to map the contours of 'cultural imperialism', which we think is questionable. Having demonstrated that it is, we will then attempt to show that these offers have a potential over and above that which has so far been imagined. They present certain positive opportunities and can positively encourage progressive features of popular cultures. The case we make is a first attempt and therefore tentative. If we do little else, we hope to provide a basis for agreeing that the offers studied are considerably more ambiguous than they are usually made to seem and that, therefore, they may be seen as contributors to change as well as conservation.

We begin making this case with reference to certain aspects of the literature on media and cultural imperialism, and, in particular, to the notion of dependency. In that literature, when the referent is broadcasting, the UK and Italy are usually placed towards opposite ends of the spectrum. The UK is typically cited as one of the more powerful source countries on the grounds that it exports not only products, but also norms of professional conduct. So far as its communications industries are concerned, then, the UK is seen as next in line only to the USA. When 'media imperialism' is broadly defined as 'the process whereby the ownership, structure, distribution or content of the media in any one country are singly or together subject to substantial external pressure from the media industries of any other country or countries without proportionate reciprocation of influence by the country so affected',[5] then Italy can appear to be a prime candidate for dependency. If we take the example of broadcasting in that country, there would seem to be considerable evidence of 'substantial external pressure'.

Writing not long after the constitutional reforms of broadcasting in the mid-70s, Fabio Luca Cavazza could state:

> Despite foreign and private competition, RAI remains the most important and almost the only source of televised information and entertainment for most Italians. Even among those who are in a position to receive other, foreign or private programmes, most end up, almost involuntarily, watching their own national television.[6]

Things are no longer quite so, even if they were when he was writing. It could be pointed out that the BBC, and then UK advertising agencies, were formative influences on the development of Italian broadcasting during the 1950s and 1960s. Since the mid-70s 'external influences' have been more overt. With the rapid expansion of the private sector, broadcasting has been transformed and worked over by privatisation to a degree not yet accomplished in the UK. There are now three major private networks: Canale 5, Italia 1, and Rete 4. There is also a plethora of smaller stations transmitting in particular regions or cities, and several of these now function as the local arm of one or other of the major outfits. These mutually competitive operations have seized the initiative from RAI and it can be argued that, in so doing, they have plunged Italian broadcasting deeper into the depths of dependency.

In advertising itself and its programmes RAI claims to produce 80 per cent of what it transmits. That this is so emphasises just how much material transmitted in Italy has been produced elsewhere. The private networks have been the main points of entry for this material. They have produced very little of their own, and when they have it is of a kind which is relatively cheap to make. Quiz games abound, as do shows that combine various elements such as phone-ins, a game, chat and perhaps a star interview. Both RAI-1 and RAI-2 have now adopted this format for Sunday afternoons with shows which run from 14.00 to 19.50 (*Domenica in,* RAI-1), and from 13.30 to 19.45 (*Blitz,* RAI-2). In addition to the elements just mentioned, these also include coverage of sport. Eco has called this type 'the hold-all',[7] and sees it as something which can confuse even sophisticated viewers about what is and is not spectacle. To this 'confusion' or, perhaps, 'deconstruction' we shall return when considering what has been said of the effects of dependency.

If we take as a focus the prime-time schedule of Canale 5, the main features of this period, the sort of foreign material and the extent of its use can be indicated. This network begins at the present time with a US telefilm (in the UK it would be classed as sitcom) *The Jeffersons* (19.00) and follows this with a quiz game *Zig Zag* (19.30) introduced and conducted by an ageing entertainer, Raimondo Vianello. 19.30 is a junction it shares only with Rete 4 which at that point also transmits a quiz show game, *M'ama non m'ama*. All the privates share the same start time for the next phase of the schedule at 20.25, five minutes or so (times are not always as announced in advance) before RAI-1, RAI-2 and RAI-3. While the private networks have been transmitting either telefilms or quiz games RAI-1 and RAI-2 have put out their main news bulletins of the day. Journalism is not something to be found on the privates' schedules. Though some of the local privates do run a news service, they transmit bulletins only during the daytime or late evening slots. There are no current affairs programmes on the privates of the type familiar in the UK, though current issues will sometimes be raised in the context of interviews in one of the 'hold-all' shows.

In the three weeks monitored (8–28 April 1984), Canale 5 transmitted, on Monday and Wednesday at 20.25, an episode from *Return to Eden* (another import); on Tuesday, *Dallas*; and on Thursday and Friday quiz games, *Superflash* presented by Mike Bongiorno (who has been presenting such programmes since the mid-1950s) and *Ciao Gente*. *Superflash* is billed as '*l'attualità della settimana*' ('the live programme of the week'). At the same point the other major private stations are offering cinema films, telefilms, quiz shows and a variety show. On Monday and Wednesday Canale 5 offers at 22.25 *Flamingo Road* and *Kojak*. On Tuesday at 21.25 there is *The Thorn Birds*; on Thursday at 23.00 another episode of *The Jeffersons* with yet another at 22.50 on Friday. Similar offerings are made on each of the other channels at about the same times. Apart from games, films and telefilms, pop magazines and talk shows begin to appear around the 22.30 mark, at the end of peak time. On Monday at 22.30, Rete 4 transmits the *Maurizio Costanzo Show*, which mixes interviews and interventions with various kinds of 'turns'. There are 'pop' magazines and sport programmes at this time and sometimes later as well. The one exception is RAI-2 which at 21.30 transmits *Tribuna Politica*, a programme in which politicians are interviewed and quizzed by political journalists from the press. Weekends do not differ much from weekdays during peak time. On Canale 5, the early part of this period is exactly the same. It begins with transmission of its main *spettacolo* (variety show) of the week, *Risatissima*, followed by the weekly sports magazine *Super Record*. Sunday runs from 19.30 thus: *Dallas* (19.30), *Return to Eden* (20.25), *Flamingo Road* (22.25) and then a cinema film at 23.25, followed by another at 01.25. Rete 4 matches this line-up on Sunday with *Dynasty* (19.30), *M'ama non m'ama* (20.25) and *Remington Steele* at 22.30.

This brief sketch reveals the heavy use of imported telefilms and cinema films during the peak viewing hours. RAI may have a schedule 80 per cent of which is domestically produced, but it is not above employing, on RAI-2, *The Streets of San Francisco* each weekday evening at 18.40 or thereabouts, presumably in an effort to engage viewers for programmes which follow. On the private networks, especially, the use of imported telefilm during the day is even more intense and includes a lot of American material from the 1960s and even 1950s. These will have been acquired by, or dumped on, the privates as part of a package that includes the more recent and glossy offerings.[8]

With this prime-time schedule of games, variety, imported telefilms and mini-series, Canale 5 claims to have ended 1983 as the network with the highest ratings, just beating RAI-1 into second place. Italia 1 was said to have been next, followed by RAI-2 and then Rete 4, said to have made losses of nearly 50 billion lire during the year and to be considering among other things dropping *Dynasty* because of its poor showing in the ratings. These claims must be regarded with caution. No one can really say accurately just how many viewers there are in Italy, since licence evasion is much more common there than in the UK. The monitoring of viewing is only now becoming a routine affair. RAI has just introduced selectively a new meter system which can record the usual sort of data. For the first two and a half months of this year meter readings placed RAI-1 substantially ahead of the other channels with an average 9.5 million viewers in the peak-time period.

Next came RAI-2 with 4.2 and then Canale 5 with 4.0, followed by Rete 4 with 2.4 and Italia 1 with an average of 2.3. As representatives of the privates have been quick to point out, the sampling details of this meter survey have not been made known. Alberto Scandolara, head of press at Canale 5, has been quoted as saying, 'Today the meter is exclusively in control of RAI, with samples that nobody knows, in places nobody knows. We accept the system but we want joint control.'[9] Meter-based readings are favoured by the advertisers on the grounds that they provide the most accurate picture of viewer behaviour available. Their use by RAI could, then, be taken as a ploy in attracting more advertising business in a complicatedly competitive situation.

This competition between RAI and the privates, but also between one RAI network and another and between each of the privates, has led to an ever-increasing dependency upon imported materials, as the peak-time schedules show. Imported programmes would seem to offer a relatively cheap way of filling the day, attracting viewers and, therefore, advertising revenue. The level of dependency might also be measured in the absence of a production structure capable of supporting the output of materials that could be successful on the international market. According to the associate director of RAI-1, Nino Fuscagni, 'Neither Italian television nor cinema has the infrastructure needed to produce television series like those which come out of America on a continuing basis.'[10] What RAI has till now opted for instead are co-productions like *La Nave perduta* (*And the Ship Sails On*) with the BBC, Network Seven in Australia and New Zealand TV, and spectaculars such as *Marco Polo* and *Cristoforo Colombo*.

The problem is not just lack of funds or of studio facilities and equipment. A recent review of the state of confidence among employees of RAI amid accusations in the press of waste, of a lack of a sense of professionalism and of unwieldy bureaucracy, quoted a programme producer as saying,

> While we in production measure our work in seconds, the bureaucracy moves in a way which gives us a substitute dancer within a week, pays fees with a slowness which is unacceptable to international artists used to a different rhythm, and, for contracts, asks for a quantity of documents that is incomprehensible to professionals, above all foreigners.[11]

While producers may be attuned to these rhythms of the international TV community, the bureaucracy appears not to be. When Fuscagni speaks of an absent infrastructure it is in this fuller sense that it ought to be understood. If models and norms of professionalism have been imported along with hardware and software, their adoption has been quite uneven, to such an extent that much about the presentation on Italian television appears amateurish in comparison with presentation in the UK. This is just what one would expect according to the arguments of the literature of media imperialism. The dependent service is a copy of the source, but a poor and pale imitation. In Italy this could be said to be all the more so in that it is caught between two models, the orthodox version of public service as developed by the BBC and the more powerful American commercial one, neither successfully reproduced.

Competition may have increased dependency and deprived Italy of the range and depth of resources and the organisation necessary to make a significant impact as an exporter, but it also seems now to be threatening that dependency and to be stimulating at least the first moves to expanding domestic production. In recent months there has been speculation that Canale 5 and Italia 1 have been attempting to arrive at some kind of agreement to modify the competition between them in order to reduce production costs, re-organise the advertising market and to halt (which seems unlikely) the ever-increasing costs of purchasing foreign product – ever-increasing precisely because of the current competition for such material. No real agreement seems to have been reached, however. Instead, there is some evidence that Canale 5 might well begin to produce more of its own material. Berlusconi has announced an intention 'to move towards the production of a larger and larger proportion of our total programming today',[12] not so much out of a sense of 'national' pride as for economic reasons. Quite simply domestic production could prove to be more profitable, especially if it provides material that can find its way to markets abroad even more economically subordinate. *Risatissima* is one of Canale 5's domestically produced programmes with which it is trying to win sales in the Spanish language markets. However, Canale 5 is far from turning its back on US imports. It has committed around 20 million dollars to the acquisition of foreign product in 1984, suggesting that any move to expand production in Italy will indeed be prolonged.

It would seem unlikely that any future domestic production in Italy would depart radically from the sorts of programmes currently attempted. Dependency is also said to be present in the absorption and naturalisation of forms that have been imposed from outside. Writing on the duplication of media systems initially developed in the source countries, Boyd-Barrett has concluded that 'the shape of communication vehicles . . . is in general highly standardised across the world'.[13] He cites as an example 'the dominant concern for maximising audiences at the expense of the alternative strategy of differentiating the audience and seeking to meet the requirements of each specific segment'.[14] This promotes the use of series formats because they offer 'a formula for securing maximum audiences over a period of time on the strength of a single major dramatic idea'.[15] There is very little about the current state of affairs in Italy which indicates independence from this standardised approach.

There have been moments of difference. Under the direction of Andrea Barbato, RAI-2 during the late 1970s attempted certain innovations in the presentation of news programmes (*telegiornali*). *Telegiornale 2 – Spazio Aperto* had an open, experimental style. The seated speaker, facing the camera, reading a prepared script in neutral tones, was replaced by one who spoke freely from notes and frequently added comments. It did not merely catalogue the newsworthy events of the day, but added interview and debate, again with a fair degree of independence permitted in the conduct of each. The opening titles showed (as is still the case) the studio with technicians, cameras and monitors, suggesting perhaps that the news did not come from nowhere. However, the experiment lasted only a few years. Barbato was dismissed for his excessive independence and the space for those journalists who did not resign in protest was considerably curtailed. Now the differences between *Telegiornale 1* and *Telegiornale 2* are minimal. The decentralisation which was proposed at the time of the reforms, intended as 'the means both of "guaranteeing pluralism" and of linking the broadcasting system to the regions, that is to say to the sources of the country's cultural practice and diversity'[16] has never really been put into effect even with the existence of RAI-3. The direction of development since the 1970s has, if anything, been to centralisation.

The proposals for domestic production seem similarly conformist, partly because the requirement is to create a substitute for increasingly expensive foreign product. At present there are tentative steps being taken to launch home-grown soap operas. Pegaso Inter-Communications have just produced two promotional episodes of a projected 30-part series called *Quarto Piano, Interno 9*, which is based upon a popular RAI radio series. Both RAI and Canale 5 have expressed an interest in seeing these episodes, and are no doubt attracted by the fact that they are cheap and quick to produce, having been recorded on video, thus minimising post-production work. There is caution, however. *Quarto Piano, Interno 9* is not intended to replace the likes of *Dallas*. It is seen rather as a qualitatively superior version of the *telenovelas* produced by TV Globo – a version that has 'a touch of Italian class and with subjects closer to our customs and mentality.'[17] (If the 'our' seems a little vague, perhaps the fact that the series is said to deal with the daily life of a middle-class Italian family – a separated husband and wife, with three daughters – specifies who might be included). Though it has demonstrated that American methods of production can be implemented, it could present something of a scheduling problem since the series is not glossy enough to compete with US imports, yet not rough enough to function as radio-for-television in the manner of the visually basic *telenovelas*.

Dependency is, then, well established with respect to what we might think of as conventional broadcasting. As an exporter, Italian broadcasting is quite peripheral. It depends heavily on imported programmes and though this is threatened by domestic competition it is unlikely that domestic production will significantly increase in the immediate future. Whatever the scale of production, it is quite likely to conform to the established international norms by adopting and in some measure adapting the formats which have met with success on international markets. The seeds of dependency have been sown with respect to the way in which 'new' technology will be introduced. Since the spring of last year, for example, RAI has been experimenting with a teletext system (televideo), providing around 600 pages of information and services compiled by a staff of 30 that includes 16 journalists. Once again RAI has looked to the BBC's approach as a model for its own. Future possibilities are typically presented in terms much the same as those that are familiar now in places where the introduction of new technology is more advanced. Recently it was stated in RAI's publicity that

> In contradiction to the apocalyptic expectations of some years ago, it will not present itself as some great 'hidden persuader' but will tend to favour the freedom of the user. The new telematic services, video recorders and video discs, in fact, will make a more personal use of the medium possible. The user will be able to decide *what* to watch *when* he wants. It will be possible, then, to move beyond that fixed mass audience . . . which has been characteristic of television's history: everybody will be able to do his own programming, choosing from an ever-increasing range of possibilities and uses of video, while, with the introduction of direct broadcasting by satellite, it will be possible to gain access to new foreign material.[18]

At the present time there is some disagreement about how to understand the relations between source and dependent units. Some will question the notion that dependent units can be seen as externally constrained, as it implies a certain innocence and passivity on the part of those supposed to be constrained. The evidence of absorption and of the active pursuit and development of courses of action derived from the outside has led to attention being directed to 'the dynamic relationship between internal factors such as a nation's class structure and history and external factors such as transnational corporations, international financial institutions and so on'.[19] The take-up of the standardised model referred to above is not best understood as the consequence of imposition. An alternative explanation would refer to the fact that there are indigenous economic forces, with the power to shape systems of communication which have adopted the standard models from economic necessity. This would follow from being so inextricably bound up with, and so committed to, the fruits that can be gained from the international corporate business system.

While there are important differences in explaining just how a certain course of action has been standardised, adopted and absorbed, however, there are far fewer when it comes to considering the consequences of it having become so. There is something very like consensus about the view that the standard model has been adopted at the expense of certain indigenous needs and national peculiarities. Clearly those forces with the capacities needed to adopt and shape models of communicative practice do so not just on their own behalf, but also on behalf of others who have little option but to consume what they are offered and of whom it has been said that their 'real' interests suffer as a consequence. The dominant local providers have only that measure of regard for local or national peculiarities that is sufficient to produce commodities which are internationally marketable as 'made in Italy' or 'made in Britain'. Only those peculiarities that register externally, in this larger international forum, will be nurtured. Those that are invisible are left either to wither away or to survive as best they can.

The activities of the private companies in Italy can then be cited for having accomplished not only what Schiller has referred to as 'the transformation of national media structures into conduits of the corporate business system',[20] but also because of the cultural effects which seem to follow from this. He puts forward the view, not at all uncommon in the literature on media imperialism, that 'the heavy international traffic of commercial products from the centre to the periphery' creates a situation in which weaker societies 'are absorbed culturally into the modern world system'.[21] The weaker the society, the more likely it is that there will be few if any countervailing forces to draw on in order to withstand this absorption. The situation in Italy is not quite like this. Recent sociological research has put together a socio-cultural map which suggests that, while there is an overall movement in terms of habits and aspirations to a pragmatic and anti-authoritarian consumerism, there are pockets of traditional resistance. The research depicts the south as a location for such resistance and with it a fairly unreceptive posture to the offers made by the media:

> In the south, therefore, we find those who have a lively sense of collective solidarity (which they demonstrate in the parish or in the

locality), those who try to resist the manipulation of the media and consumerism, and who aspire to a life which is high-mindedly strict and austere. Little by little, as you come north, other interests and forms of behaviour prevail.[22]

These other interests and activities may well be more in tune with the media's offers though, as Fejes has pointed out,[23] they ought not to be viewed as the direct and unmediated effects of the media in turn viewed as manipulative agents in the situation.

In the light of the literature on media imperialism and its effects, it can be all too easy to adopt this kind of traditionalist instance of resistance as the remnants of an authentic culture. This is especially tempting when it seems as if the international media traffic puts about materials which provide 'in their imagery and messagery the beliefs and perspectives that create and reinforce their audiences' attachment to the way things are in the system overall'.[24] Boyd-Barrett has suggested that media imperialism can be seen

> as a process which serves to reinforce existing economic and political relations between nations. The media, in other words, perform an *ideological* role. This occurs overtly in the form of explicit propaganda channels; covertly through the expression of certain values in what otherwise appears to be neutral entertainment and informational fare.[25]

But just how confident can we be that this is what the media actually accomplish and that the most sensible course of action is the defence and development of the marginal, seemingly authentic subcultures? There is little doubt that the media can celebrate consumerism and that they can win converts to it. Inasmuch as they do, they can end up reinforcing existing economic and political relations on a national and international scale. They may well do, but we want to suggest that they can do more besides. Before outlining what we think this consists of, we wish to stress again that we are dealing with objective developments. That culture which the internationally standardised media have contributed to establishing cannot be out-manoeuvred by actions on the cultural sidelines. There are parallels to be drawn here with Gramsci's observations on the development of a national language in Italy. According to his view,

> someone who only speaks dialect, or understands the standard language incompletely, necessarily has an intuition of the world which is more or less limited and provincial, which is fossilised and anachronistic in relation to the major currents of thought which dominate world history.[26]

Like it or not, the standardised media now provide 'the major currents of thought', and we risk fossilisation if we refuse to become tele-literate, to acquire a competence in the languages with which these major currents have been articulated. This is not a matter of evaluation or judgment. It does not involve questions to do with the adequacy or the acceptability of these major currents of thought. To say we must acquire a competence, become tele-literate, is simply to recognise and acknowledge an *historical* necessity.

The view that what the standardised model puts about wherever it has taken hold is ideological probably has much to do with the prior perception of its popularity. Critical attention suggests that in fact the offers made are populist, and mean by this classification something more complex than that they successfully attract the attention of many ordinary viewers. This they do indeed do, but much more besides, none of which is rated very highly by critics. With the ever-increasing pace of privatisation, the standardised model of which we have been speaking 'plays to the gallery' more and more. In the words of Philip Schlesinger, Graham Murdock and the late Philip Elliott, 'the commercial logic of the marketplace makes popularity the major arbiter of production'.[27] Indeed it does, but these authors are a little more than concerned about this *socialisation* of production. 'Serving the public', once an honourable thing to be doing in the public sector, has been transformed by the application of this commercial logic. It now rarely enables space for 'the programme makers' right to challenge prevailing attitudes and preconceptions, to provoke and annoy sections of the audience or 'for alternative and oppositional perspectives [that] are an essential precondition for an informed public, capable of making considered choices between competing policies. . . .' Now, 'serving the public is equated with giving people what they want (as measured by sales or ratings)'.[28]

In effect, then, what this socialisation of production has accomplished is the exclusion of 'critical thinking', though this is perhaps overstating the case. Some space is left within the mainstream framework, according to these authors. It is not entirely without the more 'open' investigation of issues. But, that said, the general overriding tendency is to ideological closure – at best conservative, at worst reactionary.

The populism of the offers made is manifested in a number of ways. The programmes churned out variously signal their ordinariness. Writing about the enormously attractive quiz show of the late 1950s, *Lascia o raddoppia*, hosted by Mike Bongiorno (who now hosts *Superflash*), Umberto Eco believed he saw the stereotype of the national average man, the affirmation of mediocrity and the reduction of superman to everyman. The spectator was presented with a glorified and officially blessed portrait of his own limits. Bongiorno appeared to Eco as ignorant and happy to be so, to have a petit-bourgeois sense of money and social convention, to speak very basic Italian, liberally sprinkled with linguistic and cultural errors. As his embittered polemic against what he has recently called 'neotelevision' indicates, the phenomenon has not disappeared with the passage of time but has become instead even more emphatically populist, even more preoccupied with passing itself off as 'everyman':

> The principal characteristic of neo-television is that it speaks less and less . . . of the outside world. It talks about itself and of the contact made with its own audience. It doesn't matter what it might say and of what it might speak (because the public armed with a remote control decides when to let it speak and when to switch to another channel). In order to survive this power to switch over, neo-television tries to hold the viewer, saying to him: 'I'm here, I am me, and I am you.'[29]

Moreover, there has been, both in the UK and in Italy, a set of more explicit attempts at 'fabricating' unity with 'ordinary' viewers. There has been, for instance, a run of quiz programmes of which a feature is made of their use of public opinion polling. Contestants have to guess, in some, the percentage of people who subscribe to such and such a view; in others, what 'ordinary viewers' would say or do about this or that situation. In these games it can no doubt seem to the critical that there is a kind of 'tyranny of the majority'. Authority is no longer derived from the discourses of the 'well-informed' or the 'educated' – the *really* knowledgeable. Instead it is derived from what 'most people' think, and this tends to be seen as fairly conservative.

Among popular broadcasting's commentators there seems to be general agreement that programming of this kind is both limited and limiting. In attempting to meet apparent wants rather than real needs, programmes of populist design constantly stress, celebrate and re-affirm what is already known and familiar; in short, what – at least, in the commentators' eyes – is obvious. Some have suggested that what is involved here is downright deception. Believing that sales and ratings measure nothing, or nothing useful, they see the media as constructing, perhaps inventing, certain views and then labelling them common or popular, when in fact they are nothing of the sort. Others, more disposed to accept that the media do indeed draw on popular structures of feeling and thinking, still see problems. It has been argued that these popular structures of feeling and thinking – common sense – are incapable of mounting adequate explanations. Those that are attempted are shallow or over-simplified to the point of caricature, and certainly not capable of arriving at fundamentals.

So, for instance, Stuart Hall has stated that 'you cannot learn through common sense how things are; you can only discover where they fit into the existing scheme of things'.[30] (If common sense as represented by the media does enable us to discover that there is a scheme into which things fit, it is accomplishing something, at least as much as certain synchronic structuralisms.) Catherine Belsey, in line with recent work in Europe and in the United States, stimulated above all from France, describes common sense as 'collective and timeless wisdom' which presents itself as 'non-theoretical', and which 'betrays its own inadequacy by its incoherences, its contradictions and its silences'.[31] Writing on the common-sense perspective of the TV programme *Nationwide*, Brunsdon and Morley have stated that it was 'grounded in the personal and the concrete', that it was 'practical, opposed to abstraction and theorising', and then quote Gramsci to say that it identified 'the exact cause, simple and to hand, and does not let itself be distracted by fancy quibbles and pseudo-profound, pseudo-scientific metaphysical mumbo-jumbo'.[32] But, where Gramsci was in fact approving, Brunsdon and Morley were not at all. With the assistance of the Althusserian view that ideology is the very condition of, if not the same thing as, lived experience, all this was seen as mere ideological effect which 'forecloses historical and structural examination'. Without wanting to deny that popular broadcasting can indeed be anti-intellectual and that it can resist, sometimes quite resolutely, to generalise in a legitimate way beyond what appears only to be immediate and particular, we would nevertheless suggest that it can sometimes find its way through mumbo-jumbo, that this can be useful, and that historical and structural examination can sometimes qualify as little more than mumbo-jumbo and as metaphysical.

There are, contrary to these very negative views, a number of features which seem to us positive about commercial broadcasting's populism. One Italian programme demonstrates something of what these are. Rete 4 currently transmits the *Maurizio Costanza Show* on Mondays at 22.30. It is surprisingly popular, given its transmission time. It is a kind of chat show which mixes the talk with spectacle. A run-of-the-mill edition usually finds song and dance punctuating the interviewing and the discussion. Alternatively, Maurizio will sometimes invite up on stage someone from the audience to 'do a turn'. The aura is decidedly relaxed, much more at home with everyday turns of phrase than with the discourses of experts. Maurizio conducts the show, but unlike other front men can act as a catalyst and then step back to let the protagonists get on with it. He rarely sits, is always on the move, mediating between the world of the stage and that of the auditorium. In one moment he prompts and teases a star of yesteryear into an impassioned defence of her professional life and the status of stars, then steps aside while she does battle with members of the audience who are in disagreement. In another, he confronts the minister of justice about the state's employment criteria and does so by bringing on a girl who has been fired from her state job for being too small! Then he tackles representatives of RAI and the other networks about their policies for broadcasting, during which angry interventions from the floor interrupt on the question of the fee which has been paid to Raffaella Carra.

There is here none of the well-mannered, routinised turn-taking that we find in conventional current affairs programmes. The smooth, balanced interviews of *Tribuna Politica* are quite foreign. The result is not always coherent, and it is often contradictory. But high-status interviewees do not always find themselves allowed to take initiatives or to have the last definitive words. Others can and do take on these explanatory roles. Perhaps not much is explained, if by this we mean that we learn how things have become as they are. But at the same time you feel that things are not explained away quite as easily as they can be when recourse is made to the stock responses of official discourses. The *Maurizio Costanza Show* is, then, on occasions excessive. It goes beyond these official discourses and, in so doing, presents them with difficulties that are not always contained. It is a show about which we find it difficult to say that it reproduces existing relations, for it presents some positive images not only of ordinary people as dissatisfied, but also as quite able to talk back effectively and to put alternatives.

It is obvious, however, that this show is unlikely to win much support or enthusiasm from more tutored critical viewers. Its populism would perhaps make it seem to them as sacrificing the provision of information about really alternative perspectives and as leading to an unnecessary dramatisation of issues, to emotional and irrational outbursts. Its combination of the 'serious' and the 'trivial', of serious talk with 'entertainment', would perhaps be cited as causing confusion or as compromising the possibility of developing deeper understanding. That it could be the basis for *revitalising*, for *transforming* current affairs is not seriously considered. By engaging with discourses other than official ones, this show has at least some potential to make serious discussion less moribund, something sought out by more than the minority of the 'active'.

One factor that makes this possible is that the *Maurizio Costanza Show* is not generically pure. It has many of the properties of the hold-all programme, which, of course, can be accused of encouraging a bitty rather than coherent view of the world. The advent and development of such programme types have caused Eco to suggest that even 'sophisticated' viewers become confused when watching them. According to him, there were

experiments in the 60s [which] taught us that, for many under-developed viewers, the evening's viewing was accepted as a continuum without any distinction between truth and fiction. The under-developed viewer believed that the facts in the news were a pretence just like the events of a drama, or that drama might be as true as the weather forecast. . . . To confuse things further, along came the miscellany programme. . . . At that point, even the over-developed viewer confuses genres, and suspects that the bombing of Beirut might be mere spectacle.[33]

There is a body of work in this country which would say that the distinction between 'fact' and 'fiction' is not perhaps as sharp as some think it should be. Hartley and Hawkes have suggested that television systematically imposes literary qualities on all its materials and that news broadcasts, discussions and interviews are reduced (their word) to inherited literary models.[34] Bazalgette and Paterson, in their study of the formal structures of television news and press coverage of the Iranian embassy siege, have pointed to the relation between these and entertainment forms and have stressed that many of the complex codes used to understand the real are based on fiction.[35] And, more recently Schlesinger, Murdock and Elliott, writing about television and terrorism, have pointed to

> some interesting similarities in the way particular forms of journalism and fiction handle the issues. The standard devices of the action-adventure series, for example, combine to produce the same stress on dramatic events . . . as in news coverage.[36]

There are two points about much of this sort of discussion that are open to question. At least some of the participants in it clearly do not think it right and proper that news stories 'dramatise', and perhaps this is because they continue to subscribe to the view that news, somehow, should be a literal transcription of reality which does not suffer from artifice of any kind. In addition, the discussion is haunted by a sense that cultural boundaries are being blurred illegitimately: the 'factual' and the 'serious' is being *contaminated* by the 'fictional' and the 'frivolous' with, as a consequence, the weakening of the former's explanatory powers. So worried do some commentators seem that one cannot help but feel that they think *only* the former is capable of explanation at all. In part, probably, this is based upon the perception of certain similarities between journalistic discourses, especially investigative academic ones. Each share, for instance, certain ways of deploying 'accredited witnesses'; in both, certain things are acceptable because uttered by, or backed up by, names with position or reputation. What else is shared would be an interesting topic for investigation, an investigation which would note, of course, the academic training of most journalists involved in TV current affairs. This inter-meshing is no doubt one of the reasons why there has already been considerable research in this area of television and why now there are several academics who find themselves at one with certain television journalists in lamenting the probable passing of what has become conventional investigative journalism.

Those who do would often find it difficult to accept that entertainment can not only be informative but also explanatory and educative. They would no doubt dismiss with scorn any suggestion that the quiz games referred to earlier could perform functions similar to those performed by news. Surely they do inform us, perhaps in a way less haphazard than news, of popular sentiments and views on matters which rarely find manifest representation in news but may, nonetheless, be crucial for an adequate understanding of the issues and positions that are. What is fundamentally at stake here is not only the categorisation of different cultural areas, but also their ranking. Broadly 'fictional' and 'entertainment' forms are ranked as inferior, and it is this which inspires all the concern about the increasing spectacularisation and fictionalisation of popular broadcasting. Tony Bennett and Graham Martin have been bold enough to put the matter clearly in their assertion that the process of 'defamiliarisation', which, according to Russian formalists, distinguished 'literature', embodies 'a type of mental experience that can be described as superior in relation to that produced by works of popular culture'.[37]

Before saying something about this issue, let us try to build in some context. Recent survey work in Italy suggests that, while RAI is regarded by viewers as 'serious, informative, good for news and current affairs', its leading competitor, Canale 5, is seen as 'light, varied, agile, young, supplying good films and series'. As to spectators during the peak-time slots, no easy differentiations were possible in terms of 'class'. However, there as here, women emerge as much heavier viewers than men and are more likely to watch the offers made by Canale 5. In fact, the majority of its viewers are women. We can try to imagine, then, the broad outline of a typical day for the typical Italian housewife. During the morning's domestic labours there is the possibility of some old American (or perhaps Italian) cinema film or, more often, a magazine programme with a phone-in element which is introduced by a woman. In the afternoon, ancient American telefilms and soaps are shown, with the *telenovelas* as an alternative. In the early evening, to accompany preparations for the evening meal, there are more *telenovelas*, though an increasing proportion of more recent US and UK telefilms. Given this diet, we can imagine that there will be some critical response which sees the media imperialist thesis confirmed: simple-minded women as defenceless prey to this manipulative rubbish which explains nothing, merely confirms and celebrates the obvious or the trivial.

Let us assume for a moment that 'defamiliarisation' or 'deconstruction' are what has been claimed for them, superior mental experiences to be found in the more 'serious' reaches of broadcasting, if it is to be found there at all. We should not forget that TV has frequently been cited as merely *confirming*, as a medium from which estrangement has been all but banished. Much of the popular fiction supplied by TV is thought of as *classic realist narrative*. Now, it has been said by Catherine Belsey that Barthes demonstrates in *S/Z* that classic realist narrative

> turns on the creation of enigma through the precipitation of disorder which throws into disarray the conventional cultural and signifying systems. Among the commonest sources of disorder at the level of plot in classic realism are murder, war, a journey or love.[38]

This seems very much like defamiliarisation to us. According to Bennett, defamiliarisation can 'dislocate our habitual perceptions of the real world' and 'disorganises the forms through which the world is customarily perceived'.[39] In a somewhat fuller statement he says:

> Literature characteristically works on and subverts those linguistic, perceptual and cognitive forms which conventionally condition our access to 'reality' and which, in their taken-for-grantedness, present the particular 'reality' they construct as reality itself. Literature thus effects a two-fold shift of perceptions. For what it makes appear strange is not merely the 'reality' which has been distanced from habitual modes of representation but also those habitual modes of representation themselves.[40]

If what each of these authors say is correct, we cannot any longer think of defamiliarisation as an esoteric process, but rather as a recurrent feature of popular 'classic realist' narratives. They too are then also capable of 'a type of mental experience that can be described as superior'. We do not wish to contend that there are no differences between realist and anti-realist, narrative and anti-narrative types, merely that they cannot in fact be formulated as they have been.

The notion that the classic realist narrative 'moves inevitably towards closure' may be a more solid base upon which to make distinctions, though, as has been pointed out of soap opera, closure is frequently delayed or its accomplishment is at the same time the initiation of yet other enigmas. Even when enigmas are resolved, however, it can be assumed that things are again as they were, and therefore that the overall effect can be said to be a reactionary one. As Belsey has commented, closure is also disclosure, 'the dissolution of enigma through the re-establishment of order, recognisable as a reinstatement or a development of the order which is understood to have preceded the events of the story itself'.[41] Development, change and reform are then possible in the course of the resolutions that are accomplished in popular TV fictions – surely a more productive and constructive state of affairs then celebrating a permanent state of disorder or never-ending deconstruction. In our view, then, the issue is not so much whether or not popular TV fictions accomplish resolutions; clearly they can. The important issues have to do with the nature of these resolutions, with whether they are 'magical' or not and with their practicability. When all the circumstances are taken into account, are we offered resolutions that can really be implemented?

The bare bones of our case are these. The offers made by popular television have become increasingly fictionalised and spectacular. These can and indeed do often celebrate the obvious. But, at the same time they can also be excessive: they can go beyond and stretch the familiar and the normal, and they can introduce orders of discourse other than the official sanctioned ones. They can defamiliarise and deconstruct; they can, through enigma, accomplish that 'two-fold shift of perceptions' referred to by Bennett. And, they can also be anticipatory; they can pre-figure alternative perceptions and constructions in the manner in which resolutions are accomplished. And, as popular offers are capable of this, then it also follows that they are capable of the sort of insight and explanation that structuralists would recognise. What we need now is an inventory of the processes by which all this is accomplished and this is something which could be done extending the sort of initiative that has been taken in recent studies of, for example, popular comedy.[42]

This essay has attempted to do some of the preliminaries needed to make work of this sort possible. We do not wish to suggest that, merely because the offers of the standardised commercial sector are popular, they are therefore wonderful and require no further development. Rather we have attempted to make out a case for their critical potential, and to suggest that this is greater than has till now been supposed. In popular TV the world is frequently 'turned upside down', even when its critics think it to be at its most closed, most reactionary or conservative. When it does, and precisely because it thrives on drama and enigmas, other alternative worlds are glimpsed. Commercial TV may not offer *particular* kinds of alternatives, but it does not follow from this that it denies that alternatives are possible.

The expansion of the standardised commercial sector on an international scale should not, then, be the cause of the sort of pessimism we have outlined at various stages. Certainly it sweeps aside cultural formations, some of which deserve to be dispensed with. There are many features of life in southern Italy which, in comparison with the offers made by the commercial sector, seem unqualifiably reactionary, and if that commercial sector can act as something like an 'opinion leader' there, this ought to be welcomed rather than regretted. The offers are, of course, ambiguous, never as clear-cut as we may wish them. While they may be progressive in one respect, they are anything but in another. Just what they are capable of can, however, be decided only when they are viewed in context, when, for instance, the images of women constructed in glossy US soap operas collide with those daily enforced by the rituals of southern Italian catholicism. This essay has said very little about this collision or, more generally, about how the offers circulate and are received by those not critical of them, who share their universe of concerns, sentiments and desires in some measure at least. This too must be work for the future, but it is pressing work indeed.

References

1. P. Golding and G. Murdock, 'Privatising Pleasure', *Marxism Today*, October 1983, p. 36.
2. J. Tunstall, 'The Media are Still American. . .', *The Media Reporter*, vol. 5, no. 1, Summer 1981, p. 35.
3. The Adam Smith Institute, *The Omega File: Communications* (London: ASI (Research) Limited 1984).
4. C. Curran, 'The Problem of Balance', in A. Smith (ed.), *British Broadcasting* (Newton Abbot: David and Charles 1974) p. 191.
5. O. Boyd-Barrett, 'Media Imperialism: towards an international framework for the analysis of media systems', in J. Curran, M. Gurevitch & J. Woollacott (eds.) *Mass Communication and Society* (London: Edward Arnold/Open University Press 1977) p. 117.
6. F.L. Cavazza, 'Italy: From Party Occupation to Party Partition' in A. Smith (ed.), *Television and Political Life* (London: Macmillan 1979) p. 78.
7. U. Eco, 'Stravideo!; guida alla neotelevisione degli anni '80', *L'Espresso*, 30 January 1983.
8. See G. Richeri's essay on pp. 21–35 of this volume.
9. Quoted in D. Doglio, 'Expenditure and Ratings Anxiety', *TV World*, vol. 7, no. 4, April 1984, p. 36.
10. Quoted in S. Dembner, 'Debut for home produced soaps', *TV World* vol. 7, no. 4, April 1984, p. 30.
11. See 'Ore 20, in onda una malattia chiamata RAI', *La Repubblica*, 17 April 1984, p. 25.
12. Quoted by S. Dembner in 'New Strategies Clarified', *TV World* vol. 7, no. 4, April 1984, p. 38.
13. Boyd-Barrett, op. cit. p. 121.
14. Ibid. p. 127.
15. Ibid. p. 127.
16. F. Iseppi, 'The Case of RAI', *Media, Culture and Society*, vol. 2, no. 4, 1980, p. 345.
17. Paolo Lombardo (Director of Production, Pegaso Inter-Communications), quoted in Dembner, 'Debut for Soaps', cit., p. 30.
18. G. Cingoli, 'Come abbiamo cominciato', *Radiocorriere*, 15 April 1984, p. 8.
19. F. Fejes, 'Media Imperialism: An Assessment', in *Media, Culture and Society*, vol. 3, no. 3, 1981, p. 286.

20. H. Schiller, 'Transnational Media and National Development', in K. Nordenstreng and H. Schiller (eds.), *National Sovereignty and International Communication* (Norwood, New Jersey: Ablex 1979) pp. 25–6.
21. Schiller, op. cit. p. 26.
22. See *La Repubblica*, 3 May 1983, p. 5.
23. Fejes, op. cit. p. 284.
24. Schiller, op. cit. p. 28.
25. Boyd-Barrett, op. cit. p. 132.
26. A. Gramsci, *Prison Notebooks* (London: Lawrence & Wishart 1971) p. 325.
27. P. Schlesinger, G. Murdock, P. Elliott, *Televising Terrorism* (London: Comedia, 1984) p. 169.
28. Schlesinger et al., ibid. p. 168.
29. Eco, op. cit. p. 52.
30. S. Hall, 'Culture, the Media and the "Ideological Effect"', in Curran et al.(eds.), op. cit. p. 325.
31. C. Belsey, *Critical Practice* (London: Methuen 1980) pp. 2–3.
32. C. Brunsdon and D. Morley, *Everyday Television: Nationwide* (London: BFI 1978) p. 89.
33. Eco, op. cit. p. 52.
34. J. Hartley and T. Hawkes, Unit 4, *The Study of Culture* Course DE 353 (Milton Keynes: Open University 1977) p. 51.
35. C. Bazalgette and R. Paterson, 'Real Entertainment: The Iranian Embassy Siege', *Screen Education* no. 37, Winter 1980/81, pp. 55–67.
36. Schlesinger et al., op. cit. p. 108–9. The authors also note that 'television fiction enjoys significant advantages over journalism which make it, potentially at least, more flexible in the way it can deal with the issues' (p. 76). This does not appear to extend to more popular instances, however, where they see a tendency towards closure around 'the official perspective' and 'reactionary populism'.
37. See the rejoinder by Bennett and Martin to Hartley and Hawkes, op. cit. p. 68.
38. Belsey, op. cit. p. 70.
39. T. Bennett, *Formalism and Marxism* (London: Methuen 1979) p. 20.
40. Bennett, op. cit. p. 54.
41. Belsey, op. cit. p. 70.
42. See for example Jim Cook (ed.), *Television Sitcom*, (London: BFI 1983).

JEAN–PIERRE DESAULNIERS

Television and Nationalism: From Culture to Communication

On 28 February 1983 the CBS network presented the final transmission – after eleven years of weekly broadcasting and the production of over 250 original programmes – in the series $M*A*S*H$. Two hundred million American and Canadian TV viewers looked on as the military hospital was disbanded and the group broken up. After the transmission, some thousands of people got together in more or less spontaneous $M*A*S*H$ parties. Most of the partygoers had dressed up as the character to whom they felt closest and with whom they had identified for all these years. All at once an anonymous crowd discovered traits in common, and realised that its members shared an imaginary symbolic life made up of the humour, the psychology and the philosophy so characteristic of the series. Here, in the winter of 1983, a cultural community had sprung up from nowhere – a tribute to the creators of $M*A*S*H$, but above all an intense expression of the phenomenon of communication and *identification*.

Television has this capacity to produce new collective identities, huge shifts in the symbolic life of the community comparable to those feverish infatuations with film stars in the period of the golden age of the cinema.

Few commentators on the world of television, however, deal with this dimension. Perhaps we are distracted by the effect of isolation and of separation, with viewers cooped up in their homes. Perhaps we also pay too much spontaneous attention to the content of the TV message, which is easier to analyse, and too little to the specific form of communication that television has developed and maintained. Whatever the case, it is to try and overcome this lacuna a little that I would like to offer some remarks concerning the phenomenon of identification through television.

I am going to make a seemingly curious detour, through the notion of nationalism, in order to bring out the differences between two types of feeling and emotion to do with identification – one more to do with culture, that is, nationalism, the other more directly marked by the process itself of communication, that is, identification through television.

112

Television and Nationalism

The rise of television in the key moment of the 1940s corresponds closely to a period when the notion of nationalism was widely debated. The Nazi and Fascist powers had shaken the confidence of both governments and citizens as to the dangers of over-valuing this collective sentiment. There was henceforth a distrust of national ideologies closed in upon themselves in chauvinistic and racist terms. While wishing to maintain a national bond, the various governments henceforward looked for an attachment which was more flexible and more open to international dialogue.

Moreover the foundation of the United Nations Organisations in 1945 preceded the launch of the first American TV networks by only a few months. These two enterprises on the part of civilisation sprang from the same post-war aspirations. The former served as a global political platform, the latter fostered a direct sense of national and international democracy among the citizenry. They will probably remain the most revealing expressions of the age in their attempt to go beyond the limitations of traditional political projects.

On the other hand, governments had had the opportunity to note the force of radio propaganda during the conflict. They did not intend, therefore, to commit once more the error they had made 30 years previously by not legislating for the distribution of frequencies and in not regulating content. They therefore decided on the precise ways in which television would be introduced, and conceived a national structure for distribution well before its commencement.

By the 50s, at the very height of the cold war, all the industrialised countries had mandated national organisations to set in motion their TV distribution systems. For example, in the United States, the Federal Communications Commission only sparingly issued distribution iicences in 1945, being concerned above all to draw up a global plan of action for the entire country. This plan, the *Final Television Allocation Report*, published in 1952, stipulated that the air-waves would remain public property, and envisaged the coordinated setting-up of 2,000 TV stations across the whole country. In a similar vein, in Great Britain, the BBC acquired a monopoly over distribution, but immediately prioritised the installation, at the earliest opportunity, of a network for the whole United Kingdom.

Following the lead of these two countries, the governments of all the industrial nations decided on the development of television, reserving for themselves the ultimate right of control over the air-waves and making an early choice in favour of expansion rather than the installation of prestigious stations in areas of urban concentration. This primary territorial preoccupation was to pave the way for the establishment of television.

This intention to provide universal access to the air-waves was to be

113

translated into the objectives handed down to those responsible for distribution. In each case, they were assigned a three-fold responsibility:

1. To reassert the value of popular education; to offer a sense of continuity to the national schooling system undertaken since the introduction of compulsory education.
2. To provide access to information for all citizens; to assert the right to information recently inscribed, for the first time, in the United Nations Charter.
3. To encourage the expression of a national culture through a body of broadcast entertainment; to create a new cultural community around televised works, domestic or foreign.

From now on the triad 'Work, Family, Homeland' which characterised old-style national sentiment – a strictly territorial ideology of enclosure and protection – yielded in favour of a modern, rejuvenated equivalent, conforming more to the vision of a utopian democracy. This new triad – 'Education, Information, Entertainment' – was to represent the basic values of nations which were more open, more aware, more relaxed. Television was to enable the bridging of the gap between social obligations and the enjoyment of individual rights. In short, the leisure society was invented around television.

But today anxiety is growing on the part of these same governments. The countries concerned feel themselves more and more overtaken by the popular demand for an ever-increasing number of foreign programmes. The viewing public inclines spontaneously towards American productions or towards those based on that model. The national image is slowly effaced by these numerous imports. Nowhere, except in the USA, has there been any success in finding a judicious balance between indigenous cultural life and the consumption of foreign products. In addition, governments and intellectuals openly deplore the mediocre quality of the political consciousness of citizens who have been shaped by television, citizens who are more fascinated by images and spectacle than by forms of political logic.

In sum, they regret that the cultural development of their society should submit to the contingencies of commercialisation and that the attention of its citizens should be more captivated by sport and by popular serials than by great works. In short, the hopes placed in this magnificent system of communication give way to nagging doubt.

And this shift seems destined to continue. Currently, politics is completely in thrall to the marketing media, with their telegenic smiles and hollow responses. The most popular cultural productions look more and more hackneyed, mawkish, meaningless. As for education, it seems to be regressing, with people being content with

114

scrappy television 'digests', progressing nowhere. The challenge of new national cultures and of a new nationalism will end up in a massive depersonalised culture lacking in basic orientation. It is as though the TV viewer took in images without ever coming to any clear sense of affiliation or belonging, preferring to be carried along in a state of complacent fascination.

Have we reached a theshold which we cannot cross? Has democracy followed the wrong course? Shouldn't culture in the end remain the privilege of a perceptive elite? Are the expected social links not too tenuous, too superficial for one henceforth to consider TV not as a place where people are brought together but rather as a place where the fabric of the nation is unpicked? Otherwise, why is it that the national identity aspired to results in a sort of generalised *anomie*, bogged down in passivity before the spectacle, which only a few sporadic events, such as the finale of *M*A*S*H*, succeed in contradicting now and again?

The Case of Quebec

In the course of 300 years of history, the microcosm of Quebec saw its first major nationalist movement only a few years after the introduction of TV. One must not impute to television the entire credit for the national awakening that was experienced. But television was part of it, and clearly encouraged the development of this current of feeling.

The case of Quebec is representative from several points of view. To begin with there had been in existence, for something like a century, a nationalist current of feeling that would be shattered by the introduction of TV. Further, Quebec rapidly became integrated with the North American post-war model of development, despite a slight economic delay during the 40s. Take-off closely corresponded to the birth of television in 1952. Finally, television provided an outlet for a form of cultural expression undreamed of by its founders.

The result was that television bore, and influenced, two movements of identification on the part of the Québécois: it took part in their re-attachment to the nation state, and in their inscription in the vast movement of modernisation.

The first French colony of America, Quebec became an English colony in 1760, then one of the provinces of Canada when this country was founded in 1867. Drawn from a basically peasant stock, the Québécois are little inclined to be bellicose. The risings against the English were rare and without significant consequences. The people instead resisted assimilation by banking on a closed form of nationalism jealously guarded by the powers of the church, especially over the last 100 years. It was a reliquary nationalism, characterised by systematic isolation, refusing the English influence within the

115

country but also the French influence of a France which had become secular and republican.

Until the Second World War, Quebec had experienced a nationalism which was conservative and entrenched, and which prized the soil, large families and honouring the sabbath. It was an ideology comparable to that of Spain under Franco or Portugal under Salazar.

The Euphoria of Gratitude   When Radio-Canada launched the first television network in Montreal in 1952, Quebec was in the almost complete control of the province's first Prime Minister, Maurice Duplessis. He was an ultra-conservative and cantankerous figure, opposed to any notion of modernisation. He distrusted this thing called television, this new 'interference by Ottawa' in French Canadian culture. From 1952 until his death in 1959, he was never to appear on television, and refused to give interviews or press conferences.

By contrast, Ottawa was to encourage the recruitment by Radio-Canada of a new elite in the world of journalism, the university and the arts – the only group with sufficient energy to finally overthrow Duplessis and the clergy. This elite knew that Quebec was already behind in the post-war economic and cultural drive. They also knew that the country was in a process of rapid urbanisation and was being transformed into an industrial society. Traditional values were from that point becoming too tight a yoke for a population sensitive to modernisation, to the North American style of consumption, and to the rise of numerous anti-colonial movements across the world.

Without directly attacking the Duplessis regime, this elite seized the opportunity to present the outside world to the people of Quebec and to force the province out of its cultural ghetto. Unlike what happened in several European countries, in Quebec the intellectuals did not shun TV – they took a radical hold on it during the opening years. At the same time, television was enthusiastically welcomed by the public. This piece of equipment, less expensive than the motor car, became the first true symbol of modernity. Within three years, 94 per cent of homes in Quebec were in possession of a TV set.

Thus, not only did television give an opportunity to a youthful elite to engage in the work of civic education, but above all it enabled the people of Quebec to recognise themselves as a totality for the first time in their history. Much more than the press, or radio, with their various religious or political affiliations, television, which at this particular point consisted only of a single station, became the site of a first general and massive act of identification at the very moment when the demand for renewal, and for a reconsideration of values, became pressing.

116

The symbolism of the beginning of TV is clearly naive, but it is also generous and enthusiastic. Discussion ranged from the whole world to the internal situation. The audience recognised itself in the local serials, appreciating at last its own language spoken by figures strongly marked by national characteristics. There was also excitement during the televised hockey matches in which the Montreal club, where major stars are francophone, met clubs from New York, Chicago, Detroit or Toronto. It was therefore an act of identification with language, with the stars of the news, magazine programmes, and from the world of sport, together with the recognition of an automatically national style reaching everyone in Quebec.

During these years TV allowed Quebec suddenly to recognise itself as a total entity, and one keen to develop. It was less a simple instrument of information than the hard core of a new cultural recognition, of an act of national identification which was urban, modern and integrated by different means than the clergy's ordering of the peasantry.

But in 1958 the federal government changed hands. The new masters in Ottawa, the Conservatives, took up an attitude of profound mistrust where television was concerned, in particular a francophone television which was in their view too progressive. At the end of the year Diefenbaker's government quickly opposed the claims of francophone producers concerning the recognition of their association. A strike started, halting broadcasts; it was to last three months and mobilise all Quebec, apart from Duplessis and the clergy. Journalists, university lecturers, intellectuals, electronics technicians and finally the entire public were to stand in support of the TV producers. Huge events in support of the strikers took place almost everywhere, organised by young journalists (among them René Lévesque, the current Prime Minister of Quebec) and young artists and actors. They were demonstrations of support, to be sure, but also of general euphoria. This strike was to directly pave the way for the overthrow of the Conservative powers, first in Quebec and then in Ottawa, a little while later. Television had become the stake of a nation.

This national fever bore no comparison with the nationalistic sentiments of days gone by, with their acts of resistance, secret confinements, bitter sacrifices. The new current of feeling was closer to bravado, to self-expression, to enjoyment, to pleasure and to the joy of finding oneself complete in a period of common discovery. In favour of a nationalism which looked towards ancestry and the protection of cultural gains, preference was henceforward given to a nationalism of immediate and collective recognition, of spontaneous and dynamic communication.

Television, the media agent of the instantaneous, of the sudden event, thus exaggerated the impression of *tabula rasa*. It at once permitted the transformation of an attachment to a land, to a history, into an attachment to a collectivity which was feverish, expansive, bold and, naturally, adapted to its era. A hundred-year-old culture, with strong foundations and convictions, collapsed in a few years in the era of communication and its ideology of radiant diffusion.

But cut off from its past, from its historical context, Quebec was soon to be cut off from its future.

The Conquest of Identity　　The 1960s, that period one describes as that of 'quiet revolution' and which saw strongly marked acts of terrorist activity, got under way with a complete recasting of the major national institutions under the aegis of a new government carried to power on this revealing slogan: 'Master of our own Destiny'. It involved a recasting of education, the nationalisation of electricity, the reorganisation of the social security system, etc.

During this time, television was evolving. Before disappearing, the Diefenbaker government had taken away Radio-Canada's broadcasting monopoly, and had granted licences for production and transmission to commercial stations. The first commercial French-speaking station appeared in Montreal in 1961. The owners of Télémétropole, less concerned with the civic mission of education and preoccupied instead with the profitability of the enterprise, rapidly developed the populist market, offering easy access with a stress on simple language, hilarity, pronounced use of the Quebec accent, and American imports. Télémétropole, inside a year, won over the viewing public, who promptly rejected the *recherché* and too sophisticated style of Radio-Canada. A break occurred between the public and the intellectuals.

For ten years Quebec entertained two contradictory images of itself – the one simplified, the other idealised. For these ten years, the Québécois, while at the same time developing a conviction of their national existence, noted their differences and conducted mutual examinations through the medium of the small screen.

The apotheosis of this national discovery occurred with the World Exhibition of 1967, when Montreal played host to the whole world. It was the shining symbol of the conquest of identity, but of an identity made up of exchanges and communications both at home and with outsiders, sensitive to change and lacking any political colouration of too restrictive a kind, playing instead on the spirit of a spontaneous humanism. It was, exactly in the image of television, ready above all for the adventure of communication, sensitive to the least change, rebarbative towards political allegiances too easily detected and promoting a humanism based on dialogue.

The Consumption of Identity This regeneration of Quebec imagery entailed certain knock-on effects. New singers appeared, copying English and American styles to greater or lesser extent while trying to bring out a truly Québécois side to things. But above all, advertising seized on this symbolism in order to confer a value of authenticity upon its products. All at once, Quebec was involved in every imaginable merchandising project, and identity became a striking feature of the symbols of modern commercial domesticity. Slowly, national pride faded into consumption as it was associated with whatever product was in fashion. ('There are six million of us – we should be talking to each other' was a favourite slogan for Labatt beer.) At the end of 1970, national emotion and the marketing image became more and more confused, underlining the idea of a present time given over entirely to enjoyment through consumption, of a time strictly current mediated by a process of communication which was immediate, transparent and cared little for the future.

Simultaneously, television became less a cherished object and more the central object of daily life. With the arrival of colour TV, the number of sets multiplied as they were distributed around the kitchen, bedrooms, children's play-room, etc. TV henceforth had not only a more common presence, but a more continual and effective presence, too.

The final convulsion of the cultural desire to set up television was the foundation of Radio-Québec in 1973. This new network, with its educational mandate and jurisdiction over the province, took off slowly. It bore little resemblance to the now established model for North American TV. In addition, the ideology of culture was undermined, too widely exploited by the competition. There was too little room for manoeuvre for this new distributor, and it only succeeded in making a real breakthrough with children, with a programme specially designed for them. With Radio-Québec, culture entered its folkloric period. It was the nostalgic vision of a culture and a collectivity which had been resuscitated artificially.

After twenty years of television, the image of Quebec had to be negotiated between four partners – the provincial image of Radio-Canada, an image torn between the recognition of a regional culture within the Canadian diaspora and a desire to take part in the world-wide French-speaking movement; the folkloric image of Radio-Québec, split between Quebec's educational mandate and the American model of production; the populist image of Télémétropole, systematically copying – but at the least possible cost – the American model of production; and the euphoric, hollow image of the world of advertising. None of these images connected with a real past, but worse still, none formulated any kind of cultural project, any definition of a future to be desired. Once acquired, the sense of

119

national identity was frittered away in a surfeit of artificial symbols, and national imagery was dependent upon movements of fashion. It was scattered into imaginary space; all sense of temporality was definitively lost.

The Abandonment of National Identity In 1980 there was a referendum on the national question, a mobilisation in strength of the entire political class, provincial and federal. Everywhere it was felt that a point of no return had been reached. But television reacted gently to this event. Although it would have been possible to constitute a major debate around this question, broadcasters were happy to 'cover' the campaign moderately and to let the politicians do the running around and bustling about.

It is at this point of break between an essentially nationalist ideology, and one of communication and modernisation, that one can grasp the specific effectivity of television: the model of spatio-temporal perception proper to the medium was so built into people's ways of thinking that for many Québécois the referendum had no point. The basic issue no longer stood out alongside this new conviction that an identity had finally been conquered. Worse still, it was a case of going backwards and letting politics define bygone times, past spaces. The symbolism of an open space, as much Québécois or Canadian as North American or even planetary, is too pregnant with meaning to allow for any easy justification for the conquest of a sense of territoriality. Better a space which was vast and multiple, virtually indefinite, set within an ever-present temporality.

This is the attitude which currently prevails. The symptomatic threshold – 50 per cent of the population subscribing to cable – was crossed shortly after 1980. This percentage reached nearly 60 per cent in the Montreal area. A symbolic space of 30 channels, comprising American, Canadian and Québécois broadcasts, and even some from France, Italy, Egypt or elsewhere, relating to a multitude of disparate subjects, became the dominant model of television. The Québécois became accustomed to this spatial explosion and to the abstraction of space and time performed by the mass media, to an exploded world, without temporality or history, without any continuity other than TV itself, day after day.

Thus, in Quebec, television richly stimulated the national cultural image. But meanwhile it turned a political cultural identity into a consumer product which was as ephemeral and perishable as any other product. What we will have witnessed is the consumption of a national identity. Who will lose most? Probably politics itself. For, little by little, the very criteria of differentiation between nations are dissolving, and credibility in respect of politics and, consequently, politicians, will thereby suffer. Moreover the wrangling between

120

Ottawa and Quebec appears henceforward as a risible anachronism, especially since it is now possible to follow the American electoral campaign instead. There, at least, it's a good show.

Television and Research into New Forms of Affiliation
Let us repeat that we cannot consider television as the sole agent in the transformations of our era. It is part of an ensemble. But the role of research consists precisely in specifying its exact pertinence in this period of change. It becomes more and more clear that its influence has less to do with the precise content of messages, broadly borrowed from the literature or from the radio of yesteryear, than with a specific and novel manner of cutting up time and space, and hence of affecting the symbolic relays between individuals and communities. Television directly establishes new landmarks which allow the individual the possibility of gauging the similarities and differences around him. For 30 years, the work of television has, above all, been on the side of identification, of 'joining up', of affiliation, and of the opposite, of rupture.

For if culture has the function of structuring the forms of knowledge of a society and of their efficient distribution, it has the further role of situating this knowledge within an operational space-time ensemble which can be assimilated little by little by each member of the group. It is just as much an agent of culture in the traditional sense of the term, an agent for the development of knowledge and for the delivery of information, as an agent of socialisation in the sense of communicating this information with the intention of exposing it to acceptance or rejection by the members of a group or between groups.

In contrast with the book, which favours a form of socialisation based on the acquisitions of history, the book as privileged agent of social memory, television favours an immediate form of relation, freed from the constraints of distance. We are passing from a civilisation of time to a civilisation of space. The radical transformation of national feeling in Quebec offers a disturbing illustration. A civilisation committed to open-mindedness, to mobility, to travel, designed for a perpetual youth (fashion). Television introduces the vertigo of boundless space, including stellar space; in the face of this vertigo, any territorial boundary, including national frontiers, appears as the relic of a bygone age.

The first promoters of television, the political agents who wished that it should become a new instrument for cementing the nation together, following on from the schooling process, were inevitably descended from a civilisation of the book and of history. They therefore envisaged a medium in their own image, a medium of culture, a medium which promoted national cultural values and the progress of knowledge, developing in the process a new reading of the

121

world about them. In fact, television only held on to this second feature. It became the perfect medium for continual renewal, albeit artificial, of the excessive consumption of symbols, in a giddy whirlwind of perpetual motion. Television imposed its own utopia, its own vertigo, the sense of an 'immediate' space.

In such a context, identification with acquired knowledge, that of our predecessors, that of the school, counts for less and less. It is more worthwhile to travel in a few minutes or hours to Los Angeles, Chicago or London, even in the company of Michael Jackson, Kojak, or Benny Hill. Television accelerated the breakdown of traditional, familial, religious, local and henceforward national relays, replacing these poles of identification by others which are more abstract – but with which it will henceforth be directly concerned.

The reactions of intellectuals to television belong to those for whom the demands of identification are directed towards the experience of culture. They will therefore long reproach television for maintaining a cultural vacuum in the face of all that now seems novel. But that's to miss the point. One should, rather, consider television with regard to its utopian aspects, one should be interested in the potential of abstract, distant identification offered by the medium, and work out its boundaries. And, if necessary, one should directly reassert the value of history.

When our societies have become more stable, it is conceivable that television may return to a broader sense of temporality and become more effective in relation to the growth of knowledge. The development of educational television, moreover, points in this direction. But it is certain that for a while yet the process of encyclopaedic scanning of the image will dominate, and the audience will let itself be carried away by the play of new affiliations. We have not yet gone beyond the period of ever more disconcerting identification, like watching *Dallas* in Algiers or dressing up as Boy George in Caracas.

Translated by Phillip Drummond

PART II

American Television

WILLIAM BODDY

'The Shining Centre of the Home': Ontologies of Television in the 'Golden Age'

Historians of American television have organised its past into distinct analytical periods according to successions in network regime ('The Silverman Years'), dominant programme formats ('The Golden Age of Live Drama') or a characteristic set of economic relations among television sponsors, producers and networks. But such historical moments also need to be considered as the intersections of these features of the network television economy with the historically specific trade and critical discourses which constituted and addressed television as an aesthetic and cultural object. Of particular interest to historians and theorists of the medium may be the record of the earliest years of television in the USA when the new industry created and consolidated its economic and regulatory structures and its dominant programme forms while the trade and critical discourses constructed an essentialist identity for the medium.

In the period of the early 1950s, still embedded in popular television literature as the medium's 'Golden Age', writing on television emerged from popular science books on the development of techno-logy, practical manuals on writing and directing for the medium and from the practice of television journalism. The theoretical speculation which emerged was frankly amateur and produced a number of dubious and poorly-argued essentialist claims for the medium. Nevertheless, such early writing on television reflected a remarkable critical consensus not only among television writers and critics but among many leaders of the television industry. Little of this quasi-theorising has been subjected to subsequent analysis, and this blindspot of television historiography, as much as the dearth of empirical studies on early television, has contributed to the surprising longevity of the myth of the medium's 'Golden Age'.

A reappraisal of the critical and ideological constituents of the discourse of the 'Golden Age' would examine the aesthetic hierarchies built from the over-determined critical oppositions which pitted live programming against film; New York against Hollywood production centres; the drama of character (specifically, a version of theatrical naturalism wedded to an agenda of liberal humanism) against genre entertainments and the drama of plot and spectacle; the unique work in an anthology series against the continuing-character episodic series; even the 60-minute programme against the 30-minute programme; and a construal of television authorship on the high-culture model of the theatre playwright against the image of writer as corporate employee. The oppositions in turn owed much to larger reigning critical constructions of an undifferentiated, pre-auteurist Hollywood and received notions of the realist aesthetic and the social responsibilities of the popular arts.

An analysis of the critical discourse of the 'Golden Age' would also need to address the appropriation of such taste hierarchies and ontological claims for the medium in the mid-1950s by the most powerful sector in the commercial television economy, the two dominant networks, NBC and CBS. Challenged for monopolistic business practices in their relations with affiliates, programme producers and national sponsors, the two networks made tactical use of the critical status of the nationwide live broadcast – a network monopoly – as the privileged ontological and aesthetic television form. History did not treat this strategic alliance between television's cultural critics and the networks kindly, however. Within a few years of NBC proudly reading *New York Times* television critic Jack Gould's praises of live television into the *Congressional Record* in 1956, the networks' live anthology drama programmes from New York were nearly extinct. The decline of the critics' privileged programme forms at the hands of their one-time network allies caused a crisis in television criticism in the late 1950s. The critics' tone of hyperbole and betrayal that marks the half-decade passage from television's 'Golden Age' to the 'vast wasteland' has stamped much of the subsequent consideration of the commercial medium.

At issue in this essay are similar intersections and appropriations of theoretical speculation about the nature of the television medium with the strategic aims of the industry's major economic actors during the period *before* the beginnings of network television in the late 1940s. That is, the manner in which television was constructed in the dominant discourse as an aesthetic medium – its artistic and ontological specificity, its essential conditions of production and reception, its relations to other media and its proper programme forms – while the new industry was simultaneously being positioned in relation to its significant economic 'others' – the electronics industry, radio broadcasting, the motion-picture industry, federal regulators and the advertising industry.

Television as 'the shining centre of the home' was offered by NBC network head Pat Weaver in a *New Yorker* profile in 1954.[1] Weaver was a privileged observer of the new medium, not merely as director of NBC programming from 1949 to 1956 but also in his background as advertising director of the American Tobacco Company, a major broadcast advertiser in radio and later television, and as director of broadcast advertising for Young and Rubicam. NBC's interests in the early years of television reflect the vertical and horizontal integration of the new industry; Weaver's 'shining centre of the home' was to be lit with programmes broadcast not only from NBC's five owned-and-operated stations in major markets in the USA, but from the network's group of affiliated stations too (until 1953 a *majority* of stations operating in the country were affiliates of NBC). Moreover, NBC's status as a subsidiary of RCA, which not only was the chief manufacturer of television receivers but also received 3.5 per cent royalties on every television set sold in the United States, clearly helped direct Weaver's programming strategies at NBC in the early 1950s. It was in the intersections and negotiations of the interests of broadcast sponsor, advertising agency, television manufacturer and patent holder, network operator and station owners that the system of commercial television emerged in the USA.

The beginning of network television in the late 1940s was not technologically determined in the sense of awaiting a discrete technical invention or innovation. The story of television's commercial exploitation is one of patent battles, commercial campaigns and regulatory decisions more than one of technological breakthroughs taking industry, government regulators or the general public by surprise. In fact, commercial television had been widely prophesied as 'just around the corner' since the late 1920s.[2] While the mechanical scanning systems embodied in such early forecasts were supplanted by electronic scanning in the early 1930s, by the second half of the 1930s the technical standards of the eventual system were largely in place. Nevertheless, the period 1939 to 1946 produced a number of further 'false alarms' of failed commercial exploitation, while the trade press speculated on the grounds for the medium's mixed commercial success.

Moreover, while many of the early researchers in the technology of television – radio amateurs' low-definition two-way communication, AT&T's early research in the video telephone, John Baird's and others' experiments within large-screen theatre television – pursued non-broadcast uses of television, by the late 1920s television research in the dominant firms in the American radio manufacturing industry was consolidated and shifted to RCA which pursued a highly rationalised and largely single-minded application of the technology as an advertiser-supported, network-distributed broadcast service to the private home on the model of network radio. With the exception of theatre television, which did receive industry attention in the late 1930s and 1940s, the alternative, non-broadcast uses of television did not receive wide public attention or debate. Hardly a case of a technological innovation upsetting existing commercial structures, the history of commercial television is the story of the deliberate shepherding of a technological apparatus by powerful established interests in electronic manufacturing and broadcasting, especially RCA. The vice-president of Philco, James C. Carmine, told a group of industry leaders in 1944: 'Probably never before has a product of a great new industry been so completely planned and highly developed before it was offered to the public as has television.'[3]

In this regard television presents a very different case from that of the beginnings of radio broadcasting in the early 1920s. Then, the major radio patent holders and manufacturers (United Fruit, General Electric, AT&T), pooling their interests in the patent cartel RCA in 1919, looked to radio chiefly as a means of point-to-point communication. Broadcasting was, as the first president of RCA put it, the 'surprise party' of radio.[4] Moreover, RCA and other large commercial interests in the early radio industry faced a community of frequently hostile radio amateurs, wide competition and an improvised regulatory apparatus.[5] Patent and economic barriers to entry to the radio-manufacturing industry in the early 1920s were weak enough to permit the proliferation of what RCA termed 'mushroom manufacturers'.[6] In addition, lacking the licensing barriers to competing radio broadcasters before the 1927 Radio Act, the large commercial-station operators saw the airways crowded with amateur, philanthropic and publicly supported rivals.

Given the economic and popular resistance to the idea of commercially supported broadcasting in the early 1920s, it is not surprising to find in the broadcasting industry rhetoric during commercial television's prolonged incubation in the late 1930s and 1940s the repeated wish to avoid the 'mistakes of radio'. The newly formed Television Broadcasters Association (TBA) warned in 1944:

> The pitfalls, indecisions, and wild adventures that characterized radio's birth will not be duplicated in television. . . . A prime objective of the TBA is to avoid any repetition of the errors that marked radio's beginnings in the roaring 1920s.[7]

The would-be commercial architects of the new television medium viewed the lessons of early radio broadcasting in a negative fashion, and their aims involved avoiding radio's low patent, economic and regulatory barriers to competitors as well as the wide and spirited resistance to broadcast advertising. As early as 1928, RCA, in an application for a commercial television licence, told the Federal Radio Commission:

> In the interests of saving both the vision and the television of the public, only an experienced and responsible organization, such as

the Radio Corporation of America, can be depended upon to uphold high standards of services.[8]

While the often bitter rivalry between commercial broadcasters and radio amateurs in the early 1920s was part of a larger and more profound public debate over the social uses of broadcasting and its economic support, the public debate over similar issues in television in the 1930s and 1940s was narrow and muted. Broadcast critic Gilbert Seldes, writing in 1937, lamented the lack of public debate over the medium and warned: 'Twenty years from now will be much too late for complaints.' Eleven years later, Bernard Smith called out in a 1948 *Harper's* article:

> For if, careless of television's rising significance, we do nothing now, its patterns of operation will soon become so rigidly fixed that neither the American people who own the channels nor the Congress which represents us will be able to do very much about it.[9]

As such critics feared, by the early 1950s hope of significant change in the commercial structure and premises of American television brought about by congressional or regulatory action was quickly fading. As a contemporary observer of the FCC charitably put it:

> So occupied has been the public authority with the establishment of adequate physical facilities for television, that there has been little time or attention devoted to questions relating to whom should be given the use of television facilities, undér what conditions and for what purposes.[10]

A marker of the narrowness and timidity of the 1930s and 1940s debates over television's social uses in comparison with those waged over radio broadcasting in the early 1920s are the contrasting discussions of the place of broadcast advertising. When AT&T began broadcasting commercials in 1922, the move provoked loud and sustained protest from radio listeners and amateur broadcasters, as well as from many within the broadcast industry and from Secretary of Commerce Herbert Hoover, who directed broadcast regulation until the 1927 Radio Act. Continued reservations about the use of broadcasting for advertising were voiced by the Federal Radio Commission in its 1928 annual report:

> Broadcasting stations are not given these great privileges by the United States government for the primary benefit of advertisers. Such benefit as is derived by advertisers must be incidental and entirely secondary to the interests of the public.[11]

The record of television as an advertising medium is very different. The trade journal *Sponsor* pointed out in 1948: 'Radio had been operating all over the nation for years before advertising entered the field. This is not, of course, true with television. Stations have commercials during the first week of operation.'[12] Despite scattered objections in the popular press to television advertising, few serious economic alternatives were proposed in the early literature on television. Likewise, the federal regulators of television never questioned its role as an advertising medium; a 1965 FCC retrospective study concluded that, since the 1930s the fact 'that the basic television structure and the programming provided the American home would be paid for by advertising revenue was taken for granted by the Commission.'[13]

Instead of the larger public or regulatory debates over advertising in television, contemporary discussion of the issue remained concerned with the narrower issues of appropriateness and with strategies of persuasion. These debates, in turn, often were fought over competing essentialist notions of the television medium. Proponents of television advertising in the 1930s and 1940s argued the medium's analogies with radio and urged broadcasters and advertisers to adapt radio advertising forms to the new visual service. These proponents could find support for their position in general assessments of the medium like this judgement from 1948:

> People will look at and listen to television programs for the same reason that they now listen to the radio: the television set is placed where it will form a part of the living habits of the American people. They will accept a much poorer level of entertainment in their own homes than they will demand if they have to leave the house or apartment to attend a public performance.[14]

Others in the early trade debates over television advertising were less sanguine about the acceptability of televised advertising and pointed to advertisers' repeated failures in their attempts to exploit theatrical motion pictures for advertising, either in the form of advertising shorts shown in movie theatres or in direct promotional tie-ins with theatrical features. These sceptics argued for television's decisive aesthetic analogies with motion pictures and warned that the television audience would resent the presence of advertising in the new medium. The debates about the suitability of television advertising turned on notions of the unique aesthetic demands of the medium, and it is telling that such aesthetic speculation about television in the 1930s and 1940s is found chiefly in the trade debates over advertising strategy, not as part of a general public discussion of the medium.

The positions in the debates over television advertising and their essentialist rationales in the 1930s and 1940s often proceeded from competing assertions of the situation of the television audience

130

compared to the radio audience in the home. Objections to the intrusive quality of broadcast advertising entering the private home uninvited were widespread in the early years of radio broadcasting, with advertising's opponents arguing for a ban on broadcast advertising or limitations to indirect or goodwill advertising messages. However, to the surprise of some in the radio industry, sponsors and broadcasters in the 1920s succeeded in developing popular forms of commercial programming that did not depend on continuous and complete attention from the radio audience that seemed characteristic of radio's earlier listeners. Radio listening could accompany other activities in the home, from the housewife's daytime chores to the family's evening in the parlour. Broadcast advertising was considered less intrusive, more acceptable, when integrated into this situation of distracted radio listening. Nevertheless, a sceptic of television advertising, Philip Kerby, warned potential television advertisers in his 1939 *The Victory of Television*: 'Experience gained through radio will be of little avail. . . . In television, it is doubtful if the audience sitting in a semi-darkened room and giving its undivided attention to the screen will tolerate interruptions in the programme.' Kerby, like Seldes, argued on these grounds for a return to indirect, goodwill advertising for television, where sponsors refrained from interrupting programmes with sales pitches.[15]

The central distinction in the early debates over television advertising were the different demands of television and radio for audience attention and concentration. Seldes wrote of television in 1937: 'The thing moves, it requires complete attention. You cannot walk away from it, you cannot turn your back on it, and you cannot do anything except listen while you are looking.'[16] Irving Fiske wrote in *Harper's* in 1940: 'Television, like the motion picture or the stage, and unlike the radio, requires complete and unfaltering attention. If the eye wanders for a moment from the television screen a programme's continuity is lost.'[17]

The unique demands on its audience imputed to television made some early observers of the medium cautious about the possibility of television taking radio's place in the home for a mass audience. Philco vice-president Carmine worried in 1944:

> It is not known how many hours a day people will be interested in watching television. There is already a certain amount of evidence to indicate that some people's eyes tire out after watching it for fifteen minutes – others after watching for one half-hour.[18]

An article in *Fortune* magazine in 1939 predicted: 'Considering the necessity for close attention from the viewer, it is doubtful that there will ever be more than a twenty-five per cent coverage of the available

131

audience, except in very special cases.'[19]

The marketing significance of television's aesthetic demands on viewers turned on strategic concepts of the home as the arena for broadcasting and market for the new appliance. Both NBC and CBS through the mid-1940s predicted that, for at least ten years after the fully-fledged start of network television, the only profitable sector of the industry would be in direct receiver sales.[20] Those most deeply involved in planning television's commercial development – the electronics manufacturers and the commercial broadcasters – sought to define television simultaneously as a consumer appliance for the home and an audio-visual showroom for advertisers' goods. As in radio in the 1920s, RCA and the other manufacturers and broadcasters in television aimed their marketing and programming strategies directly at the housewife and family. Again, some in the new industry expressed doubts about the viability of the radio model; Philco executive Carmine, for example, worried in 1944 that 're-tuning a television set is far more difficult than a standard broadcast set. Women may not like the mechanics of television tuning.' He also noted anxiously that 'no clinical tests have been made to determine whether the father of the house would be willing to have the lights turned out in the living room when he wants to read because his children want to watch a television broadcast of no interest to him.'[21]

Of chief concern to the leaders of the new television industry was the challenge of integrating television programming into the routines of the housewife's daily chores as radio had done. The development of television on the model of commercial radio – widespread receiver sales to the private home with programming supported by direct advertising – was seen to depend on the housewife as 'household purchasing agent' and as target of advertising messages. Given television's special demands on audience attention, the crucial question for the successful exploitation of commercial television became, in the words of Philco's Carmine, 'the degree to which housewives would drop their housework to watch television during the daytime'.[22]

The feared conflict between television's perceptual demands on spectators and its commercial tasks as object and agent of consumer sales in the private home was addressed in a 1945 CBS monograph, *Television Audience Research*. While acknowledging the problem of 'eye fatigue' for television viewers and the fears of some observers that television broadcasting to the private home on the radio model would disrupt the housewife's routine, CBS pointed out that radio broadcasters had adapted daytime programming to serve as 'background activity' to domestic chores. Admitting television's special demands on the viewer, CBS nevertheless argued: 'Television's daytime programmes, however, can be constructed so that full attention will not be necessary for their enjoyment. Programmes requiring full attention of eye and ear should be scheduled for evening hours when viewers feel entitled to entertainment and relaxation.'[23]

Just as CBS called for the reconciliation of television's audience demands and its task as sales agent in the home by constructing programmes such that 'full attention would not be necessary for their enjoyment', the opposing aesthetic analogies to radio and the motion pictures were realigned to serve the existing broadcast model. The leaders of the broadcasting and electronics manufacturing industry did urge potential television advertisers to attend to television's aesthetic analogies with the motion picture, but construed the affinities as instrumental to television's promotional tasks in a commercially supported broadcasting system. An RCA executive told a group of businessmen in 1944:

> How can you prepare yourself for the coming of television? I recommend that you begin to study its use right now by examining the methods employed by the motion picture to convey ideas. The motion picture producers are experts in the art of visual selling.[24]

A contemporary trade journal told its readers:

> Go to the movies; analyze everything you see in the picture, every product, be it dress, real estate, transportation; think of it then as if you were trying to sell it. Study your reactions to the pictures of automobiles, food, women's fashions or men's fishing rods. Does the picture show them persuasively, with sales appeal? If it does, then memorize the particular technique as far as you can.[25]

Where some sceptical observers had seen a conflict between television's aesthetic and perceptual analogies with motion pictures and its role as object and agent of consumer sales in the home, the dominant interests in television's commercial development succeeded in linking the two views in a' instrumental way. Achieved was a synthesis of radio's programming and merchandising goals with the persuasive tools of Hollywood film-making, ensuring that the new television medium would not shirk its sales-making responsibilities in the general economy.

References
1. T. Whiteside, 'The Communicator: Athens Starts Pouring In', *The New Yorker*, 16 October 1954, p. 60.
2. For a useful discussion of the period, see R.H. Stern, 'Regulatory Influences Upon Television's Development: Early Years Under the Federal Radio Commission', *American Journal of Economics and Sociology* vol. 22, no. 3, 1963, pp. 347–62.

3. City College of New York, *Radio and Business 1945: Proceedings of the First Annual Conference on Radio and Business* (New York: City College of New York 1945) p. 136.
4. J.G. Harbord, 'Commercial Uses of Radio', *Annals of the American Academy of Political and Social Science* vol. 142, March 1929, p. 57.
5. For a discussion of these contexts, see W. Boddy, 'The Rhetoric and the Economic Roots of the American Broadcasting Industry', *Cinetracts*, vol. 2, no. 2, Spring 1979, pp. 37–54.
6. P. Boucheron, 'Advertising Radio to the American Public: An Exposition of the Part Played By Advertising in the Development of the Radio Industry', (Cambridge, Mass.: Harvard Business School 1928).
7. Television Broadcasters Association, *Television*, Spring 1944, p. 9.
8. Quoted in R.H. Stern, *The FCC and Television: The Regulatory Process in an Environment of Rapid Technological Innovation* (New York: Arno Press 1979) p. 56.
9. G. Seldes, 'The "Errors" of Television', *Atlantic*, May 1937, p. 535; B. Smith, 'Television – There Ought to be a Law', *Harper's*, September 1948, p. 34.
10. Stern, op. cit. p. 5.
11. Quoted in US Federal Communications Commission, Office of Network Study, *Interim Report: Responsibility for Broadcast Matter* (Washington DC: Government Printing Office 1960) p. A19.
12. 'Sponsor – Agency – Station: Who Is Responsible for What in TV?' *Sponsor*, January 1948, p. 53.
13. US Federal Communications Commission, Office of Network Study, *Second Interim Report: Television Program Procurement*, Part II (Washington DC: Government Printing Office 1965) p. 157.
14. Smith, op. cit. p. 37.
15. P. Kerby, *The Victory of Television* (New York: Harper and Brothers 1939), p. 84.
16. Seldes, op. cit. p. 535.
17. I. Fiske, 'Where Does Television Belong?' *Harper's*, February 1940, p. 268.
18. City College of New York, op. cit. p. 136.
19. 'Television II: Fade In on Camera One!' *Fortune*, May 1939, p. 162.
20. For RCA's prediction, see '1939 – Television Year', *Business Week*, 31 December 1938, p. 17; also see W.R. McLaurin, *Invention and Innovation in the Radio Industry* (New York: Macmillan 1949) p. 235.
21. City College of New York, op. cit. p. 137.
22. Ibid.
23. CBS, *Television Audience Research* (New York: CBS 1945) p. 6.
24. T.F. Joyce, 'Television and Post-War Distribution', speech to the Boston Conference on Distribution, 17 October 1944.
25. J. Black, 'What Television Offers as a Selling Medium', *Printer's Ink*, 30 March 1939, quoted in J. Allen, 'The Social Matrix of Television: Invention in the United States', in E.A. Kaplan (ed.) *Regarding Television: Critical Approaches – An Anthology* (Frederick, Maryland: American Film Institute/University Publications of America 1983) p. 112.

ELLEN SEITER

The Hegemony of Leisure:
Aaron Spelling Presents *Hotel*

Aaron Spelling is perhaps the most powerful person in American network television. Since 1968 he and his associates have produced a string of television series which have been extraordinarily successful in the US and abroad. At the time of writing, Spelling series occupy seven of ABC's 22 prime-time hours; in some cities in the USA it is possible to see as many as 26 hours of Spelling programmes every week. His companies have produced over 100 made-for-TV movies. His exclusive contract with ABC guarantees the purchase of two new pilots from his production company every year. His relationship with the network is so close that even experienced television writers bring Spelling their ideas to produce, as Richard and Esther Shapiro did with *Dynasty*. Since 1968, Spelling and his associates have produced a string of television series which have been phenomenally successful in the United States and are distributed internationally.

The publicity about Aaron Spelling which appears in magazines and newspapers recounts the classic American success myth, where every biographical detail signals the destiny of a millionaire. Spelling's image merges the television producer with the genius businessman, the paragon of entrepreneurial spirit. *Newsweek* reports that Spelling 'works like a scrooge' and 'toils like a fiend', that 'the son of a sweatshop tailor' began writing at the age of seven, that as a struggling actor he went home every night to write scripts.[1] The *Wall Street Journal* estimates Spelling's personal fortune at over $100 million, although Spelling 'remains deeply affected by the poverty of his Texas childhood', and reports that 'far from the swaggering mogul one might expect, he is frail and nervous'.[2] The most salient feature of Spelling's biography is the sheer number of television programmes he has produced. The quantity of Spelling's output makes him a classic 'idol of production',[3] and places television in the realm of other fortune-making industries of mythical status such as oil or automobiles.

A positive image of Spelling as a businessman has persisted despite an investigation of Spelling-Goldberg Productions in 1980 on charges of criminal fraud, conspiracy and conflict of interest. In the course of the investigation, The *New York Times* reported 'dubious payments' amounting to $75 million in 1979 from ABC to Spelling's production companies. Spelling's relationship with ABC president Elton Rule was also revealed: that they own a real estate corporation together, that they share the same lawyer and business manager, that Rule's three children are employed by Spelling. The investigation failed to produce any indictments, however, and *Time* magazine sympathetically concluded that, 'By refusing to pick up the full costs of new shows they [the networks] virtually force producers into some kind of inventive bookkeeping'.[4] Spelling feels comfortable enough within the industry to refer to ABC as 'a marvellous little family store'.[5]

In this essay I comment on the ideology of the Spelling system. It is an ideology made up of strict notions concerning family, class, and law and order. I begin by examining this ideology at work in the Spelling series dealing directly with the third of these – the police series *Mod Squad, The Rookies, S.W.A.T.* and *Starsky and Hutch.* Then, using *Charlie's Angels* as my pivot, I suggest that Spelling's fiction is equally concerned with the policing of the personal, a notion which leads me finally to an examination of the 'hegemony of leisure' at work in Spelling's series *The Love Boat, Fantasy Island* and, especially, *Hotel.*

Cop Shows
Aaron Spelling's first success, *Mod Squad*, was produced by Spelling-Thomas Productions and broadcast on ABC from 1968 to 1972. The ABC publicity announced the series this way: 'The police don't understand the now generation and the now generation doesn't dig the fuzz. The solution: find some swinging young people who live the beat scene. And get them to work for the cops.'[6] The show's premise involves the stern but kind-hearted Captain Greer offering three young people who had been arrested the option of working for the police instead of going to jail. This configuration of characters – a team of attractive, pleasant and dedicated workers who are unfalteringly loyal to their boss – has been a central element in nearly all of Spelling's productions. On *Mod Squad*, the team – all in their teens or early twenties – consists of a rich white man arrested for car theft, a poor white woman arrested for vagrancy, and a poor black man arrested during a riot. Each of them works in strict subordination to the police captain, who allows them freedom in terms of movement around the city, dress code and working hours, and with whom they form an affectionate, co-operative working unit. By supplying a number of different 'types' in each series, television narratives give the appearance of variety of characters, negate class difference, gloss over the existence of racism and obscure sexism. Each member of the

Mod Squad is characterised under the general type 'kids in trouble' and each of them is rehabilitated instantly through contact with the captain, who represents paternal discipline and affection – thus effectively reducing all of their problems to generational and family issues. For the purposes of the narrative, the characters' problems – poverty, race relations, delinquency – are equivalent, because they can be resolved in the same way. It is symptomatic that such a series could be produced in 1968, when poverty, racism and sexism were subjects of so much public protest. *Mod Squad* is a testament to the ability of television to incorporate new characters into old stereotypes and generic patterns, for the programme was a perfectly straightforward cop show.

Spelling's following success, *The Rookies*, exemplifies the same formula, this time a 'variety' of first-year police officers. The rookies are all male and include a white college graduate, a white veteran and a black identified, like *Mod Squad*'s black character, as 'from the ghetto'. As in *Mod Squad*, the characters are united in their allegiance to an authoritarian, middle-aged police officer and in their dedication to law and order. The ideological content of the programmes is clear in the spectacle of the working class and the middle class, blacks and whites, banding together to defend 'the good of society' – a concept which is already understood, instinctively felt, in precisely the same way, by each of them. Defining social unrest as the result of generational conflict, *Mod Squad* and *The Rookies* turn authority and the law over to young people who are ready to enforce it among their peers.

In 1975 Spelling introduced two new cop shows with even more explicitly reactionary content, *S.W.A.T.* and *Starsky and Hutch*. Spelling's associate Goldberg described their cop shows as featuring police officers who don't try to understand the criminal, but try to punish him.[7] *S.W.A.T.* features the group of officers working for the Special Weapons and Tactics Unit in Los Angeles, using particularly violent means to deal with terrorists. *S.W.A.T.* simply extends a kind of plot frequently featured on *Mod Squad* and *The Rookies*, involving psychosis as the source of crime (like many American detective and cop shows, mental illness appears as the modern representation of evil). Terrorists and psychotic murderers are 'incurable', represent the gravest threat to society, and are therefore deserving of the greater-than-usual violence with which they are treated. Starsky and Hutch, two plain-clothes policemen in Los Angeles, routinely violate the rights of the accused in order to inflict their own punishments, a pair of slightly subdued Dirty Harrys. The casts of both programmes are racially integrated: one member of the *S.W.A.T.* team is black, as is Starsky's and Hutch's superior officer. Since a major theme in *Starsky and Hutch* is rebellion against bureaucracy, its heroes

137

therefore frequently deviate from the superior officer's instructions, the authority of the black character being undermined. The character of Hutch carries the cultural markings of a hippie and a pacifist, eating health food and practising yoga, but these signs of a social type are dissociated from any oppositional ideological content.

All these Spelling programmes were widely criticised as among the most violent on American television. Yet it is not only the violence which is troubling about them; the particular strength of their authoritarian messages, and their appropriation of working-class and black characters into the struggle for law and order, are also worrying. As Umberto Eco pointed out about the heroic feats of Superman, their work is frequently restricted to the defence of private property.[8] The responsibility for the exceedingly violent and reactionary content of Spelling's cop shows is, however, attributed to the desires of audiences; Spelling remarks that he would not let his own children watch these shows and makes statements like, 'If I could do anything I wanted, I think I'd make shows for children like *Dumbo, Snow White*, and *Black Beauty*.'[9]

Policing the Personal: The Leisure Sphere
In 1976 Spelling-Goldberg Productions introduced *Charlie's Angels*, which featured three white women (one educated, one middle-class, one a 'former showgirl') working as private detectives for the rich and powerful Charlie Townshend. In this series the boss is never seen and the women take orders from him over the phone. On screen they are supervised by an affable, middle-aged, asexual character named Bosley, who is used for comic relief. Charlie's assignments frequently send the women to hotels, casinos, spas or night clubs in search of crime and corruption. While the women are presented as competent detectives, the threat of sexual violence against them is the primary narrative source of the show's suspense.

Charlie's Angels closely imitates Spelling's past successes, like *Mod Squad*, with some important changes. While authority appears to be less controlling because Charlie remains off-screen (a gimmick which was reportedly Spelling's own idea), the programme accentuates, even eroticises, the particularly patriarchal character of that authority. Charlie's voice-over in the programme's title sequence – 'Once upon a time there were three little girls who went to the police academy. . . . But I took them away from all that and now they work for me. My name is Charlie' – emphasises ownership of the 'Angels' and identifies them as child-like.[10] The detectives are privately, not publicly, employed, and they operate primarily in the leisure sphere. Glamour, consumption, travel and voyeurism are the programme's definitive signifiers.

Conspicuous consumption is prominent on Spelling's other private detective series such as *Vega$, Hart to Hart* and *Matt Houston*, but it is associated with places of particular corruption or perversion. Matt Houston and the Harts are independently wealthy and routinely pressed into service as detectives while going about their private lives. While criminals in Spelling's detective shows are reminiscent of the psychotics who populated the cop shows, the detectives, freed from any official capacity as police, can take a more light-hearted attitude towards their work. Their heroism has more to do with facing danger than assuming civic responsibility, and the spectre of economic motivation for crime is entirely removed. *Charlie's Angels* can be described as escapist, owing largely to its setting in a leisure context, but the series includes the same authoritarian theme and cast of dedicated employees found in Spelling's cop shows.

In the case of *The Love Boat, Fantasy Island*, and *Hotel*, the characters are not police or detectives, but they devote themselves to the policing of personal life. These 'anthology' shows, as Spelling describes them, deal with three sets of guest stars and three independent plots in each episode. In *The Love Boat*, which Spelling originally co-produced with Douglas Cramer, the creator of *Love American Style*, over 100 guest stars appear each season. The plots are typically romantic comedy and melodrama and concern the formation or stabilisation of the family unit. The crew of *The Love Boat* devote themselves to offering friendly counsel to their guests. They patrol the ship like a team of vigilant friends, happy to observe others falling in love. Captain Stubing presides over the staff and the guests like a benevolent but strict father. The message of *The Love Boat* is romantic in fixed terms, focusing on heterosexual relationships among people who are already married or plan to do so by the end of the cruise. *Fantasy Island*, a show designed to capitalise on the success of *The Love Boat* and aired immediately after it for several years, is set on a mysterious tropical island where guests may realise their most compelling fantasy, as arranged by the supernaturally powerful Mr Roarke. While the reaffirmation of the family is central to most of the plots, they often take the form of Gothic or horror tales. Mr Roarke's relationship to his guests is punishing as well as benevolent. Like Charlie Townshend, he frequently sends his guests into dangerous situations in the realisation of their fantasy. The outcome of each fantasy involves learning a moral lesson, that of contentment with one's lot, and rejecting the fantasy which was so obsessively desired. Mr Roarke rules his staff of assistants, the guests, and the natives who populate the island in a way disturbingly reminiscent of colonial mastery.

The maintenance of hierarchy and authority is naturalised in these series because they take place within a narrative interested in romantic love and the family. Unlike the police or detective shows which deal with authority and discipline in a more open way, Captain Stubing and Mr Roarke assert their dominance unnoticed in these worlds of love and leisure. The pleasure cruise and the tropical island seem to be quite apart from the everyday demands of society, yet authority asserts itself there persistently, and characters assume their roles in the social hierarchy quite willingly and happily.

Spelling's most recent co-production with Douglas Cramer, *Hotel* – the only new series of the 1983–4 season to be ranked among the top ten shows in the ratings – deserves a detailed analysis as the latest 'recombination' of the cop/detective show format with the business of leisure.[11] *Hotel* takes place in San Francisco, at a smart hotel called the St Gregory. It is an anthology show which duplicates the format of *The Love Boat* exactly. The title sequence consists of tourist views of San Francisco and the introduction of the main characters in close-up, their images appearing in the gold-bordered mirror in the hotel lobby; in *The Love Boat*, shots of the cruise ship sailing the Pacific lead to the images of the cast superimposed over graphics of the ship's life-preserver. Temporal transitions are indicated by location shots of San Francisco. When guests leave the hotel, they visit recognisable San Francisco landmarks such as Union Square, Fisherman's Wharf and Coit Tower. The St Gregory's glass elevator, where characters stand before a rear screen projection of the San Francisco skyline, is repeated in every episode, just as in *The Love Boat* characters adjourn to the deck to stand before the rear screen projection of the ocean by moonlight. The composition of the shots in *Hotel* copies those of Spelling's other productions exactly. The close-ups, two-shots, three-shots and long-shots follow invariable formal rules of symmetry and high-key lighting. The guest stars arrive in the lobby, where they are greeted by and begin indicating their problems to the staff; their narratives unfold in the hotel's bars, restaurants and private rooms; at the end of the programme, the staff watch them leave through the lobby and comment wisely on their predicaments.

The staff of the St Gregory consist of the general manager, Peter McDermott (played by James Brolin who brings to the role the humanitarian authority he practised on *Marcus Welby, MD*); his assistant, Christine Francis (played by a former model); the guest-relations director, Mark Danning; the house detective, Billy, who is black; the bellhop, Dave; and two desk clerks, one white and one black, both young women. In the penthouse lives the overseer/owner of the St Gregory, Mrs Cabot (played by Anne Bancroft; Bette Davis played the role as Mrs Trent in the series pilot). Mrs Cabot is reminiscent of the matriarchal figures in daytime soap operas. Many of her friends and relatives visit the hotel to speak to her about their troubles and she frequently intercedes on their behalf. This configuration of characters, white and black, working-class, middle-class, upper-class, working together as a team to help others and cheerfully devoted to their work, has characterised nearly all of Spelling's productions since *Mod Squad*.

The plots which appear in Spelling's anthology programmes can be divided into three categories: (1) comedies about the problems of the staff; (2) love stories involving the guests; and (3) melodramas involving the guests, and often the upper echelon of the St Gregory staff, which deal with social problems or mental illness and the triumph of good over evil. The first type of story involves situation or slapstick comedy: Billy tails a guest at the hotel lobby who is determined to injure himself there so that he can collect insurance; Mark Danning's blind date turns out to be a go-go dancer, or his old high-school lab. partner. Other plots confirm the high level of job satisfaction: the black desk clerk decides to apply for a position as administrative assistant but can never find Mr McDermott (she finds him, but concludes that she wants to stay in the job she has, rather than be 'cooped up in an office all day long away from my friends'); Mark Danning thinks he is going to be fired after asking for a rise because no one will speak to him, but instead he gets the rise and a surprise birthday party from Mrs Cabot. When problems on the job do arise, all of them can be solved by the sensitivity of the management at the St Gregory.

The second type of plot is the love story, which further reinforces the charity of the institution and the affectionate concern of the staff. The interest of the St Gregory Hotel, like that of its staff, is in human happiness, not money. An elderly couple, who have escaped from their nursing home, vacation at the hotel while charging everything to the man's son's credit card, which has been sent him by mistake. When the clerical staff discover the problem, after watching the couple fondly for several days, Mrs Cabot tears up the bill herself. When a professional woman staying at the hotel for her sister's wedding has no date for the weekend, Christine Francis arranges one for her by bribing the loading-dock foreman into taking her out. They fall in love on their first date, and he teaches her to 'believe in herself'. Romance knows no class boundaries on Spelling's shows, and frequently occurs between professional women and working-class men. Other love stories have concerned a thirteen-year-old reuniting her divorced parents; a deaf mute young woman, whose domineering mother is about to have her hospitalised, falling in love with a mime; a widower celebrating his wedding anniversary alone but pretending his wife is with him ('The St Gregory is proud to have you both,' the staff reassure him).

The third type of plot involves the greatest amount of suffering and the strictest moral judgments. Peter McDermott frequently intervenes, often using force, to banish villainous characters, as when

141

a Ku Klux Klan-style convention register at the hotel and begin terrorising an elderly black couple. The hotel has to uphold their right to register as guests and are only able to expel them after they become violent towards other guests. Many of these stories have to do with feminine duplicity: McDermott has an affair with a woman who is assisting her father, an obsessive jewel thief, and she steals his master key; a former girlfriend tries to convince McDermott that he is the father of her child; his ex-wife, an alcoholic, tries to reconcile with him; a schizophrenic woman who appears alternately as a beautiful seductress and as a shy, plain woman tries to befriend, then seduce and then kill him. Like *The Love Boat, Hotel* offers a narrative pretext for limitless promiscuity, at the same time that it incessantly reaffirms monogamy. McDermott, however, is permitted to sleep with a whole series of beautiful women before discovering that they are unsuitable longer-range partners, without any loss in moral credibility. The consequences of female sexuality are, on the other hand, the subject for narrative scrutiny in several plots – where women are being blackmailed using pornography, in a story involving partner-swapping in order to impregnate the wife of an infertile man, in an unwed mother's handing over the baby to adoptive parents, and in the reunion of a married couple after the husband has beaten the wife, has had a nervous breakdown and has been hospitalised, while the wife has begun an affair.

Class conflict has intruded into the narrative world of *Hotel* in the form of a kidnapping of Mrs Cabot, McDermott and Christine by a poor family from Stockton. Shelley Winters plays the hysterical widow of a man who dies in a worker's accident at the hotel. She convinces her two sons (one a gun-waving psychotic, the other submissive and dull-witted) and her brother-in-law to hold their own trial of Mrs Cabot on the charge of murder. During the trial it is revealed that the deceased, Ellis Ellsworth (a name carrying the connotation 'hill-billy'), was part of a sandblasting crew who had orders from Mrs Cabot to continue working through the night until the job was finished, that he fell off the scaffolding, and that the family received only $1,400 from the hotel, just enough for a coffin and a burial plot. When confronted with this, Mrs Cabot (wearing a satin blouse, pearls and a fur-collared jacket) is contrite: 'I have been haunted by that since the day it happened.' Before she can sign a confession at gunpoint, McDermott, acting as her defence attorney, elicits the truth from the brother-in-law, the only witness to the accident. Besides the fact that the foreman did not tell Mrs Cabot that the work would be dangerous, it is revealed that Ellsworth had been drinking all day long, was seeing another woman, had reported to work late, was roughhousing at the time of the accident and did not wear his safety belt. The family, completely dejected, hands over the

142

gun to McDermott and Mrs Cabot generously offers to drop any charges against them with the stipulation, suggested by McDermott, that the unruly son enlist in the Marine Corps. 'I'd like to begin his rehabilitation right away,' says McDermott, throwing a punch which knocks him to the ground. 'Maybe I deserve one of those, too,' says the mother, approaching Mrs Cabot. The plot typifies a recurrent theme of American television: that when all the facts are known, the rich and powerful are blameless; that they operate on a superior level of sensitivity and consciousness of their responsibility. On the side of Mrs Cabot are the law, the intelligence and strength of McDermott, even the military. McDermott's role associates physical punishment with authority, and reinforces the idea that the Marine Corps are primarily a character-building institution rather than a military force.

The invariable role for the plot resolutions in *Hotel*, as well as for *The Love Boat* and *Fantasy Island*, is the preservation of the status quo. Where romance is concerned, all present relationships are salvageable: the husband who beat his wife is accepted back by her; the unwed mother is miraculously reunited with the baby's father and the adoption is halted; the divorced couple decide to give their marriage another try. Every employee of the hotel accepts and is satisfied with his or her role in the strongly hierarchical structure. Social problems can either be controlled by McDermott's personal force or assigned to the realm of the psychological, where the cast's repeated mouthings of self-help slogans act as cures. Female sexuality is brought under strict patriarchal control. Women characters undergo suffering or punishment and leave the hotel heading for marriage. In the exercise of authority, McDermott is not hampered by the technicalities of civil rights which plague Spelling's police officers – he can use his pass key to walk into any room of the hotel at any time. McDermott is a match for any of the shocking realities of modern life which turn up at the hotel, and the staff and guests stand in awe of his courage and moral rectitude in tackling such difficult situations.

Television and Hegemony

> In this process, that consent-to-hegemony whose premises and preconditions are constantly structuring the sum of what individuals in society think, believe, and want, is represented, in appearance, as a freely given and 'natural' coming together into a consensus which legitimates the exercise of power.[12]

The concept of hegemony, with its emphasis on the interdependence of direct political control and ideology, elucidates the case of Aaron Spelling Productions on several levels. Hegemony, articulated by Antonio Gramsci as the negotiated predominance of one class over another, operates in two spheres: the institutional and the psychological. In Spelling's case we can see this exemplified at the institutional level by his sweetheart contract with ABC and his dominance within the US television industry; and at the psychological level by the way that the audience is represented as controlling television, and the way that television programmes are matter-of-factly referred to as trash. The psychological level of hegemony, framing the exercise of power in terms of common sense, also operates in television content. If *Mod Squad*, *The Rookies* and *Starsky and Hutch* dramatise coercion by force, *The Love Boat*, *Fantasy Island*, and *Hotel* dramatise coercion by consent.

In Spelling's fantasies the power of authority, the maintenance of the social hierarchy, the control of sexuality are exercised over and over again. *The Love Boat*, *Fantasy Island*, and *Hotel* present hegemonic fantasies, described by Julia Lesage in these terms:

> The character's desires and needs make up much of the content of their speeches and are the 'stuff' that impels the action. But each narrative also has ways to contain and limit its consideration of women's desires and needs: through what is not allowed, through negative example characters, through the connotative manipulation of the *mise en scène*, or through a narrative more important than others.[13]

Lesage argues that hegemonic fantasies have been particularly important in narratives set in the domestic sphere, and in defining 'what women want' in patriarchal terms. Spelling's escapism takes us out of the domestic and the everyday into the leisure sphere, only to reassert the same limitations. These fantasy worlds are indistinguishable from the home and the workplace, where the boss is always right, where gender roles are rigidly defined, where voyeurism substitutes for sex, where punishment for transgression is swift. Only the employees in this fantasy are unreal. They are happy because they accept positions of subordination (especially women and blacks), relinquish ambition, maintain an ever-cheerful attitude towards their jobs, respect the wealthy, and avoid questioning authority. The television audience is certainly capable of fantasising a more pleasurable leisure than this.

References

1. D.K. Shah and J. Huck 'The Hit Man', *Newsweek*, 6 November 1978, p. 104.
2. J. Mayer, 'Fantasy King', *Wall Street Journal*, 12 August 1982, p. 1.
3. The term is Leo Lowenthal's. See Richard Dyer's discussion of idols of production and consumption in *Stars* (London: BFI 1979) p. 46.
4. G. Clarke, 'A Bombshell Case Goes Phfft!', *Time*, 15 December 1980, p. 49. The woman who brought the matter to light was fired for 'unfinished and sloppy work', her supervisor was promoted to vice-president of business affairs at ABC.
5. Quoted in G. Esterly, 'The *Love Boat* Phenomenon', *TV Guide*, vol. 30, no. 23, 5 June 1982, p. 29.
6. Quoted in R. Meyers, *TV Detectives* (San Diego: A.S. Barnes 1981) p. 142.
7. Goldberg was head of programming at ABC when *Mod Squad* was bought by the network. For a thorough discussion of network practices see T. Gitlin, *Inside Prime Time* (New York: Pantheon Books 1983).
8. U. Eco, 'The Myth of Superman', in *The Role of the Reader* (Bloomington: Indiana University Press 1979).
9. Quoted in Mayer op. cit. p. 1.
10. For an excellent analysis of *Charlie's Angels* see C. Schwichtenberg, 'A Patriarchal Voice in Heaven', *Jump Cut*, no. 24–5, pp. 13–16. A detailed discussion of the patriarchal themes in *Fantasy Island* is offered in M. Budd, S. Craig, and C. Steinman, '*Fantasy Island*: Marketplace of Desire,' *Journal of Communication*, vol. 33, no. 1, Winter 1983, pp. 67–77.
11. The term is Gitlin's. See 'The Triumph of the Synthetic: Spinoffs, Copies, and Recombinant Culture', in Gitlin op. cit.
12. S. Hall, 'Culture, the Media and the "Ideological Effect"', in J. Curran, M. Gurevitch and J. Woollacott, *Mass Communication and Society* (London: Edward Arnold/Open University Press 1977), p. 339.
13. J. Lesage, 'The Hegemonic Female Fantasy in *An Unmarried Woman* and *Craig's Wife*', *Film Reader* 5, 1982), p. 84.

E. ANN KAPLAN

A Post-Modern Play of the Signifier? Advertising, Pastiche and Schizophrenia in Music Television

It was the sometimes extraordinary and innovative avant-garde techniques of MTV, the American all-music cable channel, that first drew the attention of the critical establishment. These devices were automatically taken as serving similar functions to those they served in what is now 'traditional' modernism, and they masked the promotional and commercial aspects of MTV. It is the tension between MTV's context of production and its avant-garde techniques that I want to explore here, together with analysing the company's ideology and the nature of its address to teenagers.

MTV is arguably a post-modern phenomenon in its effacement of key boundaries and separations, such as that between popular and avant-garde art, and that between different genres or artistic modes.[1] I will discuss these issues both on the level of the individual videos and that of MTV's 24-hour flow, which flattens out the previously historically distinct aesthetic modes, replacing them with a surface appeal to nostalgia. Beneath this, however, lies the basic address to adolescent desire, to his/her 'imaginary repertoire', which now takes precedence over any overt political stance towards dominant culture.

MTV: The Context of Production
Owned by Warner Amex Satellite Entertainment Company, MTV is an advertiser-supported, basic cable service for which subscribers do not pay extra. Begun in 1981 as a kind of gamble, with an initial cost of $20 million, MTV garnered $7 million in advertising revenue in the first eighteen months, and had more than $20 million by the end of 1983.[2] Latest figures cite more than $1 million a week in advertising revenue during 1984, and an audience that has grown from 18 million to 22 million, aged between 12 and 34. In August 1984 MTV became a public corporation and announced that it had agreements with four record companies for exclusive rights to new videos. In addition, in response to Turner Broadcasting Company's announcement that it was to initiate a competing 24-hour music television station, MTV will open a second 24-hour channel (intended for what Robert W. Pittman, the company's executive vice-president, calls 'an untapped

146

new audience', i.e. that between 25 and 49), for an initial cost of $7 million.[3]

The bulk of the programming is promotional videos provided free by the record companies, on the model of providing radio stations with free records. Exactly how the videos are produced (by what video artists and financed by whom) remains unclear since artists' names are not usually mentioned. The bands may or may not be involved, and record companies generally are at least partially responsible for financing.[4]

In MTV's short history, artists and bands have already been in conflict with MTV management and the record companies. There is a built-in contradiction, familiar from Hollywood, between the interests of the artists and performers, and of those creating a profitable enterprise. In a predictable cycle, the more tapes were adapted to what would please the largest audience, the more successful the channel, and the greater the urge to censor material. Wary of both parental objections to the cable and those of white audiences in racist parts of America, MTV censored explicit sex and black bands in a controversial move that pressure has done something to alleviate.[5]

Artists and performers are naturally implicated in the contra-dictions because the increased success of the channel means their increased exposure and sales. As Stephen Levy notes, 'MTV's greatest achievement has been to coax rock into the video arena where you can't distinguish between entertainment and the sales pitch.'[6] The 'sales pitch' has two objects, first that of selling the MTV station itself; second, that of selling the bands (or their song/album). In each case, the enunciative stance is that of advertising, in which there is always a slippage from the signifier that addresses desire to the commodity involved.[7] The signifiers used to sell the MTV station address the desire for (1) power/virility and (2) nurturance/community, neatly combining appeals to both male and female spectators. The signifiers for power/virility are the huge rocket plunging explosively into outer space followed by images of the men on the moon, exploring new territory; and the TV monitor, scrawled with the letters 'MTV' into which a globe drops (i.e. MTV *is* the world!); those for nurturance/community are, first, the plaintive child-like voice of Peter Townshend saying 'I want *my* MTV' (i.e., 'I want my mommie, my milk'), and second, the veejays and their ambience.

This second appeal is central to the entire conception of MTV. Robert Pittman hit upon the desire for a pseudo rock-and-roll 'family', very much along the lines of the appeal of programmes like *Good Morning America* to adults;[8] but in this case, the 'family' was to be a one of peers, very deliberately lacking adults. The informal, easy and relaxed style of the veejays was supposed to conjure up the natural

147

ambience of teenagers gathered in a room to listen to music without their parents. (The decision not to include any news except that relating to music further ensured the absence of adult authority figures.) MTV constructs a (false) sense of addressing a unified teenage rock 'community', fulfilling young people's desire to belong in a world without parents.

In addition to selling itself, however, MTV also sells the music and the bands featured in its videos. Here the signifiers that address desire (for sex, violence, freedom, love) are fastened on to the commodity that is, in this case, the band and their music contained in the purchasable album. The desire is cathected on to the album which then promises to satisfy it in the familiar manner of advertisements.

Some of the videos focus almost entirely on the members of the band, betraying here their origins in TV tapes of live performances, or even in live transmissions. Here the star phenomenon is instigated, performers and their managers in effect promoting identification with band members that will bring teenagers out to live concerts.[9]

Avant-garde Techniques in MTV

MTV's avant-garde techniques often provoke the casual critic to celebrate its subversive elements. But are the deconstructive, modernist devices in fact transgressive? How are we to explain them, given MTV's commercial context of production?

Let me briefly survey the devices involved that *appear* avant-garde. First, there is the abandonment of the traditional narrational devices of most popular culture. Cause-effect, time-space and continuity relationships are often violated, along with the usual conception of 'character'. Second, videos are frequently self-reflexive. For instance, we may see the tape we are watching being played on a TV monitor within the frame; or the video sets used in the production room in which a rock video is being made, which may turn out to be the one we are watching (for example, the Rolling Stones' *She Was Hot*; Rick Springfield's *Somebody to Love*). A familiar image is the clapper-board in front frame, coming down on the action we are watching about to be filmed. Tapes often focus on photographs (of the protagonist as a child; or in the present), or set up the image in a series of photograph-like frames.[10]

All kinds of framing within the frame are common. One video sets up a proscenium-arch type of frame, with perspective, and the images are played on all three sides of what is essentially a box.[11] There is increasing use of a large screen (within the frame) above the performers' heads, on which we see not only the greatly enlarged images of the players but also the narrative involved. Sometimes the screen-spectator relationship within the video is disrupted, as in Duran Duran's *Reflex*, when a huge wave overflows on to the crowd. Def

148

Leppard's *The Photograph*, as its name implies, uses the whole concept of frames within frames to structure its narrative.

The sanctity of the image in illusionist texts is completely overthrown in MTV. No image is stable or solid for very long. Often the image is turned around as a flat, two-dimensional surface, or swept off into space (as in *Leave It*, by Yes); or it is scrunched up into a ball that then circles around in space, splitting into many pieces in the process (as in Cyndi Lauper's *Girls Just Want to Have Fun*). But perhaps the most outrageous and daring play with illusionist deconstruction is in the Cars' *You Might Think*, when all manner of surprising and unexpected operations are performed on the image, very much in the surrealist style of René Magritte.[12]

Now, how are we to understand these anti-illusionist devices? If we followed the aesthetic discourse dominant in Western culture from the late 19th to the mid-20th century, we would be forced to posit an untenable contradiction. For this discourse polarised the popular/realist commercial text, and the 'high art' modernist one, making impossible a text that was at once avant-garde and popular.

The discourse of contemporary film theory has tended to make the same distinction, if for different reasons. The classical Hollywood text, for example, has been seen as bringing about the 'reality-effect' specifically by an effacement of the means of enunciation. Devices like shot/counter-shot, continuity editing, etc., give the spectator the illusion of creating the images, suturing him/her into the narrative flow. These devices, together with the context of their production, apparently explain how such realist texts embody dominant ideology. Avant-garde texts, on the other hand, have been seen as transgressive of dominant ideology because their strategies are set up in deliberate opposition to dominant bourgeois forms. The self-reflexivity of modernist texts together with the self-conscious play with dominant forms often included (at least in the *political* modernist text) a critique of culture and dominant ideology.

These aesthetic discourses are obviously inadequate to deal with the MTV phenomenon. Arguably, two new things are going on in terms of the avant-garde devices, only one of which, however, turns out to be really new. First, the self-reflexive devices may signal not so much a complete abandonment of story (as at first seems the case) as the initiation of a new kind of story that reflects a changed relationship of self to image. The new story is about technology, about the processes of performance and filming that have come to dominate people's lives in unprecedented ways. People are not only routinely involved in image-production as their profession, but are also routinely bombarded with their own images on TV monitors. The pervasive use of the Polaroid camera, with its instant image feedback, further ensures our constant awareness of the imaged self, which has now become an accepted part of our visual environment. It carries to an extreme a process that began at the turn of the century with consumer capitalism and the initiation of the 'culture of the spectacle'.[13]

The self-reflexive strategies of many MTV videos thus turn out to be not so much an attempt to defy dominant ideology through a deliberate transgression of illusionism, but rather simply an embodiment of the new story about what the machines can do. The representation of a representation is no longer inherently transgressive; it is not that all illusionism has been given over so much as that the expectation of *traditional* illusionism has gone. Viewers are now caught up in the illusion of video production as before in that of the reality-effect.

Modernism is itself partly responsible for this: its strategies have become assimilated into the dominant culture, so that the spectator cannot be shocked any more in the old ways. The 'shock' thus has to inhere in the constant image-change, and in the use of excessively unusual images. The new technological era has produced its own narrative modalities.

Now for Jameson, the post-modernist form and the effacement of key boundaries, like that between high and low art, are largely negative. Jameson is concerned about the 'disappearance of the sense of history',[14] and the living in a perpetual present, together with the fact that 'there is very little in either the form or the content of contemporary art that contemporary society finds intolerable and scandalous'.[15] For Jameson, the modernist parody has been replaced by mere pastiche, 'a neutral practice of mimicry . . . without that still latent feeling that there exists something *normal* compared to which that which is being imitated is rather crude'.[16] If one accepts Jameson's argument, MTV's preference for pastiche reveals its lack of orienting boundaries; in this case, like much post-modernist art in Jameson's view, rock videos incorporate, rather than quote, other texts 'to the point where the link between high art and commercial forms seems increasingly difficult to draw'.[17]

What seems most disturbing to Jameson about post-modernism is the lack of any clear position from which a text is enunciated – any clear recognition of the previously sacred aesthetic boundaries. Again, MTV exemplifies this type of text: images from German expressionism, French surrealism and Dada (Fritz Lang, Buñuel, Magritte and Dali) are mixed together with those pillaged from the *noir*, gangster and horror films in such a way as to obliterate differences. For Jameson, such eliding of forms indicates the end of any critical position, a dangerous lack of the ability to speak from a particular place and to make distinctions.

While there is obviously some justification for this kind of concern, as will be noted later, the post-modern effacement of hitherto sacred boundaries need not be seen only negatively. Arguably, in many cases, video artists are quite self-consciously playing with some of these standard images, creating a liberating sense by the very fact of defying traditional boundaries. Images from both high and low art are arguably now clichéd – thin, threadbare and, in addition, archaic in the computer and space age. Rock videos arguably revitalise the dead images by juxtaposing them; they represent a necessary short-term strategy for young artists struggling to discover their place in a society that has still not found its own images through which to express its new condition. But I will return to this larger issue later on.

Ideology in MTV: The Nature of Its Adolescent Appeal
MTV embodies many of the contradictions evident in contemporary youth culture. This is precisely what makes it so interesting. One of the main contradictions, already alluded to, is that between the new artists (performers, video producers) trying to express how they see the world through forms/images available to them, and the context of a work's production and exhibition, namely the 24-hour television flow, addressed to a generalised, mass rock audience, and 'managed' by Bob Pittman in the interests of a large business corporation.

This is arguably a very different positioning from that of many artists/performers in previous rock periods. While some commercialisation was always inevitable, we are talking about an altogether different and more encompassing level with MTV. For ultimately the earlier promoters were manipulating *bodies* and sounds; now, they are manipulating *images* and sounds (at least after a certain point in a video's production). The contact with the 'bodies' earlier at least offered performers the possibility of some resistance to manipulation; but now, once the tape is released, it becomes an object in a continuous commercial circulation that has, as its base, adolescent desire.

Nevertheless, a certain important tension remains, manifesting the remaining contradiction between the original resisting impulse in the creation of certain tapes and their context of display. What is effaced by the 24-hour flow is the original address to specific delimited audiences. What MTV does is to gather up into itself the history of rock and roll, rendering the originally distinct subject positions merely nostalgic reflection on earlier periods, which are not experienced as distinct from the present. Thus, videos no longer (or rarely) make specific political/ideological comment: rather, they represent a manifestation of contemporary American youth culture's quest for a position from which to speak. Meanwhile, working in a different direction, the managers of MTV are attempting to bring rock into mainstream culture, entailing, inevitably, a dilution of the original often oppositional stances. What remains as the unconscious motivating element in the videos is what always ultimately structures mass media works – namely, unresolved oedipal conflicts. MTV is particularly fascinating, however, in specifically addressing *adolescent* desire.

There are three basic types of video on MTV, which roughly correspond to the three types of rock music that have been developed over the past twenty years, i.e. romantic (soft rock), 'modernist' (acid rock) and post-modernist rock (punk/new wave). (See the chart below.)

Modes
(all use avant-garde strategies –
self-reflexivity, play with the image)

		Romantic (pastiche, narrative, character)	*Modernism* (elements of both the romantic and post-modern)	*Post-modernism* (pastiche, anti-narrative, focus on performance)
Predominant MTV themes (all have to do with desire)	Love/sex	**A** Loss and reunion Narcissism	**B** Struggle for autonomy Love as problematic, contradictory	**C** Sadism/masochism Homoeroticism
	Authority issues	**D** Parental figures (often positive) Oedipal issues	**E** Parental and public figures (usually negative) Cultural critique (mainly re sex roles)	**F** Nihilism Anarchy Destruction

The Romantic Video   This type looks back to the 60's soft rock, tends to address the female spectator, and often uses conventional narrative strategies. It is the overall nostalgic, sentimental or yearning quality that defines romantic videos. A love relationship (not only male/female but also child/parent – or parent-substitute) is presented as the central problem-solving element in the protagonist's life. The few female soloists and song writers on MTV often make this kind of tape (for instance, Cyndi Lauper's *Time After Time*; Stevie Nicks's *If Anyone Falls in Love*). Often the protagonist is female (even when the band is all-male, as in Eurythmics' *Here Comes the Rain Again*), and her troubled love and yearnings are focused on. (The male version of unrequited love generally lacks the sentimental quality and thus falls into one of the other groups; Lionel Ritchie's *Hello* is an interesting exception.)

In the romantic video, the signifiers are linked in a narrative chain that reproduces the song-lines about love, separation and the yearning for togetherness, keeping the time/space relations intact. Cyndi Lauper's *Time After Time*, for example, begins with a typical

152

moment of pastiche, as the heroine is inspired to leave her lover by the poignant, bitter-sweet parting on the television screen of a mock Dietrich and her lover. Catching her in the act, Lauper's lover takes her to the station, the heroine stopping by to wish farewell to her working-class mother. There is a poignant parting scene at the station.

The close mother-daughter bonding in this video (quite the opposite of that in another Lauper tape, *Girls Just Want to Have Fun*) is significant in that videos generally follow the common narrative pattern of making close parent-child bondings either between mothers and sons (for example, Deniece Williams's *Let's Hear It For the Boy*) or fathers and sons (for instance, Lee Carey's *A Fine Fine Day*, where the close son-father bonding is set off by a cold inadequate mother). The tapes in this category generally idealise parent-child relationships, manifesting the oedipal yearnings underlying the urge to merge with the loved one, or to return to an early mother-child closeness.

The Post-modernist Video At the other extreme are the post-modernist videos, which retain some of the original nihilist positions of recent punk and new-wave rock, and are most often associated with the 'heavy metal' bands. Lawrence Grossberg has focused on the negativity of punk ('It reveals a self-reflexive affirmation of difference, a decathexis of any affirmation,' he notes[18]), but what impresses me is the overall vitality and creative imagination (manifested in the music and visuals of the tapes) that is para-doxically in the service of a nihilistic ideology. Good examples of such tapes include Frankie Goes to Hollywood's *Relax*; Scorpions' *Rock You Like a Hurricane*; Mötley Crüe's *Too Young to Fall in Love*; Devo's *Whip It*; Rod Stewart's *Infatuation*; and Billy Idol's *Eyes Without a Face*.

These, and other tapes like them, share some or all of the following characteristics. First, tapes show their origins in live band peformances by focusing on the figures comprising the band, seen playing their instruments in often hectic style. Second, these videos differ from romantic ones in their aggressive use of camera and editing. Wide-angle lenses, zoom shots, rapid montage (with one image rarely having much to do with the next) typify devices used. Lighting techniques derive from *film noir*, as does the general mood of the visuals. As in *film noir*, the world of these videos is unstable, alien. A common image is the sudden, unmotivated and unexplained explosion, shattering the filmic world and underscoring the violence that always lurks beneath. The male performers stand in darkly lit, strange, often deserted landscapes, hanging, as it were, in outer space, unconnected to any recognisable environment. The intensity and

153

concentrated shock-effects of these videos produce images that violate those in dominant culture.

A third characteristic of the post-modernist video is that gender representation changes. Representation of the male performers also differs from that in romantic videos in its aggressivity. To begin with, male dress here is punk – tight leather pants, spiked leather straps over bare chests, spiked hair and heavy boots, all of which reproduce bondage-style iconography. The camera will typically cut in on male bodies, isolating, deliberately garishly (effects made more strident by wide-angle lenses) faces, crotches, buttocks, widespread legs. Instruments are unabashedly used as phallic props (in a manner that was recently excellently spoofed in the movie *This Is Spinal Tap*). The camera often sways with the male bodies (as in Scorpions' *Rock You Like a Hurricane*), and figures are filmed in slow motion, often jumping in the air, spreadeagled.

Meanwhile, the female body is either set up as reviled erotic object or as bitch-like and rejecting. The woman, often vamp-like in tight leather dress, high heels and long spiked hair, heartlessly abandons or betrays the male protagonist (Rick Springfield's *Somebody to Love* or ABC's *Poison Arrow*).

Significant here is how the address in these videos is ultimately androgynous. The iconography for both male and female figures is surprisingly similar, at least in terms of spiked long or short hair, leather dress, boots, straps, etc. Women performers typically use the microphone as a phallic prop or, indeed, turn their high-heeled, stiletto shoes into such props. The alienated, hostile stance is equally characteristic of male and female figures; both are equally rejecting, faithless and violent. This androgynous iconography and eroticism indicates yet one more sphere, namely that of sex difference, in which the post-modernist video effaces traditional boundaries and separations. The videos construct an androgynous spectator, refusing the viewer a clear gender-position, blurring male/female distinctions and producing a generalised eroticism. (It is, however, obvious that these videos validate traditional male qualities of aggressivity and violence, bringing the females into this terrain, just as the romantic videos bring the male into the traditionally female terrain.)

In post-modern videos, then, the love theme turns from the relatively mild narcissism and merging of the romantic tape, that focuses on the pain of separation, into sadism, masochism, androgyny and homoeroticism. And the anti-authority theme moves from mere unresolved oedipal conflicts with parents to explicit hate – nihilism, anarchy, destruction.

Having said this, however, it is important to note that it is largely isolated images that convey these stances and emotions. In general, what is quite interesting about post-modernist videos is their refusal to take up a position vis-à-vis their images, their habit of not communicating a clear signified. In post-modernist videos, characteristically each element of a text is undercut by others: narrative is undercut by pastiche; signifying is undercut by signifiers that do not line up in a coherent chain; genres are mixed, as noted, blurring the pop/high art distinction. Yet this is usually all to no specific end, as it would be in modernist texts (Eisenstein, Brecht, Godard). The text is thus flattened out, creating a two-dimensional effect, and the refusal of a secure position for the spectator within the narrative. This leaves him/her free to cathect to the individual image or to the performer-stars, as will be seen later on.

Devo's *Whip It* is a good example of such a video. The band are presented in outfits that are a mix of iconographies. In black sleeveless tops, knee-length pants and inverted flower-pot hats, the groups stand in a deliberately artificial TV-set plot of land. Intercut with shots of the performers are shots of a cabin-style, 'out-West' house, where a fat 'momma' sits stirring her bowl (a common MTV image, by the way). In between momma and the band is a woman, dressed western-style, so immobile that at first she looks like a waxwork. The video consists of this woman being whipped by the performers (in between their playing), in such a way that her clothes are gradually removed. Momma goes on stirring unconcernedly, but occasionally comic-strip word-bubbles appear from her mouth, saying, 'Oh, that Alan!'.

Beyond the obvious pastiche of the western, children's television, and comic strips, what are we to make of the video? What position is it taking toward what it shows? Is it meant to be funny? Does it 'approve' of the whipping? It is difficult for the spectator to know: the signifiers have been pried loose from their usual meanings in the forms mimicked, but they have not been re-ordered so as obviously to express something else. If the signifiers conjure up the concepts 'sexism', 'violence', 'stupid/indulgent mom' (all of which carry intense emotions), the video does nothing with them.

Queen's *Radio GaGa* is similarly difficult to read: in this case, an argument could be made for Queen self-consciously playing with images from Nazism and Germany in the 1930s, setting off Fritz Lang's version of the future (in the footage taken from *Metropolis*) against contemporary *Star Trek* futurist imagery. The intent, then, could be to link Lang's foreboding of fascism with the present.

On the other hand, this is a sophisticated reading, only possible within the framework of knowledge about Lang, and about fascism and 30s Germany. The video does not itself construct a clear position for the spectator, or even seem to raise questions about its images. The video does not say whether it is for or against fascism, hedging along that line of not letting us know what we are to do with the images of proto-fascism (the rally scenes pastiche Leni Riefenstahl's *Triumph of the Will*, the figures looking like a cross between those in her film and those in *Star Trek*). The easy, regular beat of the music, with its haunting tune, sweeps the spectator along in a way that is pleasurable rather than disjunctive or questioning. If there is irony, rather than pastiche, it takes work to grasp it.

The Modernist Video   The bulk of the videos fall into one or other of the extremes on the chart. This is naturally in itself significant, in that the vacillation between the romantic and post-modernist types characterises the phenomenon of post-modernism. While polar opposites in overall mode, both the extreme types share a tendency to be heavily oedipal (about inner psychic dramas rather than about the social/political level of things). The middle category (that I had difficulty finding a label for, defining and collecting examples of) is the category that has characterised 'high art' in the West, at least since the Industrial Revolution and the rise of Romanticism (as a literary movement). The great nineteenth-century realist novel provided one level of critique of bourgeois society, followed by the post-romantic, modernist kind of critique. While the very category 'modernism' is again under debate, I am using it here to stand for the type of art that is in deliberate reaction against what are perceived as dominant, established forms. Modernism is, then, a counter-art form, defining itself by what it is opposed to; so that, whether taking a position to the left or to the right of the establishment, modernism (in this sense) is a largely *political* art, looking from a particular *critical* position. In this way, it is set off against both the romantic work in the sense of a sentimental/idealising text, and the post-modernist (anarchic/nihilist) one.

The chart shows how 80s culture has, as it were, squeezed out the critical middle as the 60s recede into the background. It shows the kinds of discourse that establishment culture organises (permits) because it is not ultimately threatening. What is left is merely a mild reflection of the far more vehement critique that could be found in some 60s rock music (for example, that of Dylan or The Grateful Dead).

Modernist or alternative videos differ from the previous two types in taking up a particular position vis-à-vis hegemonic culture. It is often hard to categorise them as either progressive or reactionary, and they may have elements that work in either way. These videos are most explicit about the adolescent fears, fantasies and desires that underline all MTV tapes and constitute their deepest appeal. While romantic videos represent the fantasy of effacing ego boundaries in merging with the other (a regression to the lost mother-child idyll), and the post-modernist ones provide escape into the detached

156

signifier, alternative tapes rather illustrate moments of disruption, conflict, rejection, alienation. Three themes in particular are constantly repeated.

There are first the anti-parental, anti-authority videos, revealing the adolescent disillusionment with, and distaste for, parental and governmental authority. Protagonists are shown as totally obliterating authority, or else as painful victims of it. One tape, for example, uses imagery that equates Friday liberation from the work-week with an escape from prison. Secretaries are imaged in chains that tie them to the desk, the boss (fat and ugly) as in turn bound by the liberators in ticker-tape. The performers, in their anti-establishment punk clothes, are imaged as freedom-fighters, who destroy the office and the oppressors, liberating the employees.

Jo Boxers' *Just Got Lucky* contrasts the happy-go-lucky band, in their working-men's clothes and box-cart, with a stuffy, over-weight and quarrelsome parental couple in their swanky car. The car and the box-cart overtake each other a few times, until, finally, the miserable couple are seen going merrily along in the box-cart, while the band sit comfortably in the swanky car. A similar tape is the Stray Cats' *Look at that Cadillac*, only this time there is a nostalgic 50s iconography. John Cougar's *Authority* video perhaps sums up the whole type. Here the protagonist is seen as victimised by figures representing all the types of authority in society, from parents to policemen to reporters and sports managers.

A second group of videos focuses on adolescent vulnerability to rejection. While this theme is present in romantic videos, the emphasis is different. There the usually female protagonist yearns to merge with the loved one, or bemoans the lover's absence. In the middle category, the protagonist is usually male (Madonna's *Borderline* is an exception), and the male lover victim of a faithless seductress. In one video, the rejected male lover spies on his heartless mistress as she goes out on dates with her rich lovers, who pick her up in their expensive cars. In one typical shot, the lover is lying on the floor when the woman enters; the image shows her standing threateningly over his body, her shapely legs in stiletto heels filling the frame.

ZZ Top's sexism is more playful (partly caricaturing itself), but still offensive. *Legs* deals with the transformation of a homely woman, jeered by the men, into a dazzling seductress in mini-skirt, with shapely legs, ankles and feet. In classic Hollywood style, shots again fragment the female bodies. In another tape, ZZ Top depict a garage attendant's fantasy about three *fatale* types who stop by in their spoofed-up, vintage-model car. The camera picks up leather-tight hips, stockinged legs, stiletto heels, shapely necks and arms in what are by now on MTV conventional images of women. Seduced in his

157

fantasy by the women, the attendant is later thrown out of the car on to the dusty road. Later, the line between fantasy and reality is questioned when the attendant finds the ZZ Top car key back at the garage.

The fears and fantasies being addressed here, while in many ways similar to those in classical Hollywood cinema, additionally represent a backlash against the recent women's movement. Male adolescent fears of impotence and of explosive, aggressive female sexuality are increased in a period when women are permitted to express their sexual desire openly. The male protagonists often appear emasculated, passive and unable to prevent their victimisation. They do not resist seduction in the manner of earlier macho Hollywood heroes (cf. especially *film noir*), nor are the sexual women punished.

If these videos of male rejection may be said to move in a reactionary direction, particularly in terms of the image of the female body, a few tapes by female writers and performers open up more progressive space. Cyndi Lauper's *Girls Just Want to Have Fun* (already briefly noted in relation to avant-garde strategies), while in many ways a typical anti-parental video, has the added element of the sassy female protagonist defying her stuffy/fat/ugly parents' wish to make her into a hard-working, conventional girl. The exuberant experimental devices here are not inserted, as so often, for mere technical virtuosity, but geared to the end of figuring the concept of female liberty and joy.

Donna Summer's *She Works Hard for the Money* is a more serious critique of woman's exploitation at work and her double duty of work plus domestic chores. Summer herself conducts the spectator through the images with the repeated warning phrase 'Better treat her right.' The video ends with all the workers previously imaged joining together and dancing in the road, in a gesture of defiance and united strength.

Pat Benatar's *Love is a Battlefield* addresses the issue of prostitution from the woman's point of view. Sent away from home by her fat/ugly/ unsympathetic parents, the protagonist ends up a prostitute in a city bar, hassled and pawed by the men.[19] We have shots of several of the prostitutes being hassled, and then of one particularly persistent man going too far with one of the women. The tape has already established the women's sympathies with one another, and at this point the heroine steps in to confront the man. The prostitutes all band together behind her, creating a powerful mass that sends the man into the corner. The women then join together in a threatening, war-like dance outside the bar, eventually dispersing with fond farewell gestures, and going their separate ways.

Finally, Pati Wilson's *Bop Girl* uses stop-motion photography and surrealist devices to convey the oppressiveness of the conventional wedding for the woman; and Bette Midler, in an unusual video with

Mick Jagger, manages to entice Jagger into a dance routine in which she clearly has the upper hand.

It is important to note, in concluding here, that despite the often-progressive *thematic* positioning of women in these videos, iconographically the female body is usually presented in the traditional patriarchal 'feminine'. We have another example of the constraints of working within commercial forms, which always insist upon the culturally defined 'ideal' feminine. At a deeper level, we are also confronted with the difficulty of presenting any alternate 'feminine' (any feminine outside patriarchy) while remaining, as do these videos, within conventional ways of filming the female body (i.e. as object of the male gaze).

This group of alternative videos shows a wide variety of styles and themes, and a series of differing positions vis-à-vis dominant culture. Narrative is usually more evident than in the post-modernist videos, yet cause-effect, time-space and continuity relations are typically violated. Some tapes use very avant-garde strategies, others are more conventional. What links the videos is the kind of inner adolescent dramas that they reflect, from anti-family/anti-authoritarian fantasies to male fears of female sexuality, to female images of solidarity and freedom.

While the tapes grouped as 'alternative' may in their four-minute span speak from a particular position, the 24-hour flow of MTV is such as to represent, as a whole, a possibly decentring experience. The constant change from one video to the next prevents the individual experiences from being absorbed on any other than the perceptual/emotional level. If the post-modernist video itself has elements that undercut one another, this is true of MTV as a whole: each of the three types of video undercuts the others, so that the spectator experiences constant alternation, a series of different subject-positionings that cancel each other out.

It is in this sense that MTV may be seen as a paramount post-modernist form. However, it is necessary to distinguish between post-modernism as a radical philosophy, and as recuperated aesthetic. In its radical, Derridean form, post-modernism embodies an attack on bourgeois signifying practices. As a critical theory, post-modernism exposes how these practices, claiming to speak what is 'natural' and 'true', in fact set up a transcendental self as a point outside articulation. But the practices conceal this point of enunciation, so that in an effect typical of bourgeois hegemony the spectator is unaware of being addressed from a particular position. The post-modernist critic and artist use radically transgressive forms in an effort to avoid the illusionist position of a speaker outside articulation. The 'freeing' of the signifiers is in this case really a kind of strategy – that is, a way of preventing their usual linkage to mythic signifieds.

159

The decentring of the spectator/reader, then, has a radical effect in releasing him/her from predictable, confining signifieds.

A recuperated post-modernism, such as that of MTV, has to contain its decentring effects so as to ensure the ultimately *pleasurable* viewing experience (which, in turn, will ensure repeated watching). MTV arguably contains the decentred experience in two main ways.

The decentring is, first, contained by in fact not permitting the signifiers to remain totally incoherent. In the less traditionally narrative videos, the signifiers (as noted) ultimately all refer to the performer-stars. These are culture heroes/heroines with whom adolescents identify, and who can be securely 'possessed' through the album. So, whatever is disturbing in a video can be controlled by the reassuring figures of the band.

Second, within the context of reassurance, the rapid flow of the images is exciting and pleasurable. Pittman recognised this when he talked about creating 'IPMs' ('Ideas Per Minute'), in order to 'hook' the spectator.[20] While each signifier must have a signified, the flow is so rapid that the spectator can barely associate any meaning, let alone perceive a coherence with the images before and after any one image. Usually, the spectator does not even try, but deliberately surrenders expectations of narrative, becoming hypnotised by the rapid flow, in a state of suspended incoherence that is pleasurable because partly chosen. He/she is temporarily coaxed into what Jameson has called the post-modernist, schizophrenic stance – the state of being fixated on the detached signifier, isolated in a present from which there is no escape.[21]

Conclusion
This analysis of MTV has attempted to expose the overlapping and contradictory discourses in which it is embedded. The rock video station exists in perpetual tension between complicit and transgressive aspects that are the result of the extraordinary combination of a potentially disruptive form, critical of bourgeois hegemony, embedded in a commercial, profit-making institution. The original dissenting, resisting stance, first of the blues, and then of (especially British) rock and roll in the 60s and 70s has been slowly transformed in the 80s America into the commercialised, popular forms of MTV. In exacerbating the already ongoing trend of bringing rock and roll into mainstream culture, MTV inevitably participated in diluting the original oppositional stances. The Top 40 video format, the introduction of Friday night videos on regular TV, the censorship and much-discussed racism of MTV all point to the severe constraints rock artists must endure.

A pessimistic conclusion from all of this would be that contemporary youth culture, as manifest in MTV, is post-modernist in its inability to see an 'outside' any more. Lawrence Grossberg takes this position when he notes that rock and roll in the 80s 'is no longer able to constitute itself a powerful affective boundary between its fans and those who remain outside of its culture. . . . Survival for this new youth seems to demand adaptation to, and escape from, the hegemony rather than a response to the historical context in which they find themselves.'[22]

The address to a decentred spectator, the refusal of many videos to take up a position vis-à-vis their images would seem to corroborate Grossberg's analysis of the inability of 80s youth to find a stance from which to critique hegemonic culture.

But, as I hope I have shown, the position ignores a positive underside to MTV. As in many commercial forms, rock videos address some need, some gap left by hegemonic culture and high art forms. The effacing of old boundaries between high and pop culture may be seen as transgressive. The very heteroglossia of MTV is exhilarating, if viewed in this way. Rock videos respect nothing and take nothing for granted, embodying a lively, vital desire to encompass all. As a form addressed specifically to a teenage audience, the videos allow expression of fears, fantasies and desires for which hegemonic culture has hitherto had little sympathy. The energy and creativity of many videos manifest the refusal of youth to be silenced, the desire to be heard, seen and given attention.

If capitalism utilises adolescent desires for its own commercial ends, adolescent desire is also having an effect on hegemonic culture. What precisely this effect is (or will be) is hard to say: but it is clear that the imagery, iconography and styles of rock videos are moving out into advertising, fashion and films. Advertisements begin to look like rock videos, in a reversal of rock videos' function as advertisements. Where rock videos first copied live performance films (such as *Woodstock, The Last Waltz, The Wall, The Rose*), now commercial films copy rock videos (cf. particularly *Breakin', Beat Street, Streets of Fire, Purple Rain, Body Rock*, not to mention the spoof, *This Is Spinal Tap*).

What will most likely continue is a dialectical play between the diluting forces of hegemonic culture, seeking to co-opt rock for its own consumerist ends, and the energy, vitality and creativity that are the sources for much rock and roll. As long as the tension remains, so will Jameson's pessimistic vision of a completely negative post-modernist culture be kept at bay. But Jameson's vision stands as an important warning for the future, and is indeed already partially there in the inability of rock culture to articulate *ideological* positions against dominant culture. The vitality and imagination of most American rock videos arise from unresolved oedipal desires that have not been transformed into cultural stances. The British influence,

161

quite pervasive on MTV, is useful in providing a political resonance, but it seems that the 'critical middle' has been lost in the shuffle from the 60s to the 80s. Whether or not the pendulum is still swinging remains to be seen.

References

1. cf. F. Jameson, 'Postmodernism and Consumer Society', in H. Foster (ed.), *The Anti-Aesthetic: Essays on Postmodern Culture* (Port Townsend, Washington: Bay Press 1983) p. 113.
2. cf. G. Sobczak, 'MTV, Radio and Unit Sales', unpublished paper, Rutgers University, 1984, p. 12.
3. P. Kerr, 'MTV plans 2d music channel', *New York Times*, 22 August 1984, Section D, pp. 1, 14.
4. Sobczak, op. cit. p. 13.
5. This issue is often referred to in popular articles on MTV. See S. Levy, 'Ad Nauseam – How MTV Sells Out Rock and Roll', *Rolling Stone*, 8 December 1983, pp. 36–7; A. Zeichner, 'Rock'n' Video', *Film Comment*, vol. 19, no. 4, July/ August 1983, p. 45; Sobczak, op. cit. p. 7; R. Gristgau, 'Rock'n'Roller Coaster: The Music Biz on a Joyride', *Village Voice*, 7 February 1984, p. 43.
6. Levy, op. cit. p. 33.
7. Allon White discusses this phenomenon in his unpublished paper. 'Why Did the Signifiers Come Out to Play?'.
8. cf. J. Feuer, 'The Concept of Live Television: Ontology as Ideology', in E.A. Kaplan (ed.), *Regarding Television: Critical Approaches – An Anthology* (Frederick MD: American Film Institute/University Publications of America 1983) pp. 12–22.
9. For the recent phenomenon of Michael Jackson's concert tour cf. P. Hillmore, 'Jacksons Launch a Plastic Thriller', *Observer*, 29 July 1984, p. 14; M. Kakutani, 'Why These Pop Singers Have Risen to Superstardom' (on Jackson and Prince), *New York Times*, 2 September 1984, Section 2, pp. 1, 14.
10. A recent *New York Times* Sunday supplement on women's fashions is interesting in revealing the dominance of the 'frame' (as pictorial device) in new advertising copy. Women's bodies are isolated in film strips, or juxtaposed on a page in frames; often there is a screen-spectator image, either literally a couple in a movie house, looking at the imaged-woman selling the clothes; or a painting on a wall (in realistic photography) of a woman's body.
11. Recently, Channel 4 News's *Dateline* used the proscenium-arch type of frame for its stories.
12. Interestingly enough, this video won the first MTV Award for being the best tape. The clip showed the hero in full frame, followed by the face being cut away to reveal the whole group sailing down rapids on a boat, within the cut-out face.
13. cf. White, op. cit., and R. Bowlby, *Just Looking* (London, New York: Methuen forthcoming).
14. Jameson, op. cit. p. 25.
15. Ibid. pp. 117–19, p. 124.
16. Ibid. p. 114.
17. Ibid. p. 112.
18. L. Grossberg, 'The Politics of Youth Culture: Some Observations on Rock and Roll in American Culture'. *Social Text*, Winter 1983–4, p. 112.
19. Recently, a clothing commercial shown in the USA imitated the opening of Pat Benatar's video, showing a young girl packing to leave home, her stuffy parents

162

watching powerlessly. Enter the lover taking her away, and cut to the clothing, which is now said to be appropriate for 'growing up'.

20. Levy, op. cit. p. 75.
21. Jameson, op. cit. pp. 120–1.
22. Grossberg, op. cit. pp. 110–11.

MICHÈLE MATTELART

Education, Television and Mass Culture: Reflections on Research into Innovation

Until now, there has been very little analysis in France of the possible relation between the mass production and distribution of entertainment and the educational system. However, the advent of new television channels and cable networks, by multiplying enormously the need for programmes and by transforming the conception of the audience, is likely to put this problematic on the agenda in France. Whereas the present audio-visual system is undergoing a serious production crisis, these new infrastructures make it urgent to provide for new programmes and to innovate in terms of audiences and uses. The linking of television, education and mass culture will surely figure among the openings favoured by the new networks – openings that imply new production structures, new centres of creation, new exchanges between the public and private sectors (notably multimedia groups with a pedagogical calling) and between 'light' and 'heavy' structures.

This problematic appeared in the United States as early as the end of the 1960s when, in a perspective of social and cultural innovation, certain university groups and scientific circles posed, on the margins of commercial television and within the framework of an alliance with educational foundations, the following questions: how can the potential of audio-visual technology be used for educational purposes? How can the obvious attraction that commercial television has for a young audience be channelled? How can educational television escape the ghetto of tele-education which seems to prolong the boredom of the school system and disdains the mechanisms of enjoyment so efficiently implemented by mass culture?

The Importance of Re-examining a Prototype
I would like to make two introductory comments in relation to the idea of looking back at *Sesame Street*, a pedagogic product developed in the United States in the late 1960s, from the perspectives of the present day, from France in the 1980s. These points are to do with the relationships between the apparatuses of education, and of mass media, in different national contexts; and with the historical

164

specificity of any educational initiative such as *Sesame Street*.

Firstly, then, the fact that this educational TV programme appeared in the United States (and the corollary fact that it could not have appeared in France) is explicable, amongst other reasons, by the place occupied by the mass culture apparatus in the United States in the formation of national society, that is, in the mechanisms of hegemony, which are particular to each historical formation.

We know that, historically, a society such as the United States required its mass communications system to play a role which could not previously have been played, in the interests of binding together the States of the Union, by other apparatuses concerned with socialisation and with the formation of national identity. *Sesame Street* trades on this unifying drive within mass culture, and on the hegemonic role which it has occupied since the end of the last century in the United States, as an agent of socialisation and national integration.

In France, the hegemony of the schooling system has remained unchallenged for longer than in other countries in relation to the mass media. French critical research on social reproduction has privileged the role of the schooling system. In so doing, it reinforced the notion of the school's pre-eminence over other cultural apparatuses.

Is this to say that this hegemonic character is intangible and not susceptible to being relativised, in the French context, by the importance assumed by other cultural apparatuses? Today, given that the extraordinary development of communication technologies has been clearly identified in France as a formula for escaping a crisis, is the redistribution of the apparatuses of socialisation not to be envisaged? When Jean-Luc Godard produces a video, *France/Tour/ Détour Par/Deux Enfants*, isn't he suggesting that the integrative character of the manual used by schoolchildren in the Third Republic corresponds to that of today's television?[1]

My second point is that *Sesame Street* is an historically situated product. Today the context in which the relationships of education and television, education and audio-visual technology, must be handled has changed considerably. Sixties expansion justified a massive effort on the level of education. Today, in a period of recession, education appears to be a costly luxury. The industrial nations currently recognise that no model of growth within the framework of capitalism can allow for the indefinite growth of participation in created wealth and services. *Sesame Street*, produced at the end of the 1960s, was an expression of the policies of the welfare state: within the United States, the policy of aid for social minorities; beyond, the policy of aid for the Third World. Today the liberal democracies are restraining their social expenditure. A pedagogic series such as *Sesame Street* represents the first fruits of a utopia which believed that democracy

165

had a broader capacity for nurture.

The introduction of new technologies, implying the discovery of new forms of organisation, marks a further change in relation to the late 1960s. Handling the relationship of education and technology at the level of a centralised apparatus such as television is not the same thing as dealing with the level of the micro. Today the problem of innovation lies at the heart of this tension between the need for the micro, for the small, and the massifying, universalising necessity of the multi-national, the trans-national.

The question one may ask oneself is then: what is today at stake in returning to a programme like *Sesame Street*? *Sesame Street*, as I've already stated, is the first educational undertaking to administer for an industrial market the threefold relationship of education, audio-visual technology, and mass culture. As such, *Sesame Street* remains an important symbolic matrix.

If it strikes me as important to return to this example, it is in order to make critical sense of the pedagogic choices around which the model is articulated, because these choices refer us to the contemporary prospect where such programmes are concerned, a prospect which is highly analogous in its determinations. And what interests me in particular is whether the pedagogic choices which defined this series cannot be found today in the particular conceptions of the learning process brought into play by the pedagogy of electronic leisure and its 'small machines'. From the outset, I will be defining *Sesame Street* as a system, and systems theory will be a central reference. In deciphering the mechanisms of techno-modernist thinking, we will also be engaging in the study of power.

This series in fact marks a decisive moment when a new rationality is introduced into the sphere of education, a new state of mind, served by a battery of management techniques characteristic of the current phase of capitalism and converging on what is captured by the term 'systemism', or the expression 'systems theory'. With *Sesame Street* educational television makes a brilliant entry into the new logic of the 'system'.

We might say that, if education and culture are traditionally, and quite correctly, established as fields of social reproduction, *Sesame Street* seems on the other hand the off-shoot of a tremendous effort on the part of society to 'produce' itself and not merely to 'reproduce' itself. It in fact bears witness to this society's typical conjunctions of theory and practice as characterised by the arrival of the 'system' as a way of managing theoretical production and the material process of production according to the logic of the articulation knowledge/power.

The wealth of scientific knowledge built up by the Ford and Carnegie educational foundations, government agencies and the centres of university research into the education potential of audio-

166

visual technology, the importance of early stimulation for the child's abilities, and knowledge of the learning process become the *inputs* for achieving a particular *output*. That is, at stake is the elaboration of an avant-garde pedagogic model that could be used *in domo* in order to overcome the handicap borne by young children from minority groups in relation to the schooling system.

Sesame Street seizes upon audio-visual technology whilst analysing the nature of the television medium. Not content to regard it as a simple channel of diffusion for educational contents, it prefers to reflect on its mode of operation as determined by the institutionalisation of leisure and mass culture. The creation of this prototype remains one of the only sites, and only moments, when the institutional quality of mass culture has been thought through in an attempt to remedy what its creators regarded as the commercial mediocrity of this culture, the levelling down which it effects. It is interesting to note that the opportunity to reflect on the organisational principles of the media and of mass culture occurs when a vantage-point appears outside the media and mass culture, in this case education. Let me now enumerate certain characteristics of the *Sesame Street* model.

A Prototype and a Model: The Significance of the Options

Television and Organisation   Under the new logic to which I have just referred, television is implicitly engaged as an apparatus of control and organisation. A better understanding of the point of view adopted by the rationality which characterises the system of *Sesame Street* in relation to the way television operates can be found when one compares it with the conception of a functionalist Marxism for which television, as an Ideological State Apparatus, only has power, politically and socially, at the level of content and of discourse. What is primary, in the logic of *Sesame Street*, and also in critical theories of television as an instrument of power which continually attempt, without always succeeding, to avoid falling into technological determinism is the organisational character of television. Picking up, in this specific domain, what Michel Foucault says on a general level concerning the need to go beyond juridical theories of institutions in favour of theories of strategies and techniques of power, one French writer insists on the importance of the organisational-managerial dimension of television:

> Of course, television functions in the dimensions of the symbolic and the imaginary through an entire interplay which is favourable to normative injunctions, to the processes of identification, for narcissistic, or more exactly, socio-narcissistic conflicts. But isn't this effective only at the heart of its reality as a mega-machine [*au*

167

sein de sa réalité mégamachinique] and of its more fundamental managerial-organisational functioning?[2]

Organisational surplus value precedes ideological surplus-value. Transposing the situation described by Orwell in *1984* (where a television screen is installed in every home for surveillance purposes), this same author attempts a description of the mode of control allowed by the television mega-machine, control through fascination with what happens on the screen, a sort of 'electronic *agora*', control through simultaneous, instantaneous and globalised centralisation:

> It is not Big Brother who watches us, it is we who watch Big Brother and yet it is he who, by that very fact, organises and controls us.[3]

McLuhan's famous formula, 'the medium is the message', needs analysing at several levels, an essential one being that the medium is an organiser of mass (social) space-time through its technological dimension, which allows instantaneity, globality and simultaneity. The message is the instantaneity-simultaneity-globality of the organising and integrating medium.

The panopticon is a model of communication often referred to, in this perspective, to describe the mass of control exerted by television. The image is borrowed from Michel Foucault[4], who himself borrowed from the economist Jeremy Bentham's description of a machine for surveillance whereby, from a central tower, one can check with perfect visibility the entire circle of the building, divided into cells and where those being spied upon, lodged in their individual cells and cut off from one another, are seen without seeing. Adapted to the characteristics of television – which reverses the direction of vision, permitting those who are being spied upon to see without being seen, and which functions no longer by disciplinary control but by fascination and seduction – the panopticon becomes the inverted tele-panopticon.

It should be said straight away that such an assimilation of television to the 'panopticon' model of surveillance and control entails the risk that critical analysis will renew, this time from an 'organisational' variable and no longer from an 'ideological' one, a dualistic theory of power which has so strongly marked the Althusserian approach to communication apparatus. Once again there is very little opportunity for response on the part of the receivers, who are conceived of as inert before the gaze of power. Once again, one risks perceiving the space of television as monolithically taken up by a hegemonic power and not as a space where, at the very least in the liberal democracies, social relations express themselves, alliances are negotiated, and the movements of civil society filter back and forth. Once again it amounts to a refusal to see the individual and the social in their contradictory capacity as sites of resistance, of negations of power.

A 'machine for' something does not necessarily guarantee the effect for which it has been programmed. From the internal logic of the model one cannot deduce the one-dimensionality of its effects. Indeed, it is the reduction of reality to the logic of a model that characterises systems theory.

The *Sesame Street* model brings into play another conception of creation, confronting it with social projects demanding that leisure become a productive space, a space for instruction. In this perspective creation can no longer depend upon the isolated creator, the unique consciousness. *Sesame Street* presented itself as an explicitly organised, planned intervention, responding to social needs as identified by groups who, to a greater or lesser extent, through the domains of politics, the economy, science, determine the way a society develops, choose its forms of growth, channel its processes of education. This presumes that creation will need to rest on a preliminary programme of research which on the one hand uncovers, gathers together and objectifies these needs, and on the other defines its particular goals, its specific objectives, the technical and methodological instruments by which they are to be attained. A whole scientific and technical apparatus of management was brought to bear to achieve a specific objective by reducing as far as possible the margin of risk, that uncertain factor which continues to define the market in cultural commodities more than any other.

The project was to benefit from the time allowed (eighteen months of preparation prior to the launch), from all kinds of support – technical, financial, scientific – and from marketing and public relations. What is striking at first sight is the drive for coherence, the concern for quality – a quality sanctioned by the high degree of professionalism of all those invited to collaborate – the care taken over the planning of the work, over the clarification of methodology. Nothing was left to chance. In this regard, and by comparison with the customary examples of work produced for children,[5] it was a revolution in communication. The series is poles apart from that 'inspired' improvisation, that form of creativity associated with the solitary individual genius of an author, of a scriptwriter, of a director, of an entertainer. The work of an interdisciplinary team to co-ordinate areas of knowledge and to map the educational initiative with all the instruments of science and the techniques for management and organisation is evidence of this high degree of organisation. Close collaboration was to come from creative people from the world of television and people from the world of scientific research (notably psychologists, sociologists, specialists in testing and in techniques of measurement and evaluation).

169

In the course of summer 1968 five seminars were held to assist with the development of the curriculum of the Children's Television Workshop and to draw up the programming of the series, define its goals, and specify the forms of collaboration between television people and specialists in the social sciences. The first step had been a preparatory report, commissioned by the Carnegie Foundation, and undertaken by Joan Cooney, the future director of the Workshop and of the series. From across the United States it drew upon the advice of specialists in child psychology and of communicators experienced in educational television.

In order to ensure the permanent scientific supervision of the series, two research groups were created, responsible for two types of research – *formative* and *summative*. The first, the *formative* research group, was intended to calibrate the programming of episodes of the series by supervising the work of evaluating these episodes, and of the schema for the evolution of learning upon which they were based, with a view to their possible redefinition in the light of the reactions of the young audiences tested. The second, *summative* form of research, aimed to evaluate effects, to measure – representative samples having been established – the knowledge gained by children who had experienced the series. The work of evaluating effects was assigned to ETS (Educational Testing Service), who delivered copious findings on the first two years of the project.[6] We should mention that in the countries to which the series has been exported (notably Mexico, where the Latin American version was prepared with the assistance and supervision of local psychologists and educationalists), the same task of evaluation was to be carried out.[7]

It is this regime of planning, of scientific professionalism, with which this rigorously codified project forearmed itself against the intrusion of the arbitrary, that we must attempt to analyse. We must decipher the meaning of this model, that is to say, we must attempt to uncover the aims and goals of the educational process to which it refers. We will choose to carry out this reading by 'making speak' the choices which were made at that time. Indeed, a model is uncovered not only through what it institutes, what it includes, what it recommends, but also through what it excludes. It announces its meaning through what it chooses not to be. The choices made amongst the various options entertained before this final definition of the series are rich in lessons on this subject.[8]

Choosing the site   Accepting the importance of the years between three and five in the child's development, and taking the decision to approach this hitherto neglected audience with an educational programme, the team faced the problem of a pedagogic site. In the preparatory report submitted to the Carnegie Foundation by Joan

Cooney – then a producer of documentaries for New York's public television station Channel 13, greatly exercised by the problems of children from the 'disadvantaged communities' – the criterion of cost prevailed over any consideration of a pedagogic kind. This report stated that an educational television series would cost $5–10 million to reach the *whole* of the country's three to five age range, whereas it would cost $2.75 billion to organise the access to school of *half* this audience. In view of the patent lack of kindergartens and other pre-school institutions (creches, nureries), the future director of *Sesame Street* emphasised the promised expansion of the television market: there might be a reduction in the number of classrooms, but there would be no reduction in the number of television sets.[9] This constraint had weighty implications for the pedagogic project, for it enclosed it within the rationality of profit which imposes its dynamic upon the market for industrial goods. In relation to the young child, destined to be one of the spectators most subject to these, the dynamic of their expansion is not a matter of much debate. (Let us note that it cannot be, since one of the preconditions upon which educational TV is based as a system is the demand to render profitable, for educational ends, the expansion of audio-visual technology.) There was no significant appreciation of the way the educational experience differs according to whether it unfolds in the context of a creche, allowing for the building of a pedagogic relationship as much upon the rapport amongst the children themselves as with the adult responsible for looking after them, or whether the experience is delivered to the child by television. The essential difference introduced by the screen and the machine as forms of mediation went unexamined.

The criterion of cost was to exercise a perpetual sovereignty. The success of *Sesame Street* as an educational enterprise was never clearer than when its promoters were able to announce that, given the number of TV-viewers assembled by the programme throughout the country, each programme only cost one cent per head.

Cognitive Development   Initially, the educational aims of the series covered three areas:
1. The child's cognitive development (learning the alphabet, numbers, certain academic competences);
2. His/her moral and social development;
3. His/her affective and emotional development.
Only the first area outlined above was actually taken into consideration. In his preliminary plan, Gerald Lesser, professor at the Harvard Graduate School of Education, educational director of *Sesame Street* (and organiser and director of the summer 1968 seminars), had proposed that the three areas should be equivalent; his initial project regarded as of equal importance the child's cognitive

171

development and his/her social and emotional development, which brought him close to certain so-called 'traditionalist' educationalists and psychologists. Over and against those who supported the development of the 'total' or 'integral' child – a school of thought centrally represented by Martin Deutsch, founder of the University of New York Institute for Developmental Studies – and made up of those who were concerned with the identification of the social and psychological factors which retarded and inhibited not only the mental faculties but also the emotional, affective and physical development of children from the 'underprivileged' milieux – preference was given to the cognitive school of thought. This school saw mental development as a priority, in particular the line of thinking represented by Carl Bereiter of the University of Illinois, who focused his experiments on the processes of language acquisition, performances at the level of language, as performances necessary for success. The Carnegie Foundation, as we have seen, had taken a close interest in the psychologists, educationalists and child-specialists of the cognitive school who had been dubbed 'modern' by comparison with the 'traditionalists'. To attain their goals, they suggested – amongst other pedagogic strategies – the technique of 'verbal bombardment', on which they had experimented with children from underprivileged milieux. In their book *Teaching Disadvantaged Children*, Carl Bereiter and Siegfried Engelman draw up a list of the basic skills of which a child should be capable before entering the first year of school.[10] These items became a programming guide for *Sesame Street*. It is worth emphasising that it is this codified scientific framework, already organised in the form of a sequential programme, which revealed itself to be the most useful, tailor-made for the serialised format of *Sesame Street*.

'Hard' knowledge (represented by the mental operations involved in the useful and concrete acquisition of letters and numbers) won out, equally, against the 'soft'. The 'soft', which occupied a privileged place in the early discussions around the series, represented those basic forms of knowledge which would have allowed the child to 'grow culturally; in his appreciation of arts and crafts, his familiarity with basic music concepts, his general knowledge about the world'.[11] Henceforth it was merely regarded as a reinforcement for the acquisition of letters and numbers.

Evaluation as Law   One of the essential factors in this displacement of the affective and the emotional by the cognitive, of 'soft' by 'hard', was the pressure exerted by the institutions responsible for evaluation. The tests and the methods of analysis involved in the processes of evaluation were shown to be unsuitable for measuring the effects of the programme in this domain of the *affective*, the domain of

172

what was known as 'soft'. The stress placed on the 'hard', that is, the goals of cognitive development, responded to the evaluative method's greater facility for registering the quantifiable and, notably, for drawing up scales of acquisition in the learning of letters and of numbers. Lloyd Morrissett, one of the then principal directors of the Carnegie Foundation, and generally considered to be the father of *Sesame Street*, made no bones about it:

> The affective goals were not those the project was formed around, although obviously you could get quite a few in, and it made great sense to combine a number of them with the cognitive goals. When it came to thinking about evaluation, we hypothesised that it would be very difficult to find any effects at all. Because we didn't know how much time the child would spend in front of the television set, and we knew that the sensitivity of the tests that had been developed was not great. And the reliability at those ages was not particularly good.
>
> For all those reasons, we were concerned about having any effects to show. We decided that the evaluation should concentrate heavily on those areas where we were most likely to be able to measure effects. The affective job is even tougher. That is why that was omitted as a set of goals.[12]

It is here that we uncover the relation of dependence which the various parts of a system maintain amongst themselves, moving, link by link, towards the consolidation of the whole. Furthermore, the anxiety to demonstrate results, and the importance given to the evaluation of effects, stemmed from the fact that the publication of results and the evaluation of effects contributed directly to the continuation of the programme. They made up a feedback which was directly reinvested in programme-value to the extent that, by demonstrating its efficiency where cognitive gains were concerned, they renewed its popularity. The tests formed part of the system of marketing the series.

The results of the studies and evaluations carried out by the ETS were widely circulated in the popular press. When a counter-appraisal was performed, one was perhaps in a position to gain a better understanding of the extent to which these results had served the promotion of the series. In 1975, the Russell Sage Foundation, in the course of a huge study aiming to analyse methods of evaluation and of survey, carried out a verification of the results produced by ETS. This study, published as *'Sesame Street' Revisited*,[13] showed that ETS had performed its evaluations with children who did not represent the typical profile of the *Sesame Street* viewer. The children tested had been encouraged to watch the series in a very particular way and had benefited from pedagogic support of all kinds (pedagogic materials such as books, etc.; the concern of parents who knew that their children were the subjects of an experiment, etc.). The gains which testified to the effectiveness of the series seemed to owe more to these forms of encouragement than to the series itself. This rigorous re-evaluation of the early conclusions of ETS showed amongst other things that the divide between advantaged and disadvantaged children, which the programme was believed to have bridged, had probably grown deeper. The counter-appraisal peformed by the Russell Sage Foundation was passed over in complete silence by the press.

The original project of *Sesame Street* did not foresee that the series would undergo the audience research represented by the ratings, and even expressly forbade such an eventuality. But more than a decision taken from a position of principle, more than an axiological choice when faced with this procedure on the part of commercial television, it seems very much as though it was a reaction of prudence. In fact, the programme was going to be launched on the public television network which drew a fairly small audience – incomparably smaller than that for the commercial channels – and an audience drawn from the more elevated socio-economic milieux (*Sesame Street* had a complete plan of action for reversing this situation and attracting to the broadcasts children from the most popular social milieux). At the preparatory stage, the originators of the series stated that more important than the number of children reached would be the effectiveness of the programme's stimulation of the children who were watching. The rating was repressed as a means of survey in favour of the scientific procedures of the summative phase of research. But once it became clear that millions and millions of children from all socio-economic classes were watching the programmes, the attempts at evaluation undertaken by an institution such as ETS were displaced in favour of audience surveys.

We know that the institution of the rating is eminently congruent with the mercantile dynamic of mass communications. The rating serves to reinforce the legitimacy of a system of production and distribution of cultural goods founded on the rigorous dissociation of production and consumption. A critical reflection on communication finds it difficult to do without a procedure based on this traditional means of understanding the audience as represented by audience surveys. Intended above all to adjust the mercantile rationality of the distribution of cultural consumer goods, they are also intended – although it would require considerable skill to discern which of the two demands is more important – to assert the democratic value of contact with the audience. Meanwhile, thanks to this mechanical reduction of audiences united by their membership of the category of consumers, it is the 'universal' value of the programme which is

174

justified, supposedly responding to the desires and needs of popular demand. The rating annuls the dialectic of subject/programme as the principle of production, whereas the procedures of formative and even summative research problematise this dialectic on several accounts and in a more or less contradictory manner. Replacing a form of feedback reinvested in the programme, intended to modify its approach in response to the reactions of a clearly defined and targeted audience, we find a form of feedback directly reinvested in the principle of the anonymous circularity of commodities.[14]

The Authority of the Programme   The same avoidance of the subject, parallel to the enshrinement of the programme as a closed product, is to be found in the meagre attention given to the playful bodily expressions of the child spectator. It was observed, in fact, that some children clapped hands, laughed, danced, or talked back to the screen. But no study was undertaken by the Workshop's research department to determine which aspects of the child's make-up, or of the television programme, were the stimulus for this activity. The reason for this is that the active/passive problem – a dilemma which appears daily more crucial for pedagogic practice in that it conditions not only the quality, but the very nature of the learning process – was not of interest to the Workshop.

It would not, however, have been without interest, in the latter's essentially cognitive perspective, to try to establish whether the child learned more or less according to whether he/she was active or passive. Could it not have been that the evaluation procedure in itself once again exercised its own pressures? Taking on board the active/passive dilemma clearly entailed additional constraints – as much for the procedures of formative research as for the summative procedures of the evaluation. The fact remains that the Workshop's project embraced no consideration of the advantages of the active attitude. They learned, that was enough. Thus, in practice, the recommendations were abandoned around which Joan Cooney had gained unanimous support amongst the psychologists she had met before drawing up her preparatory report: the stimulation of children's activity, their active participation, their interaction with the programme. There was no attempt to favour the production of episodes favouring this interaction. The knowledge that, actively or passively, they were learning, was regarded as sufficient.

Also abandoned was the idea of inventing strategies to encourage the child's activity at home, based on the programme. It had been thought possible to distribute to the young viewers study-aids, such as 3-D manipulative kits, so that they could become actively involved in some of the activities shown on the screen. The idea never became a reality. This was either because of the broadcasters' tendency to concentrate on more familiar methods, perhaps upon Joan Cooney's increasing opinion that the series had to stand by itself, that it could not and should not depend on the introduction of materials to be handled by viewers.[15] This reaction is a mixture of things: one is doubtless the vindication of the closure of the product, of its absolute autonomy, in order to allow it the more strongly to claim a unique authority. Pushed to its absolute limits, this logic makes the passive attitude towards reception, eyes glued to the screen, the ideal attitude. Any break in this passivity calls into question the authority of the programme. With it goes an implied recognition of the subject's freedom to attend to other things, to learn elsewhere, to find interests elsewhere. It represents an attitude of liberty which is to a certain extent felt to be a failure on the part of the programme. To accept stimuli from outside the programme is to accept – even if these stimuli are organised into a strategy of reinforcement for the programme – that the programme cannot do everything. (It is interesting to compare this attitude with that of Monica Sims, the head of children's programmes at the BBC at the beginning of the 1970s, who declared: 'We're not trying to tie children to the television screen. If they go away and play halfway through our programme, that's fine.'[16])

The demand that television series should stand by themselves also suggests a corporatist vindication by television people keen to point out the supremacy of their techniques, of their equipment, of their field of expression and of action. Any form of dependence on the outside world, any sharing of effects with elements external to the television programme, are felt, in this narrow perspective – committed to the illustration and defence of the technicist specialisation – as a chink in the armour, hinting at yet other ways of delegitimising this private territory, with its specific forms of knowledge and of power.

In fact, what is dramatically at stake in such reactions is the difficulty of living out on a daily basis the interdisciplinarity which is the lot of knowledge and of power. The originality of *Sesame Street*, as has been mentioned, lies in the encounter between those who produced the 'concepts' and the 'creators'. Is perhaps the crisis into which this formula for openness was plunged most clearly explained by the fact that it was set up the better to confirm (to exercise, establish, evaluate) a power over the child?

The exclusive character assumed by the television programme as a form of education also finds expression in the way in which the role of parents, and in general, of the circumambient community is defined. This role is not seen as useful except to the extent that it creates a context of reinforcement for the programme. It is clearly subordinated to a behavioural prescription and defined within the limits of its mechanical rationality: it works, it works less well, it works better.

176

Here, 'it works better' when the parents watch with the child, when the child is accompanied by 'sympathetic' parents who watch with him/her. A presence without content, without meaning of its own, without the power of interaction unless it be that of allowing the programme-machine to function better. It is a form of presence at the service of the programme's presence, subject to the sparkling luminosity of the television screen. A silent reinforcement, but important in creating a climate of confidence, in securing the convergence of those twin sources of authority, parents and programme – a convergence which provides a sense of security. Calmed are the tensions, the conflicts which are always liable to spring up when the child watches a programme which is not shared by others. The child, for its part, feels comforted by the support for the programme shown by the familial and communal context.

The programme claims an ecumenical ethos the better to achieve its effects, but depends more fundamentally on its technical and scientific authority: instructive and entertaining, it is the best television programme parents could dream of for their children. But perhaps the programme claims itself as the authority at the expense of disqualifying the abilities of the mother, father, older children or adults watching with the young learner? The power relations set up between the specialist knowledge invested in the programme and the knowledge of the ethnic minority children to whom it makes its chosen address stand every chance of being profoundly unequal and of provoking, at the very least, an erosion of the legitimacy of these particular sets of knowledge. It is a question to which we shall have occasion to return. Let it suffice to say here that the educational relationship between mother and child is displaced by the intervention of an authority accredited by the myth of objectivity, of scientific modernity, of technology. The maternal support is no longer required and valorised except in relation to a programme which acquires merit through the authority of the specialist.

If one also takes into account all the accompanying handbooks, texts, records, guides, magazines and printed matter which have blossomed round the programme, one can better gauge the de-legitimation of maternal knowledge which is at stake. The mother only appears as the relay for the specialist – objectively disarmed, dispossessed, of notions held 'in common' (that is to say, in the sense meant by Gramsci, belonging to the 'common sense' of one's group or one's class) about how to be with the child, to amuse it, to teach it to read and count. All these forms of knowledge, all these notions held in common which refer to the 'common sense' of one's group or class, are transposed into a seductively euphoric register whose practical mastery the programme alone is able to possess.

The Seductive Capital of Commercial Television The major
discovery of *Sesame Street*, we know, was to link educational content
with the appeal of the techniques of the TV commercial, notably the
techniques of advertising. Getting the child interested, capturing his
or her attention, teaching via entertainment, were the central
preoccupations of the series' promoters, any lack of attention
rendering the message inoperative.

This central concern for attracting and amusing the child was
clearly expressed by Lloyd Morrissett to one of the directors of the
Ford Foundation before calling together the interdisciplinary teams
for the preparatory seminars of 1968: 'In fact, I think the programme
is much more likely to fail because of lack of entertainment value than
because of absence of coherent educational content.'[17]

In fact, differently than other examples of educational broadcasting – obligatory viewing forming part of a compulsory school
curriculum – the new educational series could only rely, to draw its
audience (one moreover initially defined as a pre-school audience) on
the mechanism of pleasure, on the audience's desire to watch and to
go on watching. The first decision fundamentally coherent with this
strategy of organising attention through desire, no longer through
constraint, was the decision to use television no longer as a tool
inscribed within the schooling system, but within the space of the
private, the space of leisure, where the functioning of the television
medium is ruled by the key role it occupies in the organisation of free
time. Apparently devoid of the subjecting, disciplining aspects of
educational television, television in the household works by seduction
and motivation. *Sesame Street*, both as an alternative to school and to
conventional forms of education through television, represents the
culmination of reflections on the particular legality of mass culture
and an attempt to invest these reflections in the pedagogic field.

The desire to interest the child, to captivate its attention, was part
and parcel of a current of thought in vogue in contemporary public
opinion and held in esteem by politicians, a line of thinking that
sought alternative solutions in place of the traditional methods of the
school, seen as a place of boredom. The failure of schooling was in large
part attributed to this boredom, which was directly associated with
the inefficiency of the school as institution. In an article written in
1965 B.F. Skinner enumerated, without necessarily substantiating
them, different responses that one could give to the necessity of
gaining the child's attention, in a perspective influenced more or less
by the findings of behaviourism:

> How can we make him [the student] concentrate? The TV screen is
> praised for its isolation and hypnotic effect. A piece of equipment
> has been proposed that achieves concentration in the following

desperate way: the student faces a brightly lighted text, framed by walls which operate on the principle of the blinkers once worn by carriage horses. His ears are between earphones. . . .

A less coercive practice is to make what is seen or heard attractive and attention-compelling. The advertiser faces the same problem as the teacher, and his techniques have been widely copied in the design of textbooks, films, and classroom practices. Bright colors, variety, sudden change, big type, animated sequences – all these have at least a temporary effect in inducing the student to look and listen.[18]

The core of the *Sesame Street* method is alluded to here: the TV screen to which is attributed (by a specialist in teaching machines) an hypnotic effect, diversity, rapid changes, animated sequences. The similarity to the advertising style that characterises *Sesame Street* is also evoked.

Joan Cooney, in the course of her tour of small local educational television stations before drawing up her preparatory report, had noted and deplored the 'impecunious' state of these stations, the 'slow and monotonous pace and lack of professionalism' in the case of programmes being produced.[19] Taking a diametrically opposed position, *Sesame Street* decided to compete with the rhythms of the commercial television which had shaped the habits of children and were conditioning their expectations in relation to the television medium. 'Children are conditioned to expect of television the rapid action of film violence – bang! bang! bang! – and material with a strong visual impact, produced at considerable expense and with plenty of talent.'[20] Taking into account the child's conditioning by commercial television, and the colonisation by the latter of his/her ways of seeing, taste, expectations, the *Sesame Street* project was to capitalise upon this conditioning for educational ends. The series would explicitly seek to be the opposite of the 'poor' programmes of educational TV. Claiming a nationwide outreach, it would demand from the outset such a level of finance that all the appropriate production techniques could be used, that the best technicians could be employed. Production costs throughout the *Sesame Street* schedule were to absorb two-thirds of the budget – the costs of research, promotion, management and marketing never more than the remaining third.

The didactic method used for the learning of letters and numbers was to be directly borrowed from the techniques of commercial advertising. Its lynch-pin was the 'technical effect', or 'technical event'. The technical event lies at the heart of the discourse of advertising. In advertising it is a matter of holding the attention by creating around a minimal piece of information the maximum

179

number of 'technical events' per minute. The rate of appearance of technical events (that is, those created from visual and sound-effects, from any alteration in a natural rhythm leading to a break in the continuity of a piece of information) is strictly codified. In the United States, the rate is 20–30 technical events per minute for television advertising, 8–10 per minute in a commercial television programme, falling to 2–3 per minute in the ordinary programmes on public television.[21]

Sesame Street was to represent for the first time on public television a programme whose high density of 'technical events' would place it on an equal footing with programmes from the commercial networks. Here one can again note that the choice of public television does not exactly correspond to an axiological choice and that one can again doubt the wish to create, from within public television, a true alternative to commercial production. In their desire to make another kind of television, the creators of *Sesame Street* had recourse to the parameters of commercial television in order to create the alternative. They deployed the principle seductive feature of this commercial form of television as it is defined and constantly updated, amassed, sustained, by the sector which makes up the matrix of industrialised culture, its privileged space for creation and innovation, its mainspring, master in the art of giving pleasure, the art of selling: advertising.[22]

One cannot help but point to the contradiction between a desire to create an alternative to a commercial television saturated with programmes of violence (a phenomenon excessively documented by communications experts in the United States) and recourse to the tyrannical procedures of the 'technical event'.[23] It is as if the violence at issue in the relation between child and TV resided only at the level of explicit moral content and not in the very structure of television's functioning. Alongside that, one has evidence of the claims made by the initiators and creators of *Sesame Street* for a television which would not focus on sensationalism, which would make room for the ordinary 'life-sized' events of 'the natural environment' of 'the world as it is'.[24] Over and above the ambiguities, not to say the incoherences of discourse, over and above too the impulse to make justifications in answer to reproaches (for *Sesame Street* was reproached for looking to be effective through the use of rapid visual bombardment, just as it was reproached for operating on the basis of the schema signal/response), one may ask whether one is not here in the presence of that characteristic optimism of liberal capitalism – which dreams sincerely of being able to use 'to good ends' technologies and techniques, no matter how constraining. Is there not a considerable proximity between the approach adopted by the originators of *Sesame Street* towards communication technologies and theories of

180

behaviour, and that which, during the 1930s, characterised progressive thinkers such as Tchakhotine and which still characterises today, on the left, East and West, a good number of orthodox milieux in both research and in politics?

Both groups have an instrumental conception of technology and of science, the end justifying the means. Both talk as though these were neutral spaces, unmarked by the power relations between groups and classes, as if their use was not pre-figured by the needs and interests of forces and which stamp a direction upon society. The producers of *Sesame Street* do not seem to have measured the contradiction that exists between the 'educational' style and advertising techniques which bring to a climax of alienation the unequal relation of exchange which is the basis for a material and symbolic mode of production and distribution.

Opposing the importation of the series into Great Britain, the director of children's programmes for the BBC argued: 'Do we really have to import commercial hard-selling techniques into our own programmes because *Sesame Street* researchers tell us that in America children will not watch anything quiet or thoughtful?'[25]

It is not only the recourse to the 'technical event' which characterises *Sesame Street*, but the propensity to reinject into the pedagogic field all the stimuli of the consumer universe, all the injunctions so normative for the imaginary and sensorial dimensions of the child. Operating certainly by the seduction of rhythm, and of diversity, *Sesame Street* operates above all by stimulating the immense arsenal of signs from the universe of mercantile culture, stimulating the integration of the child with this world. In fact, what triumphs here is a modality of time fixed by industrial culture: a modality ordered on artifice, a time-dimension which no longer has anything to do with the temporality of daily life, but is instead the time of the extraordinary feat, of the exceptional, the spectacular. (It is this structural weight of the spectacular which the creators of *Sesame Street* do not wish, or are unable, to critically address.) It is a modality which, allied to technological progress, rules out other times, other rhythms. What is eclipsed is, on the one hand, the temporality of daily life, of the real – lived duration – and on the other the rhythms specific to other cultures. This trait becomes particularly important in the context of a series intended to speak to ethnic minorities, children belonging to other cultures of origin than that of this highly industrialised nation. Fighting against segregation, it agglomerates them around the timescale of technological progress, which is ineluctably assimilated to the irreversible progress of modernity. It assimilates, homogenises and agglutinates them through the instantaneity and immediacy which typify its techniques for learning and the culture of anticipation to which it refers.

181

One may legitimately ask whether the true educational message of *Sesame Street* doesn't reside in this initiation into the consumer universe with its modalities of mass space and time.

Conclusion

I would like to return in this conclusion to two or three question around which are articulated the choices made by an educational series like *Sesame Street*.

Firstly, the question of *standards*. In the conception of the education system as a system of production this question assumes capital importance. What American techno-modernity invented were the standards of knowledge, educational objectives of reference. (I may add that it also had the power to invent these standards in the domain of mass culture.)[26] As soon as one has standards, the teacher knows what he or she must do, the pupil knows what he or she must attain, the programmer knows what he or she may programme. As I have shown, the *Sesame Street* curriculum was borrowed from two cognitive psychologists who had drawn up a list of the minimum number of operations which a child should be capable of performing before entering the first year of school. It is this scientific framework, already codified, already drawn up in the form of a sequenced programme, that proved to be the most useful, tailor-made to fit into the *serialised dimension* of *Sesame Street*.

Secondly, and in the same order of ideas, what were privileged were mental operations, the cognitive, and useful learning over and above the criteria of emotional development and openness to the domain of art and creativity as defined by psychologists concerned with children's integral development. This displacement of the affective and the emotional in favour of the cognitive is in large part due, as we have seen, to the pressures exerted by the institutions in charge of evaluation. Analytic methods proved inappropriate for the *measurement* of the effects of the programme in the domain of the affective and those features covered by the term *soft*: an openness to art, to music, etc. The stress placed on the goals of cognitive development responded to the evaluation methods' greatest ability, its capacity to register the *quantifiable*, the measurable.

And it is on this point that I would like to close. For today these contradictory tendencies between which *Sesame Street* made its choice are to be found in the major currents of thought which divide the social sciences and very particularly the communication sciences. In the first school of thought the organisational element prevails, dominated by the cybernetic model, whereby the social is controllable, reducible to the quantifiable, the measurable, the commensurable, the 'hard'. In this scheme learning processes make direct reference to behavioural science, to experimental psychology, which benefit today from advances in the life sciences; certain representatives of this tendency, and not the least significant, harbour the greatest mistrust for psychoanalysis, and by the same token, for the imaginary, the unconscious, subjectivity, the symbolic. Another tendency can be detected in which there meet the findings of the new linguistics of communication, psychoanalysis and anthropology – a tendency which, by contrast with the narrow rationality of a mathematical mirage, allows for the fact that the imaginary, the subjective, and the symbolic are the components of the historic real.

It is not possible to reduce this to an opposition between black and white, between good and bad. The numerous cross-over points between one group's utopia of social control and the other's utopian return to subjectivity prevent us from so doing. It is nonetheless true that these oppositions, which are not only of a scientific order, stake themselves on the restoration of the individual as historical subject in our societies where atomisation is very much the order of the day.

Translated by Phillip Drummond and David Buxton

References
1. In this title for his television programme, Jean-Luc Godard makes direct reference, by way of a little parody, to the title of the school textbook *Le Tour de France par deux enfants (Two Children Go on a Trip Round France)*. The title, for its part, refers to the customary trip round France taken by the 'companions', young workers who have reached the end of their period of apprenticeship. The textbook presented knowledge of the homeland, of the country, and of national values, as the foundation of all true civic training.
2. E. Allemand, *Pouvoir et Télévision* (Paris: Anthropos 1980) p. 31.
3. Ibid. p. 44.
4. M. Foucault, *Discipline and Punish: the Birth of the Prison* (London: Allen Lane, 1977) Part 3, 'Discipline', chapter 3, 'Panopticism', pp. 195–228.
5. Walt Disney is, of course, renowned as 'the master of fantasy'. But this expression conceals the fact that this form of artistic production relates to the particular expectations of an audience (their cultural and moral make-up), to the economic constraints of this market, and to the aesthetic constraints of this specific domain. But there is no point of comparison between the framework which governs the Disney style of production and that which a series like *Sesame Streeet* imposes upon itself.
6. S. Ball, G.A. Bogatz, *The First Years of 'Sesame Street': An Evaluation* and *The Second Year of 'Sesame Street': A Continuing Evaluation* (Princeton, New Jersey: Educational Testing Service 1970 and 1971).
7. See R. Diaz-Guerrero et al, *Investiquacion Formativa de 'Plaza Sesamo'* (Mexico: Editorial Trillas 1975).
8. The work of the educationalist Richard Polsky, who had access to all the internal documents tracing the origins of the Children's Television Workshop, is particularly useful here. See R.M. Polsky, *Getting to 'Sesame Street': The Origins of the Children's Television Workshop* (New York: Praeger 1974).
9. Carnegie Corporation of New York, 'Television for Preschool Children: a Proposal' (1968), quoted in Polsky, op. cit., p. 41.

10. C. Bereiter, S. Engelmann, *Teaching Disadvantaged Children in the Preschool* (Engelwood Cliff, N.J.: Prentice-Hall 1966). See also G.S. Lesser, *Children and Television: Lessons from 'Sesame Street'* (Toronto: Random House 1974) and Polsky, op. cit.
11. Carnegie Corporation of New York, op. cit., quoted in Polsky, op. cit., pp. 42–3.
12. Lloyd Morrissett, interviewed by Richard Polsky (1972), in Polsky, op. cit., pp. 18–19.
13. T.D. Cook et al, *'Sesame Street' Revisited* (New York: Russell Sage Foundation 1975).
14. This shift towards the adoption of the ratings was to signify the gradual (and eventually total) loss of the recognition of a particular identity for the audience to whom *Sesame Street* was originally addressed and for whom the series was conceived: the audience of three to five-year-olds drawn from US ethnic minorities. What is revealed here is a law which governs the circulation of the products of mass culture – they tend to lose the mark of the origins at the same rate as the marketplace increases their market-value.
15. Polsky, op. cit., p. 43.
16. M. Sims, quoted in M. Winn, *The Plug-In Drug: Television, Children, and the Family* (New York: Viking Press 1977) p. 55.
17. Lloyd Morrissett, letter to Edward Meade, Jr. (1968), in Polsky op. cit., p. 63.
18. B.F. Skinner, 'Why Teachers Fail', *The Saturday Review*, vol. 48, no. 42, 16 October 1965, pp. 99–100.
19. J. Cooney, 'The Potential Uses of Television in Preschool Education: A Report to the Carnegie Corporation of New York' (1966), quoted in Polsky, op. cit. p. 11.
20. Cooney, ibid.
21. J. Mander, *Four Arguments for the Elimination of Television* (Brighton: Harvester, 1980) p. 308.
22. Advertising is a major consumer of innovatory scientific ideas. It has benefited from behaviourism, as it has done from semiotics, in order to adjust its message to the motivation of the individual and to his or her routine ways of decoding discourse. Betty Friedan's book *The Feminine Mystique* and Vance Packard's *The Hidden Persuaders*, both written at the end of the 1950s, offer many insights on the first of these. The history of the impact of semiology on the refurbishing of advertising messages remains to be written.
23. A method designed to measure the lapses in attention of children watching television, the distractor method, was used by the producers of *Sesame Street* to test each part of the programme in order to ensure that it would hold the child's maximum attention. They thus noted that cartoons and fast-moving stories were the most effective for holding the attention of the young. See Winn, op. cit. p. 55.
24. Lesser, op. cit. pp. 250–1.
25. Monica Sims, letter to the *Guardian*, 22 December 1970, p. 6.
26. I look at this question in A. Mattelart, M. Mattelart, X. Delcourt, *International Image Markets: In Search of an Alternative Perspective* (London: Comedia 1984).

PART III

Television and its Audience

ELIHU KATZ AND TAMAR LIEBES

Mutual Aid in the Decoding of *Dallas*: Preliminary Notes from a Cross-Cultural Study

There seems to be growing support for that branch of communications research which asserts that television viewing is an active and social process. Viewing takes place at home and, on the whole, in the presence of family and friends. During and after a programme, people discuss what they have seen and come to collective understandings. It is via such understandings, we believe, that the messages of the media enter into culture. We are suggesting, in other words, that viewers see programmes, not wallpaper; that programmes do not impose themselves unequivocally on passive viewers; that the reading of a programme is a process of negotiation between the story on the screen and the culture of the viewers; and that it takes place in interaction among the viewers themselves.[1]

This perspective raises a question about the apparent ease with which American television programmes cross cultural and linguistic frontiers. Indeed, the phenomenon is so taken for granted that hardly any systematic research has been done to explain the reasons why these programmes are so successful. One wonders how such quintessentially American products are understood at all. The often-heard assertion that this phenomenon is part of a process of cultural imperialism presumes, first, that there is an American message in the content or the form; second, that this message is somehow perceived by viewers; and third, that it is perceived in the same way by viewers in different cultures.

Consider the worldwide success of a programme like *Dallas*. How do viewers from another culture understand it? A common-sense reply might be that such programmes are so superficial that they are immediately understood by all: they portray stereotyped characters, visualised conflict and much repetition. But this cannot be the whole of it. One cannot so simply explain the diffusion of a programme like *Dallas* by dismissing it as superficial or action-packed. In fact, at least as far as kinship structure is concerned, the story might be considered quite complex. Neither can it be understood without words; there is very little self-explanatory action. And there are American mores and cinematic conventions to grapple with.

187

Alternatively, perhaps the programme is only little understood. In many countries, American television programmes are aired as a by-product of the purchase of American television technology – equipment, spare parts and programmes all arrive in the same package – and viewers may be satisfied to watch the lavish productions without paying much attention to their meaning. But this is also unlikely. Even children, who do not understand the meanings intended by the producer, understand *something* and shape what they think they are seeing in the light of their experience with life and with the conventions of the medium.

We are suggesting, similarly, that people everywhere bring their experience to bear in the decoding process and seek the assistance and confirmation of others in doing so. Some of these experiences are universal: deep structures such as kinship relations or relations between id and superego. Other experiences are more culturally differentiated by society and community and constitute more selective frames for interpreting the programme and, possibly, for incorporating it into their lives. Incorporation, we think, is filtered by group dynamics – in conversations with significant others – and can be done in a variety of ways: by affirmation or negation of the moral of a story, for example, or through identification with a character, or by some more critical judgement.

Social Dynamics of Meaning-Making: An Empirical Approach
To observe these processes in action, we have undertaken a programme of empirical research. We assembled 50 groups of three couples each – an initial couple invites two others from among their friends – to view an episode from the second season of *Dallas*, and to discuss it with us afterwards. These focus groups were lower-middle class, with high-school education or less, and ethnically homogenous. There were ten groups each of Israeli Arabs, new immigrants to Israel from Russia, first- and second-generation immigrants from Morocco, and kibbutz members. Taking these groups as a microcosm of the worldwide audience of *Dallas*, we are comparing their 'readings' of the programme with ten groups of matched Americans in Los Angeles. The discussion following the programme takes approximately one hour and is guided by a rather open interview guide for focus groups. The discussion is recorded and it is followed by a brief individual questionnaire that asks participants to indicate whether and with whom they normally view and discuss the programme.

If we are correct in our assumption about the social process of reading *Dallas*, the method we have chosen enables us to simulate and 'sample' the high moments of this process. The post-discussion questionnaire, as well as a preliminary inspection of some of the protocols, provide evidence that the programme is viewed in the company of others and is widely discussed; there are repeated allusions in the focus groups to such discussions. Of course, we cannot prove that interpretation is altogether dependent on such interaction, or precisely how pervasive everyday television talk might be. Even if we have overstated the 'necessary' and pervasive aspects of such interaction, the method of focus-group discussion provides a very close look at the social dynamics of meaning-making. People seem to express themselves very freely.

Of course, it is true that the statement of any individual in a group may be influenced by the statements – even the presence – of the others, and may well be different from what it might have been in a personal interview. But that's the point: if our assumption about the normality of the social reading of television is correct, it is precisely these group-influenced thoughts and statements in which we are interested.

Two other caveats need to be mentioned. This particular study cannot provide a conclusive answer to the question of whether American programmes are read with greater ease than programmes from other countries. Nor can we generalise easily from *Dallas*, or its genre, to other American genres. So we cannot say with certainty that *Kojak* or *I Love Lucy* are processed in similar ways, cognitively or socially. These questions require complex and costly comparative research for which we are not yet prepared. What we are doing is complicated enough. We are attempting to sample the interaction of small groups of different languages and cultures during and after the viewing of a television programme that has been imported from outside their own culture and language, in an effort to identify the ways in which meaning and possible relevance are ascribed to the programme.

A different way of stating our problem is to say that we are interested in the critical apparatus marshalled by lower-middle-class groups of varying ethnicity while sitting in front of the television screen. Again, we find ourselves in the midst of an almost unspoken debate over the activity level of television viewers and their conceptual powers. Most scholars and critics don't seem to give the common viewer much credit; yet, occasional research and some theories suggest that there is a native critical ability possessed even by the most unschooled viewer. One recent empirical study dares to suggest that lower-class viewers may be *more* articulate than well-educated ones in analysing popular television programmes.[2]

If we restate our basic concern in these terms, we are asking, in effect, how the viewer analyses content or performs his own structural analysis of a programme like *Dallas*. The group discussions, then, may be analysed as ethno-semiological data, in which the readings of the viewers may be compared to those of critics and scholars who have analysed the programme. Since the effects attributed to a TV programme are often inferred from content analysis alone, it is of particular interest to examine the extent to which members of the audience absorb, explicitly or implicitly, the messages which critics and scholars allege that they are receiving.

However one approaches the problematics of the study, we are, in effect, asking two basic questions: how do viewers make sense of *Dallas*?, and does viewer understanding differ in different cultures? To translate these questions into research operations, we ask, first of all, what happened in the episode, inviting group members to address the narrative sequence and the topics, issues and themes with which the programme deals.[3]

We pay particular attention to the ways in which these issues are discussed. For example, *Dallas* raises value questions about family life, living by the rules, loyalty, money vs happiness, civilisation vs 'the frontier', the invasion of the family by business and vice versa. Which of these issues will be raised in the group discussion and what concepts will be invoked to discuss them? Are these concepts taken from: universal forms (deep structures), tradition, personal experience, TV genres?

We are also interested in viewers' perceptions of the message of the programme. Do they perceive that the programme proposes a correlation – positive or negative – between money and happiness? Do they agree that business is destroying the family, or vice versa? Do they feel that the programme takes sides between the id and the superego? Do they feel that the programme is about American decadence or American ascendance?

In addition to the analysis of issues and messages we ask a second sort of question: how much 'critical distance' can be discerned between the group discussion and the television screen? Thus, some groups will gossip about the characters as if they were real people, analysing their motivations in everyday terms. At the other extreme, certain groups will discuss attributes and actions as 'functions' in a dramatic formula, groping, as critics do, towards a definition of the genre to which *Dallas* belongs. At this level of how 'real' the characters and situations are thought to be, we ask whether they apply equally to all or only to 'them', or to who 'they' are: Texans, Americans, First World?

Yet another level of analysis is embedded in the sequences of conversation. Can one perceive in the interchange among group members a direction – some 'progress' – towards a shared reading? Are there identifiable 'outcomes' in the course of mutual help in understanding a character or an episode? Is there agreement or disagreement over whether an action is justified? Is there debate over whether a certain character or situation 'could happen here'? What are the patterns of such processes of consensus-building or meaning-making? It is too early for us to answer these questions definitively. Nevertheless, we wish to share some very preliminary observations about this social process of meaning-making based on impressions from preliminary analysis of the Israeli cases.

Mutual Aid in Interpretation

First, let us look at an example of a statement which reflects the process of mutual aid in the making of meaning. During the viewing of the programme itself, group members fill in information for friends who missed the previous episode, remind each other about the past performances of certain characters who have been absent, explain motivations for actions and prepare each other for a coming 'surprise' or 'unpleasantness'. Consider the case of an illiterate middle-aged Moroccan woman named Ziviah conversing with her fellow group members, including her husband, her sister, her sister's husband and a friend:

> *Salah*: [about Dusty] It's not clear whether or not he can have children.
> *Miriam*: They talked about it in court [in the last episode].
> *Salah*: Why does she [Sue Ellen] live with him? That's strange.
> *Miriam*: Why? Because she's suffered enough. What do you mean, 'why'?
> *Ziviah*: Where's their father? Why don't we ever see him?
> *Miriam*: I think the father is dead.
> *Ziviah*: That's what they say.
> *Zari*: He died a few weeks ago, and it hardly matters.
> *Ziviah*: [indicating the screen] That's Bobby's wife. She's dying to have a child.
> *Miriam*: No, she's in a mental hospital now.
> *Ziviah*: Oh yes, yes, that's right.
> *Yosef*: Really?
> *Ziviah*: Yes, yes.
> *Salah*: She's in a hospital now?
> *Miriam*: A mental hospital.

But groups can reinforce each other not only in accurate exegesis of a text; they can also contribute cumulatively to a misreading. This process is particularly interesting when the distorted interpretation derives, apparently, from the attempt to incorporate a segment of the story into a familiar pattern of culture. Thus, in the following exchange, an Arabic group finds it culturally compatible to assume that Sue Ellen, having run away with the baby from her husband, JR, has returned to her father's home rather than to the home of her former lover and *his* father:

191

George: He's trying to monopolise all the oil in order to destroy Sue Ellen's father. He wants to use it to pressure. . . .
William: Sue Ellen's father.
Interviewer: Sue Ellen's father? Is that right?
William: Wasn't that Sue Ellen's father that was with him?
Hyam: Yes, Sue Ellen's father; that's him.
Interviewer: Where was Sue Ellen at the time?
Hyam: She's staying at her father's.

The previous example deals less with meaning, perhaps, and more with simple information. Let us look at an example of the way in which social interaction clarifies meaning. This is from a group of new immigrants from Russia, who know only a little of the English of the original and only a little more of the Hebrew of the subtitles. Yet here they are conversing in Russian, about Americans in Texas, on Israeli television. The issue is why the court gave custody of the baby to the mother, Sue Ellen, rather than to JR.

Liuba: Justice has a lot to do with it.
Misha: What justice? It was the medical certificate [attesting to the impotence of the man with whom Sue Ellen is living] that helped, not justice.
Mile: No, it's justice, not the medical certificate, that helped her to win.
Sofia: It was proven that Sue Ellen left him not to go to another man but to a sick man whom she was going to help at a difficult moment, and that was the decisive factor in the court's decision.
Misha: Nothing would have helped without the certificate.
Mile: Misha, he's not potent, this new husband of hers.
Liuba: She didn't go to a lover, but to. . .
Mile: Remember, she can't have any more children. So it's justice.
Misha: What justice? It's the medical certificate.
Mile: You're wrong.
All: You're wrong. It's about justice.

Mutual Aid in Evaluation
Additionally, there are arguments about how things *should* have turned out. Some members of the group think well of the outcome of an issue raised in the programme, while others disagree. Thus the group also sits in judgment of the values of the programme, or at least brings its own values into open debate. Here is an example of this process from a group of Moroccan Jews, most of whom are already rather well integrated into Israeli society. The subject of this conversation is why Miss Ellie refuses to be JR's accomplice in the kidnapping of the baby:

192

Zehava: She [Miss Ellie] knows how it feels to be a mother. If her own son were taken away how would she feel? She would feel it keenly. She doesn't want others to suffer that way.

Yossi: You're talking as a mother? How about talking like a father?

Zehava: That's my opinion, and that's what I said. Let me explain to my husband. He's saying. 'Why should the father be the only one to suffer? Why should we be defending only the mother?' My answer is that the mother gave birth to the child and suffered for him. She loves him better than the father because the child is of her flesh. A father is a father; OK, so he loves his child.

Machluf: And not of his flesh? Isn't the father a partner in the child?

Zehava: The child's from his seed, but not of his flesh.

Machluf: What do you mean his seed and not his flesh?

Zehava: It's not the same thing. She suffered at the time of birth, and not the father.

Machluf: Don't they have half and half in the child. . .? In the government you [women, feminists] say you want 50 per cent, but you really mean you want 75 per cent.

Another episode from this same group goes even further in questioning the wisdom of social arrangements for allocating and administering justice. Some members of the group insist that justice is too narrow in its focus. If only the judge had taken account of the whole of Sue Ellen's questionable past or the fact of her running off with the child, instead of focusing on her purity of soul, he would have awarded custody of the child to JR:

Yossi: The kind of justice we just saw is called dry law. It's a kind of impersonal law, without people. Who says that the court had to decide that the child should stay with its mother? It's only a coincidence that her friend can't go to bed with her or give her a child. She shouldn't have been unfaithful, and the court shouldn't have given her custody of the child.

Such arguments are not limited to taking side over issues within the programme. A theme in the programme as a whole is sometimes interpreted or evaluated against an opposite position which is embedded in the culture of the viewing group. Thus, one of the members of this same Moroccan group spoke eloquently, in liturgical rhetoric, of how much he did not feel allied to the values of *Dallas*:

Machluf: You see, I'm a Jew who wears a skullcap and I learned from this series to say 'Happy is our lot, goodly is our fate' [*Psalms*]

193

that we're Jewish. Everything about JR and his baby, who has maybe four or five fathers, who knows? The mother is Sue Ellen, of course, and the brother of Pam left. Maybe he's the father. . . . I see that they're almost all bastards. . . .

A similar sort of rejection of the perceived message of *Dallas* can be found in a kibbutz group:

Sarah A: When I see them, I only pity them.
Amaliah: I live better than they do.
Sarah A: And I tell myself, how terrible it would be if I were one of them.
Amaliah: With all that they have money, my life style is higher than theirs.

But rejection is by no means the universal reaction. The groups we have examined so far are not so quick as the two just cited to reject the material values in *Dallas*. Indeed, even the groups that do reject them at one point in the discussion may reconsider at some other point. More typical, perhaps, is the following exchange from a group of North Africans in a semi-rural co-operative settlement:

Miriam: Money will get you anything. That's why people view it. People sit at home and want to see how it looks.
Salah: These are special people. Somehow they get it all, and we don't.
Ziviah: Right.
Yosef: Everybody wants to be rich. Whatever he has, he wants more.
Zari: Who doesn't want to be rich? The whole world does.
Miriam: Wealth also makes an easy life.
Ziviah: It's the best thing.

Personalisation vs. Objectification: Dimensions of Critical Distance
It is clear from these examples that people are discussing and evaluating not only the issues of the Ewing family but the issues in their own lives. Indeed, much of the discussion in groups focuses on problems of conflict between the sexes, normative vs anomic family relations, money vs happiness, loyalty vs opportunism, and the like. Some of the discussants clearly use the programme to discuss themselves and their conflicts. Others do so less freely. This may turn out to be one of the important differences between the ethnic groups; namely, how much critical distance is maintained throughout the discussion. Here is an example of personal soul-searching triggered by the programme:

194

Sarah A: When they tried to kill him [JR], her behaviour was simply . . . I don't know what to call it. How could she suddenly. . .? It's true you feel guilty, so you worry about a person. But suddenly to love him? . . . That seems put on. So what? Because I feel guilty, I should suddenly sell myself, sell my personality?

Consider the following – from a Russian group – in comparison:

Sima: I'm surprised by his [JR's] attitude to his father. He must be feeling that his father is superior to him financially, as a businessman. What we see in the course of the programme is that he is constantly telling his father, 'Father, don't worry, the boy will come home, don't worry, everything will be all right,' as if he were giving a report to his father, as if he were bowing down to him.
Marik: In my opinion, he has inferiority feelings toward his father. . . .
Misha: He's a very complex person. . . . He has many contrasts. One can't say that such a person is very positive, although he does have certain positive qualities. I can't say that business for such a person, and his ambitions for achieving his goals, are negative. Without such qualities he couldn't work and make money, and making money is his profession.
Marik: Agree.
Sima: For him, everything is divided according to priorities, according to their importance. In business, let's say everything has to be organised. In a family, there has to be an heir. Everything as it should be.
Interviewer: Do you mean without emotion?
Sima: I wouldn't say without emotion. Maybe, yes. It seems to me that he wants his son not because he loves him; he's not so devoted to him. He simply knows that's the way it should be. He knows that he's his father's heir. I believe that he's living according to his father's code.

The more systematic analysis on which we are now engaged suggests that the several ethnic groups do differ, as we suspected, in degree of social distance. Certain groups use the programme 'referentially': that is, they relate the narrative to real life. Others speak much more analytically, or 'poetically', relating to the dramatic construction of the story rather than to its reality.[4] The groups that specialise in referential statements are the Arabs and the Moroccan Jews; culturally, they are probably most distant from *Dallas*. The most purely poetic is the Russian group who have much to say about genre, dramatic conflict and the like. While the oriental groups and the Russians may be said to specialise in one mode on account of the other – talking either about life or about genre – the American and kibbutz groups seem to be more flexible, speaking both critically and referentially.

While the groups differ in the extent of their use of poetic and referential statements, the form of referential statements also appears to distinguish among the groups. Thus, when discussing the relationship of the programme to real life, the Russians exceed all the others in their use of abstract or universal categories such as 'businessmen' or 'women' or 'Americans'. The others talk much more in terms of 'we'-groups. Moroccans and Arabs do this more seriously, while Americans and kibbutz members do so more playfully, as if they were 'trying on' the roles of the different characters of *Dallas*, imagining how wonderful or awful it might feel to be in their place.

While poetic statements are surely more distant than referential ones, it is not immediately clear that referential statements about general categories such as 'businessmen' or 'Americans' are less involved than references to oneself or one's we-group. In other words, it is possible that relating the programme to broad categories of persons may imply a belief in the reality and generalisability of the programme that is not necessarily present in talking about the relation of the programme to oneself. If more generalised is more distant, the Russians are the most distanced group, leading both in the proportion of poetic statements and in the proportion of referential statements that allude to abstract categories of people. According to the same calculus, the Arabs would rank least distant, or most involved.

Yet, for all of their differences, there are interesting similarities between the Russian and Arab groups. Not only are they more 'specialised' (in the ratio of poetic to referential) than the other groups, and more 'serious' (compared to the more playful role-takings of the Americans and kibbutzniks), they are also more 'evaluative'. Both groups tend to prefer the rhetorics of evaluation (good/bad) to the rhetorics of interpretation. The Arabs use evaluation in their referential statements, the Russians do so in their poetic statements.

Summary
Since we are still in the midst of analysing these very complex protocols of the focus group conversations – a mere sampling of which is reproduced here – it is too early to propose anything as pretentious as conclusions. Nevertheless, we can state at this point that we are impressed by the sophisticated ways in which very common people discuss these stories. Clearly they understand the broad outlines of the narrative; clearly they know the structure of the relations among the characters, their emotions and motivations, and are able to articulate at least some of the central themes. There is also evident

selectivity in what is discussed. The importance of family far outweighs the importance of business, as we expected. Less sophisticated groups sometimes use kinship terms to identify the characters.

Issues discussed include 'success', 'loyalty', 'honour', 'money and happiness', sex roles, the functions of children, and many others. Topics raised in the programme are generalised in the discussions so that they refer to generic human problems or immediate personal issues. The feeling of intimacy with the characters, expressed in many of the groups, has a 'gossipy' quality which seems to facilitate an easy transition to discussion of oneself and one's close associates. It is likely that the continuous and indeterminate flow of the programme, from week to week, in the family salon, invites viewers to invest themselves in fantasy, thought and discussion. The social distance between the Ewing family and the rest of the world seems far less important than one might have thought. Unhappiness is the great leveller.[5]

Altogether, we feel strongly supported in our hypotheses that the viewing process is active and social – perhaps even among those who vigorously deny it. The discussion frequently alludes to what discussants said last week or last month. This social process surely contributes to the ease of understanding (and sometimes to misunderstanding) and to the making of meaning and evaluation. Anthropologists agree, even when survey statistics do not.[6]

The focus group method has proved very satisfactory. Discussions of television programmes, as simulated in these groups, appear to constitute a forum for the discussion of basic social issues and themes. They liberate people to say playfully – among their peers – what they might say seriously only in situations of crisis or conflict. It seems unlikely that these statements would be evoked in reply to an individual questionnaire or interview.

Groups appear to differ in what we call 'critical distance', that is the extent to which characters and issues are generalised or personalised, and the extent to which statements about the programme refer to the structure of the story or to 'life'. Certain ethnic groups switch easily from discussing the story to discussing life; others keep their distance. Certain groups generalise the programme to abstract social categories such as 'women' or 'Americans'; others implicate themselves more directly.

What seems clear from the analysis, even at this stage, is that the non-Americans consider the story more real than the Americans. The non-Americans have little doubt that the story is about 'America'; the Americans are less sure, and are altogether more playful in their attitudes towards the programme.

Hegemonic theorists will find it easy to interpret the reactions of both acceptors and rejectors of the values in *Dallas* as establishment

197

messages. If the money and muscle of the Ewings are an invitation to the fantasies of social mobility and the supposed 'American way', identification with the *Dallas* characters will serve the purpose. But what about those who see in *Dallas* only a reminder of how much better off they are without power? It takes only the slightest agility to see that this is even more hegemonic. It is a message to stay down, and enjoy the better of the possible worlds, letting the unhappy few take care of the rest.

References

This is a revised and expanded version of our paper, 'Once Upon a Time, in Dallas', that appeared in *InterMedia*, vol. 12 no. 3, 1984, pp. 28–32. It includes findings from the paper 'Cross-Cultural Readings of *Dallas*: Poetic and Referential Statements', presented to the International Television Studies Conference. The project is based jointly at the Annenberg School of Communications, University of Southern California and the Hebrew University of Jerusalem, and we wish to thank the Trustees of the Annenberg Schools, Inc., and Dean Peter Clarke for their support.

1. We are here in disagreement with others who believe that the unit of television viewing is better conceptualised as background, or as a 'strip' that cuts through an evening's viewing, or as a pervasive barrage of messages about society that is embedded in all of prime time. Our argument is simply that certain programmes – some more than others – are identified by viewers as discrete stories, and that such viewing entails attention, interpretation, evaluation and perhaps social and psychological consequences. For recent relevant writings on the 'active' audience, see P. Palmgreen, 'The Uses and Gratifications Approach: A Theoretical Paradigm', in R. Bostrom (ed.), *Communication Yearbook*, no. 8 (Beverly Hills, California: Sage 1984); D. Morley, *The 'Nationwide' Audience* (London: BFI 1980); and W.A. Collins, 'Cognitive Processing and Television Viewing', in E. Wartella, D.C. Whitney and S. Windahl (eds.), *Mass Communication Review Yearbook*, no. 4, (Beverly Hills, California: Sage Publications 1983).
2. W.R. Neuman, 'TV and American Culture: The Mass Medium and the Pluralistic Audience', *Public Opinion Quarterly*, vol. 46 no. 4, 1982, pp. 471–87.
3. In their paper, 'Television as a Cultural Forum: Implications for Research', *Quarterly Review of Film Studies*, vol. 8, no. 1, 1983, pp. 48–55, H. Newcomb and P. Hirsch argue that television is a 'forum', presenting viewers with issues that need to be resolved. Their content analysis identifies three levels: topics, issues and themes.
4. See R. Jakobson, 'Linguistics and Poetics', in R. and F. de George (eds.), *The Structuralists: from Marx to Levi-Strauss,* (New York: Anchor Books 1972).
5. Content analysis finds that American prime-time family programmes consistently offer this message of consolation for those who can't make it up. See S. Thomas and B.P. Callahan, 'Allocating Happiness: Television Families and Social Class', *Journal of Communication*, vol. 32 no. 3, 1982.
6. Anthropologists are trying to show that survey research on the frequency of television talk is missing the active but subtle interpretations of programmes and applications to relevant issues that go on during and after viewing. See J. Bryce and H.J. Leichter, 'The Family and Television. Forms of Mediation', *Journal of Family Issues*, vol. 4 no. 2, 1983, pp. 309–28.

CLAUS–DIETER RATH

The Invisible Network: Television as an Institution in Everyday Life

New communications technologies not only represent a challenge to national goals for industrial production (for example, the electronics industry), nor do they merely pose a problem or a question to do with national or international investment and collaboration (for example, Eurovision broadcasts or European TV co-production). Rather, they present themselves as bearers of new forms of socio-cultural reality, which touch upon traditional boundaries – of the nation-state, but of politics itself as well. Their location is not the arena of political decision-making or of official communications between nation-states, but within the tensions between the public sphere and private daily life, between the idea of collective life and the rituals of the TV viewer. This dynamic will be sketched out in the following remarks on a particular case of mid-European 'TV reality' – the ZDF 'crime-watch' series *Aktenzeichen XY . . . Ungelöst (Reference XY . . . Unsolved)*.

In 1933 the art psychologist, Rudolf Arnheim, foresaw television as 'a means of distribution':

> It has social consequences – in that it renders the object on display independent of its point of origin, makes it unnecessary for spectators to flock together in front of an 'original' – and economic consequences, in that it takes the place of other means of distribution.
>
> Thus television turns out to be related to the motor car and to the aeroplane as a means of transport for the mind.'[1]

The scene of action is no longer travel, but everyday domestic life, that 'structure of inertia' which is 'on the surface weak, but in fact can hardly be disturbed', acting as 'a blockade against any far-reaching form of change'[2] which becomes the projection room for the synthetic, spatial, temporal, and social structures of television. In the following I would like, through the example of a particular programme, to talk about two of the structures which televisual communication projects into the everyday, namely the political-administrative and the socio-geographic.

Reference XY . . . Unsolved is a ZDF series which since 1967 has brought together an audience of approximately twenty million spectators in Germany, Austria, Switzerland and in neighbouring states, in a TV hunt for criminals.[3] This hour-long programme is broadcast every four to five weeks, produced and presented by Eduard Zimmermann. In each episode he presents the public with a number of 'actual criminal cases' – unsolved cases passed on to the programme from police press offices. The cases consist of current enquiries mixed with acted scenes of outstanding, still unsolved, crimes. 'Wanted' pictures (photos, identikit pictures) are shown, as well as clues in the hunt (the tools used, objects abandoned during the getaway, the escape vehicle, the victim's personal possessions, recordings of voices) and scenarios of the crime (reconstructions of the deed by means of puppets and so on). Recently photographs have been introduced of hold-ups in banks taken by surveillance cameras. The main cases, or the particularly 'telegenic' ones, are reconstructed in acted scenes – a kind of crime-film without the dénouement, in which the detective reveals the murderer. In order to discover the 'solution' in the next episode, the citizen must co-operate by telephoning the studio and passing on the information which is possibly in his or her possession.

In between the presentations of the individual cases the studios in Munich, Zurich and Vienna are linked up to receive viewers' calls.[4] After almost every case the police officer responsible appears in the studio to provide further clues, and at around eleven o'clock spectators are able to see, in a short survey, whether their efforts have yet borne fruit. In this sense the series *XY* is simultaneously a perverse realisation of Brecht's theory of radio, which called for the distribution-system of radio to be turned into a communications apparatus in which everyone is involved. In the 'crime-watch' drama of *XY*, twenty million pairs of eyes suddenly focus on a particular district in a city, a motorway intersection, a dwelling, a family, a person, an implement; the TV-citizen becomes a member of the police, the restorer of 'law and order', the eye of the law. The state and the police force merge into the audience, into a community around the broadcast, made up of the invisible electronic network between isolated homes and dwellings – which in the case of *XY* serves to arrest the errant and the deviant. Thus the social arena functions as a hunting-ground, the living room as a hunter's hide. Mixing documentary, fiction and live action, the show also mixes the enjoyment of TV with the denunciatory activity of a viewer who passes on advice to central office.

In the programme's second year the producer described it in the following terms as an 'invisible network':

> In the Austrian holiday resort Wald im Pinzgau, the owner of a guest house leaps suddenly to his feet. 'But those are our guests!' he

calls out to a couple of friends sitting with him watching television. The owner is looking at two empty chairs. Until a few minutes previously the two sought-after bank raiders had indeed been sitting there. They had arrived at the little guest house three days before. They were driving an Opel Kapitän with Viennese number-plates and behaved around town like wealthy playboys. On the Friday evening they first sat with the owner and a couple of other viewers in the TV-room of the little boarding house and watched the *XY* broadcast. They must have had a premonition of disaster. For towards 8.30 they unexpectedly got up and said goodnight. Shortly afterwards the host heard car doors slamming outside and the car driving away. When a little later he saw photos of the two on the screen, the reason for the hasty departure immediately became clear to him. The host got in touch with the police station in Mitterstill by phone. Thence the alarm was passed to the neighbouring ports. The road-system was cordoned off in all directions.[5]

Full of consternation, the viewer belatedly recognises his proximity to the criminal, to the moment of danger, to the possibility of himself becoming a victim. He becomes part of the social fabric through the sudden impact of the world outside upon a moment in his photographic memory; in a flash these episodes of 'public interest' add their fragments to his own life history. His life becomes a story. The shock of the encounter inscribed within the notion of 'photographic memory' undergoes a change, following the significant encounter, within the cosy living room in front of the TV where *XY* is playing. Suddenly it is no longer meaningless and merely potential, but becomes a part of social life. What emerges is a holographic social space, an electronic 3-D picture, in which the individual suddenly looms up and then disappears again. On a Friday evening, after a week on the assembly line, on the motorway, at the VDU, being rushed and pushed about, the TV viewer in his cosy home picks up the phone and sets in motion the quest for a putative offender. Whereas he spends all week glued to the set, now he plays against it: the followers of *XY* become a kind of living, middle-European computer, fed by Zimmermann.

It is less crime itself than the social totality that is at stake here:

> The TV 'crime-watch' is no magic cure for crime. The method used is reminiscent of the operation, of an electronic data-bank from which extraordinarily precise information can be called up in an extremely short time . . . . And the receptive capacity of millions of human minds, which can be checked at one and the same time with the help of the television screen, could be considerably greater than that of an equally powerful electronic robot.[6]

The spectator becomes part of a European crime-drama, to which he, as active spectator, supplies the ending. Thus he joins the throng, becomes a member – perhaps an indispensable one – both of the communal flow of information and of the energy associated with the world of crime. For while he sits before the television set, he is in a constant movement of osmosis which involves a 'flight from daily life'; he sits both on the near side and the far side of his own four walls, of the family, of the state, of law and order, of normality, and of social life at large.

Projected here into the sphere of everyday domestic life is a pattern which touches upon structures which are not only geographical but also political/administrative:

1. The television institution, which organises the production and transmission of the programme, is neither private nor belonging to the state, but is defined by law as public. Zimmermann is not a representative of the broadcasters, but rather is involved in production as an independent collaborator with his own production company. In the process he uses emblems and logos which simulate the trappings of authority through their distant similarity with police insignia. (Zimmermann's appearance has caused him regularly to be called 'the national Deputy Sheriff'.)

2. The cases which he takes on board are supplied to him by the police press office – and so from a state, that is to say, regional institution. They are cases which have been chosen for their telegenic suitability, that is to say, on the assumption that they will be successful with spectators.

3. At last, as the spectator acts, state and police merge into the public. The broadcasting organisation becomes a new guardian of the law, consisting of the invisible electronic network.[7]

4. The interrelationship of two types of mass formation is involved here – that of the political mass, and that of the 'TV mass'. One is constituted by a sense of national unity (passport, taxes, military service. . .) the other in terms of intervention in the network of TV, ignoring national boundaries – not really particular common interests or consent of a political sort, but 'simply so'.

5. Hereby emerges a new kind of criminal-geographic entity: frontiers of a national, regional, or cultural kind no longer count; what counts much more is the boundary of the territory of transmission. For instance, this is how a fugitive who had escaped over the French-German border was spoken of:

> He stayed in future almost entirely in France. In the area near the border he exercised special prudence. For example, before renting accommodation in a hotel in Metz – near the border – he asked suspiciously whether they could receive the transmissions from

German ZDF here. Only when this was denied did he stay on in the building.[8]

The 'space of transmission' thus cuts across – as a new geographic entity, which has its own sovereignty, its own guarantors – the geographies of power, of social life, and of knowledge, which define the space of nationality or culture.

New synthetic orderings of reality emerge at the push of a button: the world of TV-language, TV-geography, the TV-community. Television thus *creates* social reality – a phenomenon of a very different order than a slight improvement upon family or community life. What is at stake in the first place is not *influence* upon a reality, but the effect of constituting reality. Television – and in particular serial-format programmes like *XY* – can present an electronic platform, as only a small number of political or social occurrences are able to. The fact that, apart from this programme, almost no other so completely contains all the specific properties of the television medium should give cause, as much in terms of forms of production as in terms of the scopophilia of the spectator, for more intensive reflection than has hitherto been the case.

However, new techniques of distribution have emerged, which more radically pose the problem here referred by way of example to a single programme – satellite, cable, videocassette. While cable precisely delineates a territory of distribution (and thereby is controlled by national sovereignty), a satellite covers regions which are not identical with national territories. Insofar as its signal is strong enough, those who inhabit its electronic space can have a part in its broadcasts. The cassette market works quite differently. It makes possible an unofficial traffic in audio-visual products, which can satisfy the most eccentric and most particular interests, which is not possible for a public medium (video sub-culture, for example, as among Turks in Germany). Telematic networks can create socio-cultural realities which are indeed still difficult to think about, but can already be produced.

The part played by the phenomenon of TV-geography in traditional political calculations can be gauged from two German statements. The Christian Democrat Federal Minister for Inter-German Relations, Windelen, spoke, at the beginning of 1984, out of his concern with the possibility of a complete cabling system, but not out of a pessimism towards the media – rather 'for reasons to do with German politics'. The job of protecting the unity of the German nation, he argued, entails

the duty of taking into consideration the effects on radio-listeners and TV-viewers in the German Democratic Republic (GDR) of decisions on questions about the media. Day after day people in the

GDR receive from the Federal Republic, by means of radio and TV, a little bit of freedom which the political system in which they live is unwilling to concede.

Programmes which one day could only be diffused by satellite, distributed by cable and received by means of sets specially adapted for this purpose, could perhaps not be received in the GDR, or only in exceptional cases. Thus it is necessary to retain traditional terrestrial forms of broadcasting.[9]

His Berlin party colleague Landowsky spoke of the exercise 'to inform the population of East Berlin and the GDR via normal forms of broadcasting. Complete cabling of the city would make this task of providing information more difficult.'[10]

And in the GDR, in the zone around Dresden, not reached by any programmes from the West, is what is known in the vernacular as 'the valley of the clueless'. We therefore see facing us, in a Europe once defined in terms of nation-states, many different, floating partial continents.

Translated by Phillip Drummond

References
1. R. Arnheim, *Rundfunk als Hörkunst* (1933. Munich: Hanser 1979) p. 164.
2. H. Bausinger, 'Alltag, Technik, Medien', in H. Pross, C-D Rath (eds.), *Rituale der Medienkommunikation* (Berlin: Guttandin & Hoppe 1983) p. 25.
3. In 1977 the programme reached an audience of 16.7 million adults in the Federal Republic (51 per cent of sets received the programme; in 1979, after Channel 1 had begun competing by counter-scheduling attractive feature films, the figure was still 37 per cent). For a while the programme had a combined audience of 30 million in four countries (Holland also took part in the early days). What is impressive, however, is less the number of sets which are turned on than the quality and quantity of viewers' involvement.
4. In virtually every programme Zimmermann deals with cases from all three countries, and preferably ones involving internationally active criminals. Depending on which country the crime was committed, we go over to stories from the studios in Munich, Zurich or Vienna.
5. E. Zimmermann, *Das Unsichtbare Netz* (Munich: Südwest Verlag 1969) p. 148.
6. Ibid. p. 183.
7. According to Zimmermann, in the BRD approximately 2,000–2,500 spectators report clues for every broadcast. In Austria and Switzerland the figures are similar. One is tempted to describe the structural function of the programme as one of a 'synthetic Mafia'.
8. Zimmermann, op. cit. p. 79.
9. H. Windelen, 'Ein Stück Freiheit', *Süddeutsche Zeitung*, 17 February 1984, p. 24.
10. K.-R. Landowsky, 'Lokalfunk der Zeitungen ware Bereicherung für die Stadt', *Volksblatt Berlin*, 4 March 1984, p. 16.

JUSTIN LEWIS

Decoding Television News

[In the longer version of this essay presented to conference, Justin Lewis contextualises his interest in the analysis of television news in terms of a convergence between text-oriented semiotics and an audience-oriented 'cultural studies' approach which has contributed to the development of notions of the encoding-decoding process, particularly through such initiatives as David Morley's work on *Nationwide*.

Lewis's project began with the selection of a British TV news broadcast – the thirty-minute ITN *News at Ten* broadcast of Friday, 26 March 1982. It went on to analyse the programme through a series of 54 detailed interviews with audiences of 'decoders'. The first four groups were used to develop specific lines of questioning, the remainder to provide the basis for the analysis. A variety of educational and occupational backgrounds was sought, as well as broad age-range and gender parity.

The 200,000 words of response were then codified by Lewis under five main categories. First, units of meaning as constructed by members of the audience were regarded as 'lexias', following Barthes's model in *S/Z*. Second, 'themes' were established in terms of the audiences' perceptions of news items as wholes. Third, 'narrative contexts' were identified, in the sense of 'a particular history that gives a news item (or parts of that item) meaning'. Fourth, a range of 'critical discourses' was identified, covering a spectrum from notions of media 'bias' to specific ideological responses to particular items. Fifth, the 'residual' category of 'extra-textual contexts' was established to designate meaning-systems or contexts, other than the 'narrative' or 'critical', whose origin lay outside the text – *Eds.*]

Programme Synopsis: 'News at Ten', 26 March 1982

The British Leyland Item This story began with news of a 'new deal' between management and unions at the Longbridge plant, but concentrated in its film report upon the increases in productivity brought about by the use of robots. A manager and two workers were interviewed, both enthusing about the productivity increases, despite the redundancies involved. The story finished with the reporter stressing that BL's future success could only be jeopardised by strike action.

The Company Car Item This was a brief reference to a 20 per cent increase in company car tax.

The Pound/Dollar Item A brief report dealt with the price of sterling against the dollar, in relation to American interest rates.

The West Bank Item This report concerned disturbances on the West Bank, with Israeli troops clamping down hard on rioting among the Palestinian population. These disturbances were said to follow the sacking of three Palestinian mayors by the Israelis. After film of the disturbances, an Israeli spokesperson, Menachem Milsom, was filmed justifying the sacking of the mayors and the Israelis' new hard-line approach. The reporter, Derek Taylor, then contextualised the story in terms of possible problems with the future Israeli withdrawal from the Sinai.

[Advertisements]

The El Salvador Item This was a report from El Salvador on the eve of their elections. We were introduced to the main candidates, Duarte and D'Aubuisson, and to the political complexion of them and the other candidates. We were then told that D'Aubuisson was now being considered a possible winner, that he was on the extreme right and had been linked to the death squads. The Americans, we were then told, had shifted their position in order to accept a possible D'Aubuisson victory.

The China/USSR Item This referred briefly to China's response to friendly overtures from the Soviet Union.

The Drugs Item A fairly short item followed about the conviction of a Sussex University research student for the manufacture of an illegal drug (Bromo STP).

The Whitelaw Item Coverage was given to the Home Secretary's speech on law and order to a Conservative Party conference (see below for full transcription).

The Jobs Item This made up part of ITN's weekly look at recent job losses, new jobs and new orders in Britain. The number of jobs, the firms and the places involved were given with accompanying graphics.

The Everest Item Following the summary of the headlines, there was a fairly serious film report on the progress of a British expedition to Tibet, to climb Everest by a 'totally new route'. The film revolved around rare shots of the British team in the Tibetan capital.

Transcript of the Whitelaw Item

Burnet: The home secretary, Mr William Whitelaw, got a standing ovation today after a speech to Conservative Party activists at Harrogate. He spoke in a debate on law and order at an annual conference of the party's central council and, to judge from his reception, he has emerged triumphant again, after a week fending off his critics. From Harrogate, our political correspondent, David Rose.

Burnet in studio. No logo.

Rose: Mr Whitelaw must have been worried about what sort of reception he'd get today. There had been rumblings from the party's grass roots, and he'd been given a rough time by the party conference on this issue last year. But in the event, every speaker except one supported him. Mr Whitelaw defended his record, and contrasted it with his predecessors' and opponents'.

Film of Whitelaw walking on to platform.
Rose captioned.
Shot of audience applauding.

Whitelaw sitting with colleagues on platform.

Speaker below platform.

Whitelaw listening, smiling.
Audience listening.

Whitelaw: It was Labour home secretaries like Roy Jenkins who failed to provide the prison places, for whose shortage they now criticise us. I am tired of those, whether Liberal, Labour or SDP who, far from supporting the police, and encouraging the public to help, concentrate on criticism and complaint.

Whitelaw speaking (captioned).

Rose: He was clearly delighted by the way the debate had gone.

Zoom out, no sound.

Whitelaw: And may I once again thank you deeply for the support and help which you have given to me at a very difficult time. (Applause.)

Sound up again.

Whitelaw sits down.

Rose: And they rose to him. Afterwards Mr Whitelaw told me that he had been hurt by previous criticism, from within his own party. Many of these representatives from the Tory grass roots are worried by the crime figures – but today, few held the home secretary personally responsible.	Zoom out to reveal audience who slowly rise.
	Zoom in to Whitelaw acknowledging applause. Audience clapping.
There's no doubt that Mr Whitelaw has received almost total support from the Conservative Party workers here at Harrogate. This time last week he feared what looked like a tough week of criticism: first on Monday, from Tory MPs; then in the House of Commons yesterday; then here from party workers in Harrogate. But tonight his position looks very much stronger. David Rose, *News at Ten*, Harrogate.	Rose, to camera.

The Audience in Action – A Summary of the Research

The Process of Decoding   Two stages in the process of decoding can be identified:

1. The extra-textual contexts – particularly the narrative contexts – used by the viewer to understand and interpret a news item will significantly determine which lexias will be decoded and how they will be decoded. These meaning systems can therefore be understood as channels for access to the TV message.
2. The organisation and meaning of these lexias will then determine how the message as a whole will be read.
It should be emphasised that these two stages are separated for analytical purposes – they do not necessarily represent a chronology of the decoding process. The specific channels of access used by the viewer to understand an item may have been appropriated because of the way that item was constructed. In other words, in identifying a process in which two determinations interact, I am not suggesting which one of these determinations 'comes first'.

News at Ten's weekly item detailing the areas where jobs have been lost, or where new jobs have been created (the *Jobs* item), provides a simple but neat demonstration of this process. A majority of the decoders understood this item in relation to a story – or narrative context – about the level of unemployment and the economic climate in general. The programme's weekly report about jobs had, indeed, been created largely in response to the 'beginning' of this story – during the period when unemployment under Mrs Thatcher had begun to rise fairly dramatically. From that point on, rising unemployment became extremely newsworthy.

For these decoders, the relevant part of the *Jobs* item was the *ratio* of 'new jobs' to 'jobs lost' (rather than, say, which kinds of jobs had been gained/lost, or the areas/companies involved). In other words, the narrative context employed by these decoders gives them access to a *specific part* of the item, and gives those parts meaning. Accordingly, the item was seen to mean that: unemployment continues to rise (articulated by 15 decoders); unemployment continues to rise, but jobs are beginning to return (articulated by 9 decoders); or simply that jobs are beginning to return (articulated by 4 decoders). So, viewers using a certain narrative context to understand the *Jobs* piece are directed towards a certain part of that item, which then directs the viewer towards one of a limited range of meanings.

For those decoders who, on the other hand, used more complex narrative contexts to understand the item, the process of decoding produced quite different meanings. Some of the decoders (8 of the 50), for example, interpreted the item in terms of an extra-textual context identifying regional differences in unemployment levels (clearly a matter of some importance to people living in an industrial northern city like Sheffield). Accordingly, this opened up and made meaningful those parts of the item indicating *where* jobs were coming and going. During the interview/viewing sessions, therefore, every member of this group made references to *places* mentioned on the item. This, in turn, led them to construct meanings that either confirmed or denied regional trends in unemployment levels. In this instance, the ratio of jobs lost/new jobs became a less significant part of the item – for these decoders, it is *where* jobs are coming and going that is important in determining its meaning, rather than simply *how many*.

Another group of decoders (5 of the 50) were able to refer to a narrative context specifying the decline of jobs in manufacturing industry (as opposed to, say, the service industries). In these cases, the types of jobs lost or gained became significant. Once this happened, the viewer was forced to construct a meaning confirming the narrative context – in this case (because of the nature of the lexias involved) the item was seen as demonstrating the decline in British manufacturing industry.

The process of decoding that produces these meanings is not a matter of choice for the decoders. It is not a case of the viewer choosing, on the basis of his/her predilections, which part of the message he/she feels is important and then constructing a suitable meaning. This is a common conception of the audience to which the 'uses and gratifications' approach gave a great deal of credence. It is a comfortable model of the television audience that has provided both researchers and broadcasters with an easy and convenient view of the world – yet it is profoundly misleading. The viewer will, on the whole, have only a limited range of appropriate meaning systems (extra-textual contexts) to draw upon when watching a television news story. These contexts will give the viewer a specific form of access to certain sections (lexias) of the item, which will, in turn, force him/her towards a certain meaning (or set of meanings). Moreover, because these channels of access (as I have called them) will frequently open up only certain parts of the TV message, the nature of exactly *what* is being communicated is by no means predictable.

The news of Whitelaw's reception in Harrogate, for example, would appear, to both broadcasters and researchers, to have a fairly straightforward and clear meaning. The story was 'about' the favourable reception given to Willie Whitelaw by Conservative Party workers, following a period when he had been losing credibility with his own party's right wing. The story was, indeed, something of an anticlimax. After a series of attacks upon Whitelaw for his supposedly 'soft' approach to law and order – attacks which had become particularly vociferous during the 1981 Conservative Party conference – the broadcasting media sent teams up to Harrogate expecting the (then) home secretary to be given a rough ride. As one BBC news broadcaster put it, in one of the group discussions: 'We were there to see Willie Whitelaw get mauled, and he didn't. We'd expended all that effort, and so had they (ITN), so we still had to produce something out of it.' What resulted on *News at Ten* may not have been terribly newsworthy, but it was not, apparently, ambiguous. Not, at least, until we examine how it was decoded.

The *Whitelaw* item can be divided into three main stages. The first stage is a resumé of the story's narrative context by Alistair Burnet (briefly) and the reporter on location, David Rose. We are then shown a brief film clip of Whitelaw's speech, following the news that all the speakers in the debate, bar one, had supported him. The final part of the story sees a relieved Whitelaw receiving a standing ovation, with David Rose reporting that this support has made Whitelaw's position, within his own party, 'very much stronger'.

In terms of the story's *encoded* meaning, the second section of the item – the brief clip of his speech – was completely irrelevant. *What* he said, in terms of how the story was set up, was of little importance

210

– what was significant was *how he was received*. The footage of Whitelaw's speech was intended to signify nothing more than 'here is Whitelaw speaking'. Despite this, of the three sections, it was Whitelaw's speech that made the greatest impact upon the decodings. Of the 50 decoders, 41 incorporated references to the speech into their readings, 38 incorporated references to his reception and only 12 incorporated references to the story's context (i.e., the fact that he had been having a difficult time in his own party recently). Although the fact that Whitelaw received support at Harrogate was signified throughout the item (verbally by Alistair Burnet, David Rose and Willie Whitelaw, and visually by shots of his audience applauding or giving him a standing ovation), several decoders were unable to identify the origin of this support, or its significance. Of the 38 decoders who referred to this support, for example, 8 suggested it came not from members of the Conservative Party, but from people in general. Of the 41 decoders who referred to Whitelaw's speech, on the other hand, a large number – 31 – mentioned at least one of the two points he made, despite the irrelevance of these points in relation to the encoded meaning of the story (he begins by criticising former home secretaries for not building enough prisons, and then refers to the need to support the police and the opposition parties' failure to do this).

I shall deal with the relative impact of these two sections of the item in more detail later. Suffice to say at this point that, for many of the decoders, Whitelaw's speech was actually seen as the focal point of the story. This was made possible by the decoders' failure to incorporate the item's introduction into their readings. Without knowledge of the context of events in Harrogate, it is impossible to understand the significance of Whitelaw's good reception. This, in turn, forces the decoder to shift his/her attention towards what Whitelaw actually said.

If the decodings are analysed in more detail, we can see that the ability to absorb the item's introduction into a reading is fairly dependent upon the decoder *already knowing* about the narrative context to which the introduction refers. Of the 12 decoders referring to the item's resumé of Whitelaw's problems in his own party, 9 had detailed prior knowledge of Whitelaw's recent trials, and 3 a vague knowledge of them. (There were, on the other hand, 10 decoders who referred neither to Whitelaw's previous position nor the support given him at Harrogate, and none of these had any knowledge of the story's narrative context.) In other words, the first section of the item became meaningful only for decoders with access to the narrative context to which it referred. For the majority of the decoders without access to this narrative context, the broadcaster's encoded meaning *was simply not communicated*.

For the smaller group who already knew about Whitelaw's problems, the process of decoding worked thus:

(a) The decoders were able, on the basis of this narrative context, to make the opening lexias, the item's introduction, meaningful;

(b) The introduction to the story therefore related to subsequent parts of the item, giving *them* specific meanings;

(c) These meanings then combined to create a range of readings around the central theme – that Whitelaw, after criticism from within his own party, was now enjoying support.

For the larger group of decoders who did not already know about Whitelaw's problems, the process of decoding worked like this:

(a) The decoders were not able, on the basis of narrative contexts (or other extra-textual contexts) available to them, to make the item's introduction meaningful. They were, on the whole, able to construct readings around Whitelaw's speech and the support he received on the basis of various discourses about law and order and politicians in action;

(b) This gave Whitelaw's speech and/or his enthusiastic reception a certain range of meanings in relation to one another (or in isolation, depending on the extra-textual contexts available to the decoder). Without knowledge of the item's introduction, for example, the meaning of his enthusiastic reception is constructed in relation to the speech, i.e. it is specifically *what he has just said* that has earned him a standing ovation;

(c) These meanings then combine around a range of themes – Whitelaw supported by his party for his handling of certain law-and-order issues (constructed by 3 decoders), Whitelaw speaking about law and order (constructed by 9 decoders), Whitelaw gaining general support for his measures (constructed by 4 decoders) and so on.

Decoding Narrative   It has already been indicated how the *Whitelaw* item worked in terms of two narratives: one with Whitelaw's speech as its focal point, one directing the viewer towards the reception he received. This seems a useful place to begin, as it allows three important points to be made. First, the *Whitelaw* item demonstrates, lest we forget, that narrative structure is a product of the process of decoding. However powerful a narrative structure may be in directing the viewer's interest and concern, that power is ultimately dependent upon the availability of appropriate extra-textual contexts. Second, the two conflicting narratives present in the *Whitelaw* story reveal a great deal about the nature of narrative in television news. In their introductions, both Alistair Burnet and David Rose cite the story's introduction and attempt to direct the viewer past Whitelaw's speech towards his reception. Burnet begins with the most 'newsworthy' element of the story:

212

The home secretary, Mr William Whitelaw, got a standing ovation today, after a speech to Conservative Party activists in Harrogate.

He then refers briefly to the speech – *without mentioning its content* – before returning to the main point:

> . . . to judge from his reception, he has emerged triumphant again, after a week fending off his critics.

David Rose then proceeds to fill out the context in more detail and, in so doing, strengthens the emphasis on Whitelaw's *reception* rather than his speech:

> Mr Whitelaw must have been worried about what sort of reception he'd get today. There had been rumblings from the party's grass roots, and he'd been given a rough time by the party's conference on this issue last year. But in the event . . .

As has already been indicated, these attempts to construct a narrative, moving from a 'worried' to a 'triumphant' Whitelaw are surprisingly unsuccessful. There are a number of reasons for this (which will be dealt with in this essay when appropriate) but perhaps the most revealing is the way this narrative conflicts with the conventions of news narrative.

These conventions instil various expectations into the TV viewer. Where a news story contains a fairly brief sequence of actuality film (preceded by a newsreader's and/or a reporter's introduction), the viewer can usually expect that sequence to signify the focal point of the story. This is the case, for example, with the *West Bank* item, where the actuality film of the Arab/Israeli disturbances is not only the 'newsworthy' focal point of the story, but is also perceived as such by the decoders.

Given these expectations, the *Whitelaw* item contains two possible focal points: the speech and Whitelaw's reception (these being the only two 'events' communicated during the film report). For the majority of decoders (who were not guided by the encoded narrative towards his reception), the second is necessarily seen as a 'reaction' to the first. The traditional format of television news therefore encourages a reading based upon the least significant (insignificant in terms of the news value encoded into it) part of that item.

A slightly different example of a traditional format producing certain expectations amongst viewers of TV news occurred during the decoding of the *Pound/Dollar* item. Nearly all the decoders were aware that the level of the pound against the dollar was a piece of information that cropped up fairly regularly on the news. The common feature of this brief but regular financial news item is the level of the pound, i.e. whether it rose or fell. This information, rather than the news about American interest rates or Chicago money markets (news that, on this *News at Ten*, gave meaning to the information about the level of the pound), therefore provided the focal point for most decoders' readings of it – even though many failed to recall whether the pound had actually gone up or down. The decoders had learnt a specific structure of response. What is significant is that these responses do not necessarily facilitate an understanding of a news story, or the ability to structure it into a coherent narrative.

The third point raised about narrative by the *Whitelaw* item is perhaps the most interesting. It refers to a code of narrative identified by Roland Barthes in his analysis, in *S/Z*, of Balzac's short story *Sarrasine*. It is a narrative code that structures the relation between lexias, defined by Barthes as the hermeneutic code.

> Let us designate as hermeneutic code all those units whose function it is to articulate in various ways a question, its response, and the variety of chance events that can either formulate the question or delay its answer; or even, constitute an enigma and lead to its solution.[1]

The hermeneutic code then, is a way of establishing links within a narrative. It is, moreover, perhaps the most powerful link in televisual communication. The hermeneutic code, more than any other, draws the viewer into the narrative: once the viewer has become interested in the question, the enigma, he/she has become 'hooked'.

The code of enigma works on a number of levels. It can refer to the straightforward posing of a question, such as the one that opened the *News at Ten* under study (seen by the decoders): after the first chime of Big Ben, we were asked of Roy Jenkins, 'Is he now the alternative prime minister?' It can also refer to implicit suggestions about the future *of the narrative*, the kind of enigma/resolution structure that characterises most TV or cinematic fiction, but which is embodied most obviously in the continuous serial like *Coronation Street*. As Christine Geraghty writes:

> The apparent multifariousness of the plots, their inextricability from each other, the everyday quality of narrative time and events, all encourage us to believe that this is a narrative whose future is not yet written. Even events which would offer a suitable ending in other narrative forms are never a final ending in the continuous serial: a wedding is not a happy ending but opens up the possibilities of stories about married life and divorce. . . .[2]

The qualities that Geraghty attributes to narratives like *Coronation Street* are, in a number of ways, appropriate to TV news. Each of the main items on *News at Ten* are episodes of stories of which the viewer will, if he/she wants, hear more. The *Hillhead* item, in resolving one narrative (the Hillhead by-election) opens up others – the future of Roy Jenkins, the leadership of the SDP and the Alliance and, ultimately, the whole future of parliamentary politics. The *British Leyland* item very obviously finishes with an enigma – will strikes disrupt the progress now being made at Longbridge? The viewer is therefore referred to the future of BL, both in terms of productivity and industrial relations. The *West Bank* story refers specifically to the future of the Sinai withdrawal, and more generally to future Arab/ Israel relations and international relations; the *Whitelaw* piece, in signifying harmony, suggests the possibilities of disruptions in the future, and so on.We are witnessing the plot of history. Despite this, the continuous serial is one of the most compelling forms of television while, for most people, TV news is the least. As Patterson writes, the audience of TV news programmes is often 'an inadvertent one – which, in large proportion, does not come purposefully to television for news, but arrives almost accidentally, watching the news because it is "on", or because it leads into or out of something else. . . .'[3] Why is this?

If a programme-maker were asked to produce a narrative form that, by subverting or ignoring the hermeneutic code, failed to capture or sustain the viewers' interest, he/she might have come up with a TV news programme. Apart from occasional instances during opening headlines (like the question about the alternative prime minister), TV news pre-empts the development and resolution of enigma. It does this in two ways.

First, it orientates the news item around a focal point or series of focal points. These focal points, be they disturbances on the West Bank, or reactions of senior politicians to the Hillhead by-election, are almost never presented as resolutions or developments or enigmas/ questions. When the history of an event is referred to, the enigmatic quality of that history – what would be the reaction of the Palestinians to the sacking of their mayors? what were the circumstances of Jenkins's win at Hillhead, and what are the consequences? – is absorbed into the event/focal point itself. During the film report from the West Bank, reference is made to the mayors *after* the disturbances have (on the film) begun, while the Hillhead by-election itself is covered *after* reactions to it have been given (the circumstances of Jenkins's victory are not mentioned at all).

Second, on the rare occasions when the history of an event *is* presented as an enigmatic prelude to the focal point of the story, any enigmatic quality it may have is subverted by the newsreader's introduction to the story. This is precisely what happens during the *Whitelaw* item. David Rose attempts to set up an enigma, thereby guiding the viewer towards Whitelaw's reception (rather than his speech): 'Mr Whitelaw must have been worried about what sort of

215

reception he'd get today. There had been rumblings from the party's grass roots. . . .' This attempt has, however, already been pre-empted by Burnet's introduction: 'The home secretary, Mr William Whitelaw, got a standing ovation today, after a speech. . . .' The hermeneutic code could have worked here to shift the decoders away from the speech towards Whitelaw's reception. The newsreader's introduction robs the enigma of its power.

The role of the introduction on television news is not to set up or contextualise the subsequent report, but to summarise it. The 'main points' of the story are given before the story is properly told. If the 'main points' of *Coronation Street* or the F.A. Cup Final were given at the beginning of the programmes, only the most enthusiastic viewers would be inclined to continue watching.

TV news is not, of course, alone in suppressing the hermeneutic code. Print journalism operates in much the same way, although there is a suggestion that the tabloid newspapers are beginning to move towards a more narrational style of reporting. What makes the denial of enigma on TV news so significant is that it is virtually the only form of television to subvert this narrative structure. Even a programme like *Top of the Pops* attempts to introduce the hermeneutic code into its narrative, via the chart run-down (who will be where in the charts this week?) and the presenter's reluctance to introduce the acts other than immediately before they appear (who else will be on this week's show?).

Examples of the hermeneutic code on *News at Ten* are, therefore, relatively few and far between. It is important, nevertheless, to understand *where* and *how* the code operates in relation to decoding narrative.

The *El Salvador* item was one of the few to build up a narrative within its own parameters, and to attempt to lead the viewer along the stages of that narrative. This attempt was, inevitably, slightly pre-empted by Sandy Gall's introduction which transmitted a synopsis of that narrative. The narrative structure of Snow's report, nevertheless, seemed to have a distinct effect on the decodings. Although Snow's report communicates a great deal of information, the gist of the story revolves around the following narrative:

(a) Major Bob D'Aubuisson is a candidate in the El Salvador elections.

(b) He is seen as having a dubious reputation, because he is an extreme right-winger and/or responsible for killing Archbishop Romero and/or connected to the death squads, who are responsible for the dead bodies found dumped by the roadside (the last of these obviously involves connecting two lexias).

(c) The Americans are willing to support this man.

(d) This support is based upon a shift in the Americans' position.

216

The *El Salvador* item is clearly not reducible to this narrative, although the narrative does incorporate substantial parts of the text into it. It was, moreover, constructed by 19 of the 50 decoders. If the fourth part of the narrative is discounted, the number moves up to 25 – exactly half the decoders. This is unusually high. It compares with the 10 decoders who were able to produce a version of the more general two-stage *Whitelaw* narrative (the context of Whitelaw's appearance at Harrogate and his reception there), and the meagre 4 decoders who were able to construct a three-part narrative after watching the *West Bank* item (the causes/context of the disturbances, the disturbances, the significance of these disturbances).

The reason for this discrepancy, I would suggest, lies in the space the reporter, Jon Snow, was allowed to develop the *El Salvador* narrative, and the techniques he used to do so. The hermeneutic code can be seen to operate throughout this development. Snow begins his report by setting the scene of the election – the arrival of the observers, the distribution of the ballot boxes, the political complexion of the candidates on offer (and the enforced absence of the left). He then reports:

> Though there are half a dozen parties of the right, the battle is really between two men: President Duarte in the centre for the Christian Democrats, is Washington's candidate, but both he and the US Embassy here think he has a good chance of losing.

Having introduced the loser, the enigma 'who, then, is the likely winner?' is established. D'Aubuisson is then presented in these terms, and his 'right-wingness' is stated both explicitly and implicitly (in relation to his policies). The film then moves to a shot of Snow standing by three dead bodies. Snow briefly describes the scene, setting up the enigma – 'why are there dead bodies here, and what has this to do with the election?' This enigma is developed in Snow's next sentence, which answers the first question by referring to the death squads, but leaves the second open. The enigmatic power of the scene is intensified by two more descriptive shots of the same scene revealing close-ups of a vulture and an empty pair of boots.

The camera then focuses on Jon Snow, who resolves the enigma by referring to the evidence linking D'Aubuisson to the death squads, and to the killing of Archbishop Romero. This narrative ends with the Americans' 'new view' of D'Aubuisson, information which is, again, presented without disrupting the narrative flow – Snow tells us *first*

> until a few weeks ago, the embassy made it plain that D'Aubuisson was *not* a man with whom they could co-operate. But, last night. . . .

before detailing the nature of the new view.

There is fairly clear evidence that this narrative was reasonably successful in capturing and sustaining the decoders' attention. Of the 22 decoders, for example, who made the link between the death squads and the dead bodies, over two thirds (15) went on to link D'Aubuisson to the death squads. This comprises nearly all of those (18 decoders) who made the second link. The two lexias are therefore connected in the decodings: those linking the dead bodies to the death squads are fairly likely to make the subsequent link with D'Aubuisson, while those who made this second link were very likely to have made the first.

Similarly, the 15 decoders making both links were also likely to refer to the final stage in the narrative – the American about-turn towards D'Aubuisson. Eleven of the 15 went on to do this while, interestingly, the 4 that didn't either referred to Sandy Gall's introductory reference to D'Aubuisson as a 'pathological killer', or else had got confused at an earlier stage by muddling up D'Aubuisson and Duarte. Both would have a subversive effect on the narrative – the first because it pre-empts the enigma about D'Aubuisson, the second because it would confuse the last part of the narrative.

Of the 23 decoders who did refer to the American volte-face, a very high proportion – 19 – constructed the three substantive parts of the narrative leading up to it (D'Aubuisson as an election candidate, his dubious history and the fact that he was currently approved of by the USA).

These levels of inter-lexia relations do not occur during most of the decodings of the rest of the programme. The levels of inter-lexia relations decoded during the *West Bank* and *British Leyland* items, for example, were extremely low.

On the evidence of these decodings, then, the power of a narrative – held together by the hermeneutic code – to reproduce versions of itself in the decodings, would appear to explain a great deal.

It is the opportunity to *take part* in narrative development that affords the decoder satisfaction and pleasure. The news frequently denies the decoder this opportunity by suppressing the hermeneutic code (and therefore the enigma's encouraging the viewer's participation), subverting the developmental nature of the narrative (by directing the viewers to certain focal points and moving the viewer *around* those focal points rather than forward) or restricting access to those with knowledge of appropriate narrative contexts. It is a denial of pleasure that few other television programmes would risk.

This leads to my final point highlighting the importance of narrative in the decoding process. The hermeneutic code provides a specific way of encouraging the viewer to establish links between lexias, thereby encouraging him/her to continue watching a TV programme. From this we can deduce a less specific narrative code, a code that refers generally to the development of associations between sequences of lexias. This will be referred to, in this essay, as the code of narrative development.

Apart from the *El Salvador* story, the best instance of narrative development occurred during the item about the conviction of Paul Barker, the man who manufactured an illegal drug in a Sussex University laboratory (the *Drugs* item). Purely in terms of recall, these two items were more successful communicators of information than any of the others.

The *Drugs* item begins with news of Barker's conviction, who he was, what he did and where he did it. We are then shown a picture of the guilty man, and informed that: 'Paul Barker told the judge he knew more than his professor. The judge said he was arrogant and bogus.' The first statement – 'Paul Barker told the judge' – follows directly on from previous lexias giving the length of his sentence. Notice also the use of the active ('Paul Barker *told* the judge') rather than the passive ('The judge was told by Paul Barker'). The active form signifies the *development* of sequential actions, whereas the passive signifies the *already developed* (this point will be developed in relation to visuals and verbals). The second part of the sentence, similarly, develops the references in the first part of the story – the fact he was a 'research student' working in a 'university laboratory' (of the 10 decoders who referred to Barker as a research student, 7 went on to refer to his claim to know more than his professor).

The next sentence – attaching the descriptions 'arrogant and bogus' to Barker, reveal how important the developmental aspect of the narrative is to decoding. The first description, 'arrogant', relates directly to the previous lexia – it could be seen, indeed, as describing or responding to that lexia, i.e. the statement that 'he knew more than his professor' was 'arrogant' or provoked accusations of arrogance. The second description, 'bogus', on the other hand, bears no obvious relation to the previous lexia. Accordingly, nearly half of the decoders referred to the description 'arrogant' in relation to Barker (21 out of 50 decoders) while only two made any reference to the idea that he was 'bogus'. Of these two, one referred to the incompatibility of the two descriptions: 'What did they say he was – arrogant and bogus? I'm not sure how they get those to fit together.' Although the developmental relation between these lexias would not necessarily mean the decoder would, unprompted, refer to both, a high proportion did. Of the 19 decoders referring to Barker's claim that he 'knew more than his professor' more than two-thirds – 13 – referred to the idea that he was arrogant.

This conveniently brings us on to one of the most common and successful forms of developmental narrative – the development of 'personality'. Throughout the *Drugs* item, the significations operate in relation to the development of a central signifier – the man who

219

committed the crime. Each new lexia binds itself to this central signifier – we hear of *his* crime, *his* punishment, *his* occupation, *his* marketing manager, what *he* thought of *himself*, what the judge thought of *him*, how *he* committed the crime and where *he* got caught. The development of the narrative is the story of a man, a 29-second slice of an individual's life. This not only provides the story with 'human interest', it also helps hold the story together, giving the viewer a reference point throughout the narrative.

The use of an individual or character as a reference point for narrative development is, in fact, surprisingly rare. This is not to say that news, along with other cultural forms, does not focus on individuals – it does. News, as this *News at Ten* demonstrates, continually uses individuals from within the establishment to construct its agendas and define the meaning of items – an approach encapsulated in the well-known theory of primary definers.[4] Similarly, institutions and their effects are frequently reduced to the (prominent) individuals within them – the coverage of politics, for example, is frequently reduced to the comings and goings of politicians like Roy Jenkins or Willie Whitelaw. The way in which these personalities and individuals are used within TV news, however, far from being reference points for narrative development, actually obstructs such development. Their statements or actions, as in the *Hillhead* item, are either constructed as events or focal points, or else are used to revolve around such events, explaining or interpreting them. Apart from a brief summary of the result and the reaction from the Tory, Labour and SDP camps to Jenkins's win, the lengthy Hillhead story is a long list of quotations from Roy Jenkins, David Steel, Shirley Williams, David Owen, Cecil Parkinson, Tony Benn, Francis Pym and Michael Foot, all revolving around an interpretation of a single event.

The failure of TV news to use narrative (or enable its audience to use narrative) to communicate information clearly has an adverse effect upon its signifying power, in terms of the gap between the encoded and decoded messages. As has been demonstrated, news uses structures that either subvert or discourage development – analysis of the decodings has emphasised this time and time again. It has also been suggested that those structures create their own expectations – expectations which (as the *Whitelaw* item shows) create their own effects. There now follows a brief consideration of these expectations and their effect on decoding in relation to *News at Ten* more generally: how the items work in relation to each other and the flow and style of television news.

Flow, Refocusing and the Style of the News
Raymond Williams has described how the experience of watching

220

television can no longer be understood as the perception of a discrete set of programmes, but as the experience of 'flow'.[5]

The concept of flow can also be used to describe the more specific experience of watching TV news. The content of a news programme is potentially extremely diverse, yet we (as Williams does) will invariably lump that content into one amorphous mass known as 'the news'. The 'flow' of TV news is encouraged by programme editors – items that are in some way connected are usually juxtaposed in the running order: in the *News at Ten* under analysis, the *British Leyland* and *Company Car* items; the three foreign news items (broken up by the advertisements); the two 'law-and-order' items.

One of the consequences of this flow was to weaken the power of the introductory sections of the news. These introductions, it has been argued, often have the power to 'frame' the viewers' reading of what follows – they tell the viewer what the rest of the item is about (Brunsdon and Morley, for example, argue this point in relation to *Nationwide*).[6] My own evidence suggests that the opening sections of news items do not act as framing devices at all, but as refocusing devices.

The weakness of the introduction to the *Whitelaw* item in structuring decodings has already been demonstrated. Although it has been shown that there are specific reasons for this, this weakness was part of a general tendency by decoders to ignore the information presented at the beginning of items. This was particularly clear during the readings of the *British Leyland* item.

The *British Leyland* story was introduced in terms of a 'new deal' between management and unions in industrial relations at the Longbridge plant. This 'new deal' was said to provide 'the icing on the cake' of significant increases in productivity. News of the 'new deal' was nevertheless ignored by nearly all the decoders. This allowed a subsequent interview with two BL workers to create a significant impact upon the decodings. As has already been described, the way in which the two workers were seen was significant because they contrasted with a narrative context portraying BL workers as strikebound, inefficient and militant. Such a reading was only possible *if the introduction were ignored*, since the statements by the two workers were not at all surprising in relation to the earlier news of the 'new deal' – indeed they were entirely predictable.

The weakness of the introduction to this item (and other items) is partly a product of the flow of news item into news item. The introduction of each new item comes while the viewer is still recovering from the previous item. The function of the introduction is therefore to refocus the viewer's attention from one topic to another. The work required by this refocusing inevitably blurs any details offered by the opening sequence.

One of the decoders to recall the beginning of the *British Leyland* story specifically acknowledges the refocusing process.

Rather odd, I thought it started off with some announcement of a new deal, some new deal. . . . I was still in the shock of having watched the Hillhead story and still wanting to take that in. We certainly moved on extremely fast from Hillhead to the Leyland story, and maybe I missed something that's obvious.

The statement that the we 'moved on extremely fast from Hillhead to the Leyland story' is particularly interesting (the more so because it comes from the producer of a news and current affairs programme). News programmes invariably 'move on extremely fast' from one item to another – no sooner has one story ended than another begins. It is because he found himself thinking, while watching the *British Leyland* story, that the introduction might not have been as he'd remembered it, that he is made aware of this fact. He is suddenly conscious of the problem of refocusing.

Another item with a distinguishable introduction was the brief news about company-car tax going up. The item told us:

Up to three quarters of a million people with company cars were told by the chancellor, Sir Geoffrey Howe, today that the tax they pay will go up again next year, for the third year running – it's going up by 20 per cent, and if they get free petrol they'll pay even more.

Although this item lasted less than a quarter of a minute, the focal point of it was absorbed by most of the decoders – 37 of the 50 recalled the fact that company-car tax was going up, while 14 remembered the exact percentage of the increase. Some of them, indeed, felt the item was of considerable significance to the car industry, and should have been covered in more detail. Nevertheless, of the six lexias presented by the item – three quarters of a million people own company cars; Sir Geoffrey Howe's announcement; company-car tax will go up; for the third year running; by 20 per cent; or more if they get free petrol – the only two with no presence *at all* in the decodings were the first two. The first lexia's absence was, in some ways, the more significant. Several decoders, when discussing the item, suggested that it would have been useful to know how many people were affected by the increase, precisely the information given in the opening lexia.

It seems highly probable that the opening lexia would have been more powerful if it had been presented at a later stage. It could, for example, have been introduced thus:

The tax on company cars will go up again next year, for the third year running, by 20 per cent. This increase will affect three quarters of a million people.

222

In this version, the number of people owning company cars is freed from the muffling effect of refocusing.

The flow of one news item into another is the product of a particular style. The news is made up of a whole series of stylistic conventions that shape and structure the news so that we immediately distinguish it from other forms of television. The decoders' familiarity with the form and style of the news had a range of effects.

The news about the level of sterling against the dollar, for example, was seen by many decoders as signifying no more than 'this is the news', absorbed (like the *News at Ten*'s opening shots of the Houses of Parliament) into the flow of the news to render its specificity meaningless. Nearly half (22 of the 50) of the decoders, when prompted, remembered nothing other than that it was 'on', as usual.

The *Everest* item, on the other hand, despite its serious and newsworthy content, was seen by half the decoders as the 'light thing at the end', as one decoder put it ('you know, Mrs Smith's poodle that got lost, ate 4lb of sausages in the supermarket and then was sick'), because of its position at the end of *News at Ten*.

A more specific instance of the stylistics of decoding occurred during the *Drugs* item. The item refers briefly to the man who sold the drugs as a 'marketing manager'. This reference was thought, by many decoders, to be at odds with the language normally used to refer to the drugs subculture (terms like 'dealer' were thought to be more appropriate). As one decoder put it:

> It did strike me as an odd sort of term to use for that kind of person – in many ways he's almost an accomplice or something.

Another even put quotation marks round the phrase:

> We were treated to a very brief mention of his marketing manager who came over in inverted commas by some device or other (I don't know whether it was verbally expressed or whether we were told his 'so-called marketing manager'), but certainly the impression of inverted commas came across.

In other words, it was as if the phrase had been *quoted from another discourse*. The 'device' she refers to was no more than her ability to identify a phrase stylistically at odds with its context.

The 'marketing manager' is, in fact, fairly incidental to the narrative in which he appears. His presence in the decodings – 15 decoders referred to him – was almost entirely due to the way he was described. Almost all of the 15 decoders who referred to him did so like the two I have quoted. Significantly, none of the 6 decoders who misunderstood the nature of the drug mentioned the 'marketing manager' or, when prompted, saw anything strange about the phrase.

Verbals and Visuals   Suffice to say that, all other things being equal, the more direct the relation between visuals and verbals, the greater the impact upon the decodings. Within this context, two important areas of investigation emerged that need referring to: the link by authorship and action sequence.

The phrase 'link by authorship' is used to refer to points in a news programme when a statement is linked to a specific author. This frequently involves relations between the verbal and visual levels of television: a statement may be accompanied by a picture of its author, or we may see the author actually speaking.

The notion of authorship is fundamental to the ethos of impartiality on which the news is supposed to be founded. Broadcasters do not expect, for example, the viewer to understand a newsreader or reporter as the author of his/her statements, since he/she is, theoretically, a neutral communicator of 'the news'. At the same time, the neutrality of the news is also based upon the viewer's ability to associate the other characters who appear on the news – politicians, trade unionists, etc. – with what they say. If this does not happen, the particular views of a particular speaker will be untainted by the partiality of authorship, and will appear as news rather than views.

On the whole, rightly or wrongly, decoders did not identify reporters or newsreaders with what they said. The individuality of particular reporters went almost completely unrecognised (apart from among the broadcasters taking part in the study who knew the individuals concerned), other than by a few (favourable) references to Jon Snow. What was more serious, from the broadcaster's point of view, was that decoders often failed to link politicians and other speakers to their statements.

A good example of this failure occurred during the decoding of the news about Roy Jenkins's victory at the Hillhead by-election. This lengthy (9-minute) item consisted of a series of quotations from a number of politicians: Roy Jenkins, David Steel, Shirley Williams, David Owen, Cecil Parkinson, Tony Benn, Francis Pym, Michael Foot and a series of unidentified Social Democrats. One of the item's themes that some of these quotations were used to suggest was the notion that Roy Jenkins was now 'the alternative prime minister'. This idea was repeated seven times during the item: five times by various Social Democrats, once in the opening headline and once in a question asked by Peter Sissons. In order to maintain its impartiality (given the negative implications of the idea for the Labour Party in particular), it was essential that these suggestions were seen as originating from these Social Democrats rather than from *News at Ten*.

Two of these suggestions were, apparently, quite clearly authored by Shirley Williams and David Owen. Pictures of Williams and Owen appeared next to a visual display of their statements (which were read out by Alistair Burnet). The other three authored references to Roy Jenkins as 'the alternative prime minister' came from rather vague but nevertheless identifiable sources:

> The Social Democrats have been talking today of Mr Roy Jenkins as the next prime minister.

> Mr Jenkins arrives at Westminster on Tuesday. His friends expect him to become Mrs Thatcher's chief opponent – they say, the alternative prime minister.

> Today Mr Jenkins could have been facing the political wilderness – instead he's being talked of as a future prime minister.

Not surprisingly, given the number of references to it, two thirds of the decoders (33 out of 50) subsequently constructed this idea as one of the item's themes. What was more startling was that most of them (25 out of 33) were unable to identify the source of the idea. They felt, therefore, that it was *News at Ten*, rather than the SDP, which was presenting the idea that Roy Jenkins was now 'the alternative prime minister'.

The consequences of this for news broadcasting are considerable. If the authorship of a statement is not firmly established – say, by film of the author speaking – the partiality of these statements will go unrecognised.

The ability of the decoders to link by authorship in response to film of people speaking was, on the other hand, comparatively high throughout this edition of *News at Ten*. This was the case whether the speaker was William Whitelaw, Menachem Milsom (the West Bank administrator) or a worker at BL. One reason for this may be that this form of access comes from a broader category of verbal/visual link – the action sequence.

The way in which the active-verb form sustains a narrative more successfully than a passive-verb form has already been briefly described. It was suggested that the reason for this was that the active form signified a development, whereas the passive form signified the already developed. The active form, therefore, encourages the viewer to participate in the narrative, whereas the viewer has already been excluded from the passive form.

This distinction can be extended to the action sequence. This doesn't have to be existing in itself to encourage narrative development. The shots of Whitelaw, Jenkins or Menachem Milson speaking are all action sequences. What makes them interesting is that they appear to be happening in 'the present' of the story itself (i.e., it has not happened yet in that story) – we are not sure what is going to happen next in the sequence (of actions). The story is actually there, developing in front of our very eyes.

These qualities of the action sequence are, of course, diminished if their developmental quality is subverted by an introductory synopsis, but they do not vanish altogether. The action sequence itself will appear to be happening, as opposed to a descriptive/reported sequence of past events (like, for example, David Rose giving the background to the *Whitelaw* story).

Many of the lexias that carried weight in the decodings (during the longer items) were perceived as action sequences: the film of politicians speaking about Hillhead; the BL workers at Longbridge; the scenes of troubles on the West Bank; Whitelaw's speech and reception and Jon Snow's ingenious reconstruction of the scene with the victims of the death squads as if it were an action sequence. This fact, on its own, is perhaps not all that surprising. What I hope this analysis of decoding has shown is that our perceptions of the action sequence – or any other sequence – is a product of a number of variables structuring visual/verbal relations, narrative and, ultimately, the process of decoding.

The Alienated Viewer   There is one final aspect of the research to consider, albeit fairly briefly – a more general point about the position decoders felt they occupied in relation to *News at Ten*.

The picture presented by the research is at best depressing, at worst alarming. While the majority of decoders felt that the news was 'neutral' and 'unbiased', they rarely made connections between the world represented in the news and their own world. Many of the decoders felt that television, in a general unspecified sense, represented a world somewhere in the establishment. This was, in different ways, expressed by decoders from a whole range of political (or apolitical) backgrounds, and implied a certain alienation from the news – the world of 'them' rather than 'us' or 'our' world. This feeling was articulated fairly clearly during the *British Leyland* item, by the large number who felt it to be a 'put-up job' or 'an advertisement' for British Leyland. Behind this accusation was an assumption broadly linking television with the government and the world of management, the world of 'them'. What was perhaps most interesting about this assumption was its vague, rather indefinite quality. When questioned as to exactly why ITN should want to broadcast propaganda on behalf of British Leyland, most of the decoders could not, or felt no need to, pinpoint any specific set of relations between the two. In the following exchange, for example, the establishment is symbolised by 'government'. (It has just been suggested the two BL workers were 'plants'.)

226

Q: Who do you think planted them? The management?
A: Probably the management. I mean, they *may* have thought it [automation] was a very good thing.
Q: Why do you think television co-operated with that?
A: They're basically dominated by the government, what's on television anyway, everything, er, they have a say in what goes on.
Q: Do you mean a specific part of government, or the institution of government?
A: The institution of government 'cause, I mean, you can't blame any party, the Conservative or the Labour – it's the government in general.
Q: So that's why they would go along with management?
A: Yeah.

Another decoder linked various institutions, including, albeit implicitly, the media, as facets of 'the system'.

The whole way it was reported that, you know, Britain has got to get its industry up . . . it's just making people think that the best way things will get better, is just keep really working hard for the system, which I don't really agree with.

Her assumption that television is part of 'the system' is so deep-rooted that it remains unspoken. Despite my question, she feels no *need* to point out the link between British Leyland, television and the system. She therefore answers the question by reasserting her original point.

Alienation from television news is, in many ways, the most fundamental problem thrown up by this research. Space does not allow here an enquiry into ways of overcoming it. It seems appropriate, nevertheless, to make certain recommendations on the basis of the evidence presented. These will be restricted to problems that can be overcome without a fundamental reappraisal of the function and value of TV news.

Some Recommendations
The following recommendations are made on the assumption that the viewer is served by a news service that can successfully communicate substantial pieces of information, together with the relations between those pieces of information. This necessarily involves making the news more accessible and more interesting. It also involves broadcasters anticipating the process of decoding, i.e. the extra-textual contexts available or unavailable to the majority of television viewers.

Narrative   There are, as has been indicated, a number of problems

227

with the way television news uses (or does not use) narrative to communicate a story. Given the constraints upon broadcasting news – most obviously, newsworthy events do not offer themselves to reporters and editors in a neat package conveniently arranged into a developmental narrative – there are a number of ways of using narrative to make news stories more accessible, more comprehensible and more compelling.

First, the traditional approach of arranging various pieces of information around a focal point or points displays a sloppy disregard for the importance of narrative in communicating sequences of information. Broadcasters need to present a news story *as* a story. This means using a developmental narrative structure, where pieces of information, A, B, C, are presented sequentially, and where B relates to A, C relates to B and so on. Sequences can develop chronologically (for example, 'this happened, then this happened, then this happened,' etc.) or logically (cause of an event or problem, the event or problem, the implication of the event or problem). What is essential, however, is that they do actually develop. The focal point of a story should be presented in terms of such a sequence, it should be a *part* of the story. If this is not done, as the decodings have shown, the context or implications of a news event simply vanish into the air-waves.

One of the reasons why focal points are invariably presented far too early in a news story is because of a traditional practice inherited from print journalism – namely, the journalistic code that headlines information and then structures it in sequences of decreasing importance. The most newsworthy elements come first, through to the least newsworthy information at the end (which may then be lopped off by newspaper editors). Such a practice is thoroughly inappropriate to news broadcasting. It does not particularly facilitate the task of editing, while it makes the viewer's task in understanding the details of a story far more difficult.

Second, if a narrative is to be seen to develop, if the viewer is to be drawn from one sequence to the next, news reporters and editors should use rather than subvert the hermeneutic code. If this means withholding information until it becomes appropriate to the demands of the story, then so be it. This means that the current practice of beginning an item by introducing its focal points must be abandoned. A news event is rarely so important that the viewer needs to be told it at 10.01pm rather than 10.03pm. A reporter – like David Rose during the Whitelaw item – may attempt to introduce the focal point of his/her piece with an enigma contextualising it (for instance, given Whitelaw's problems with his own party, what would happen at the Conservative Conference at Harrogate?), but such an attempt (as the decodings show) will frequently fall on deaf ears if the newsreader has

228

already subverted that enigma in his/her introduction.

Structuring a narrative in terms of enigmas and resolutions not only gives the 'solutions' – usually the focal point(s) of the story – greater impact, but allows the viewer more easily to contextualise those focal points. In these circumstances, he/she is far more likely to comprehend what the broadcasters understand is going on in British Leyland or on the West Bank.

Third, when the viewer needs to know a particular narrative context of an item to understand that item properly, such a context should be provided. Further, such a provision should accord with the other points made – the narrative context of an item should therefore be given at the beginning of the narrative sequence, so that the following story can be seen to develop from it. Obviously there will be instances where such contexts, or aspects of them, can be assumed to be fairly well known. On the basis of this study, however, it seems likely that these instances are perhaps less common than broadcasters appear to assume.

Relating Visuals to Verbals   The arrangement of a news item into a developmental narrative cannot, of course, take place without careful consideration of the relationship between verbals and visuals. David Rose's attempt to contextualise the *Whitelaw* item, for example, was considerably weakened by the lack of any appropriate visual material to accompany it. Similarly, the sacking of the Palestinian mayors on the West Bank, or the consequences of the Israelis' hardline approach for the Sinai withdrawal, would undoubtedly have had more impact if they could have been signified visually as well as verbally.

The problem here is that direct visual/verbal links – particularly action sequences – are more difficult to set up with some types of information than with others. How, for example, can the withdrawal from the Sinai be signified visually before it has happened? What would the sacking of the Palestinian mayors actually look like? There are two points to be made here.

The first is that direct visual/verbal links only need to be used where possible or appropriate. This does not simply mean appropriate to the film footage supplied, say, by a team on location, but appropriate to the demands of the narrative. Problems relating to the withdrawal from the Sinai, for example, were an important part of the *West Bank* story. Further, it is a difficult piece of information for viewers to absorb, since its relation to the story that precedes it is fairly complex. It is, therefore, appropriate that such a piece of information is communicated as strongly as possible, i.e., using a visual/verbal link.

The second point follows from the first. Where the demands of a narrative require a direct visual/verbal link, broadcasters must use a little more imagination than hitherto in order to provide one. In the case of the future Sinai withdrawal, an easy option would have been to show library pictures of the Sinai. A more effective solution might have been to use graphics showing a map of the area with moving visual blocks, signifying the Israeli population and their potential movement. The sacking of the mayors could have been fairly succinctly signified with film of a Palestinian – preferably one involved in the civil unrest, or one of the mayors themselves – briefly describing the sackings and his/her unhappiness with them (thus establishing a fairly powerful link by authorship).

What is important, then, is not so much the links themselves, but an understanding of when and how they are used (or not used) during an item.

Quotations and Authorship   There is, of course, no reason to suppose that a viewer will necessarily construct links between the verbal and visual levels of a story – particularly where those links are indirect. This is, as has been pointed out, a real problem when people speak or are quoted during news items. The decoder will not necessarily connect a statement to its author – thus the majority of decoders during the *Hillhead* item, for example, were unable to connect statements characterising Roy Jenkins as 'the alternative prime minister' to various SDP sources, although such sources were specified *five times* during the item.

Failure to establish a link by authorship can have two quite different effects. In some cases, both quotation and author may be glossed over by the viewer. In others, such as during the *Hillhead* piece, statements that come from certain types of sources will be given a ring of 'objectivity' and authority if those authors are forgotten, i.e. the statements are no longer tainted by the partiality of authorship. This can be dangerous and misleading.

During a BBC 2 News report (23 April 1979) of the riot in Southall (where Blair Peach died), we were shown filmed highlights of the riot. During this action sequence, a fire bomb was thrown out of a window towards the police. This visual sequence was accompanied by the following voice-over:

> Roads to the meeting place were cordoned off – with reactions like this – what Commissioner David McNee called 'unprovoked violence against the police'.

This quotation, accompanied by 'evidence' centring the statement to the visual 'reality' of the riot, is made fairly powerful by the direct visual/verbal link. The link between the quotation and its author, on the other hand, is less powerfully established. The possible consequences are fairly clear: McNee's statement is given the authority of an 'objective' description of events. Such a consequence, given that his statement – that the violence was 'unprovoked' – was extremely contentious, was profoundly misleading.

The use of speakers or quotations on news broadcasts should, therefore, be dealt with extremely carefully. Moreover, I would suggest that news broadcasters use quotations – invariably from an extremely small élite of speakers (politicians, police chiefs, etc.) – far too readily. Structuring a news story around quotations from various members of the establishment – be they trade union leaders or judges – is not only unlikely to provide the viewer with a developmental narrative (i.e., it is an extremely dull way of presenting information), it is also likely to distance the viewer from the world depicted therein (it will be seen as 'their world, not ours').

There is a strong case for not using quotations on news programmes unless the link by authorship is abundantly obvious. The list of 'authors' used by TV news does not engender the viewers' interest or involvement with a new story.

Anticipating Decodings   My final recommendation is more general, although it covers a multitude of specific decoding practices, such as the refocusing effect. Throughout this research, the styles and conventions used by a programme like *News at Ten* have been shown to have consequences for decoding. At the moment, most of those who control news broadcasting have very little conception of these consequences. They are therefore either unable or unlikely to anticipate the short-term or long-term effects of the programmes they make upon the attitudes and perceptions of various sections of the population – for three reasons. First, adequate research in this area, as has been suggested, is simply not being done. Such research cannot be left to academic institutions, whose resources are very limited and whose work is frequently ignored. The research departments the BBC and the IBA need to accept this responsibility.

Second, there is a real sense in which broadcasters can become alienated from the majority of the population viewing the TV world from the other side of the screen. Because of their involvement in the encoding process, it becomes extremely difficult for them to understand the commonly experienced distance from the television product. Moreover, the well-established conventions styling and structuring television news have created their own practices of news gathering, giving them a permanence and authenticity that does not exist outside broadcasting.

Third, it will always be difficult for those working in news production to appreciate how inaccessible their work is to large numbers of people, as well as the *nature* of that inaccessibility (i.e., the effects of a partial reading of a news item). Given that the presentation of news appears to be both slick and uncomplicated, misunderstandings or misreadings can easily be dismissed as the decoders' problem rather than the encoders'. The importance of TV news in the social and political education of British people is clearly too great for broadcasters to abdicate such a responsibility.

While more research is needed in this area, it is imperative that such research has a direct link to programming. Changes in the presentation of TV news are likely to require changes in the practice of filming, reporting, editing and investigating a story. Such changes are unlikely to be made unless the understanding (of the audience) that precipitates them informs the practices of production rather than merely a few practitioners.

A Practical Recommendation   It seems appropriate to end with a brief example of what some of those recommendations might look like in practice. Even if the news values adopted by *News at Ten* are more or less accepted, the news stories it contains can be rewritten to overcome many of the problems of communication revealed by the research. The *Whitelaw* item demonstrates these points.

The main problem the decoders had with the *Whitelaw* story was a difficulty in understanding its significance. The narrative context of the story was clearly crucial to the communication of its particular meaning. Altough the reporter, David Rose, referred to the appropriate narrative context (i.e. the difficulties Whitelaw had been having in placating the party's right wing on the law-and-order issue), this was missed by most of the decoders – apart from those who were already familiar with that narrative context. Partly because of this, and partly because of its position in the narrative and its verbal/visual impact, the decoders attributed undue significance to Whitelaw's actual speech. This speech, in terms of the story the *News at Ten* team were trying to put over, was entirely inconsequential.

The failure of the *News at Ten* team to get its message across to the majority of decoders is, as has been demonstrated, due not so much to absences in the news item, but to the way that item was constructed. Most importantly, the three-stage narrative – Whitelaw's problems in his own party, his reception at Harrogate, the meaning of that reception – was not read off by most decoders for three main reasons:

(a) The subversion of the hermeneutic code, i.e. the question implied by the narrative context – 'how will Whitelaw be received at Harrogate?' – was answered before it was asked;

(b) The summary of the item's narrative context was further weakened because it was not supported by any accompanying visuals;

(c) The speech itself was made to appear as the item's focal point (rather than its reception).

All these problems have been avoided in the following version of the *Whitelaw* story.

Burnet: Speculation about the future of Mr William Whitelaw was brought to a head today, at a Conservative Conference in Harrogate. Mr Whitelaw has had a difficult few months coping with hardliners in his own party – David Rose reports from Harrogate.	Burnet in studio.
Rose: (Over background noise from the 1981 Conference.) Since his rowdy reception at last year's Conservative Party Conference, home secretary Willie Whitelaw has had a tough time fending off criticism from right-wingers in his own party.	Film of Whitelaw speaking to 1981 Conference, with graphics indicating time and place.
Both in and out of the House of Commons, Conservatives to the political right of Mr Whitelaw have been saying that the solution to the rising crime figures lies in taking tough action against offenders. They have attacked the home secretary for his more liberal approach to law-and-order.	David Rose, in the conference hall, to camera.
In the face of this criticism, the response of Conservative Party workers in Harrogate today was seen as a crucial test.	Film of Whitelaw walking on to the platform.
In the event, the party workers rallied round to give him their full support. During the debate, every speaker bar one supported him. As the party representatives rose to give him a standing ovation, Mr Whitelaw was clearly relieved.	Film of the debate. Film of Whitelaw receiving a standing ovation.
Whitelaw: And may I once again thank you deeply for the support and help which you have given to me at a very difficult time.	Film of Whitelaw speaking.
Rose: There is no doubt that, after his reception tonight, Mr Whitelaw's position in his own party looks very much stronger. David Rose, *News at Ten*, Harrogate.	Film of Whitelaw acknowledging applause.

Burnet's introduction merely refocuses the viewer's attention towards the issues at stake in the subsequent report. David Rose is then allowed space to set up the narrative context of the story, accompanied by a direct visual link. Having developed this context, Rose then firmly establishes the enigma: what will happen at Harrogate? The enigma is then resolved, Whitelaw expresses his relief and, as the applause fades away, Rose briefly confirms the significance of what has taken place. This significance has already been symbolised verbally and visually by the story's structure, moving as it does from Whitelaw under attack to Whitelaw receiving support. Pictures of the 1981 conference are replaced by pictures from Harrogate. The story, for the time being, is complete.

References

1. R. Barthes, *S/Z* (London: Jonathan Cape 1975) p. 17.
2. C. Geraghty, 'The Continuous Serial – A Definition', in R. Dyer et al., *Coronation Street* (London: BFI 1981) p. 11.
3. T. Patterson, *The Mass Media Election* (New York: Praeger 1980) p. 57.
4. S. Hall et al., *Policing the Crisis* (London: Macmillan 1978) pp. 57–60.
5. R. Williams, *Television: Technology and Cultural Form* (London: Fontana 1974).
6. C. Brunsdon and D. Morley, *Everyday Television: 'Nationwide'* (London: BFI 1978).

PETER DAHLGREN

The Modes of Reception:
For a Hermeneutics of TV News

The reflections in this essay derive from an ongoing project my colleagues and I have been carrying out in Stockholm, entitled 'Sweden's Hegemonic News Media: Their Role in Defining and Framing Reality'.[1] The aim of our work on TV news has not been to make an inventory of the manifest content, nor to engage in a critique of its ideological dimensions, though some aspects of both do appear in our study. Rather, we have been trying to elucidate *how* TV news contributes to the ideational process, that is, to probe the elements and dynamics by which TV news communicates meaning. Working on the premise that the 'net' meaning left with audiences must involve some active construction/interpretation from their side, we have also begun to explore the ways in which audiences 'make sense' of programmes.

This has led to two attempts at conceptualisation. The first used a modified 'social construction of reality' approach as a prelude to our ethnographic work with audiences.[2] The second, presented here, seeks to develop a non-technical way of talking about the cognitive activities of the audiences and to specify some of our assumptions about the reception process. As researchers trying to investigate both the possible meanings of TV news broadcasts (from the standpoint of the social order as a whole) as well as audiences' activities of meaning production, we needed to clarify our thinking about reception. This would provide us with a better frame for our inquiries into programming as well as for our ethnographic work.

To enter into discussions about the TV news reception process, as well as about discourse analysis of audio-visual texts and the general question of meaning, is to confront an array of traditions, approaches, tendencies and trends, with varying sets of basic assumptions and goals. However, I can state here at the outset that I feel that a certain degree of eclecticism is appropriate, given the somewhat exploratory nature of the work. Also, I am trying to develop a perspective on TV news reception which could stimulate some discussion among producers and journalists. Hence, my long-range aim is to emphasise the heuristic and the practical, even if the exposition here, for reasons of precision and economy, makes some use of academic jargon.

In what follows, I shall briefly summarise some of the main features of the perspective that emerged from our preliminary research into TV news, and then present what can be called the 'hermeneutic' attitude which guides our current inquiry. From there I take up reception as an analytic category, and introduce what I see to be its three major modes for TV viewing.

Probing the Programming: Some Lessons

After an initial effort to conceptualise and plan our research, we took a step back and sensed that there was something lacking in our perspective. It seemed that we had some kind of 'knowledge' about TV news that was falling by the wayside and not becoming incorporated into our work. We realised that this was the knowledge we had gained about the phenomenon not as researchers, but rather in the role of culturally competent viewers who watched rather regularly and responded to the programme from the horizon of our own everyday lives. While the knowledge we had from this angle of vision was no doubt in part coloured by our work as researchers, we felt that it could be instructive to us.

We devised what we call the 'discrepancy method' whereby we would watch a transmission with as much of the horizon of everyday life as possible – the naiveté, the associations, the references, etc. The spontaneous impressions, unreflecting impulses, common-sense understandings and unaided recall capacities from that experience would be culled and later compared with the results of detailed study of the videotapes and transcripts. While a far from rigorous method, it provided some instructive contrasts for us. Our own experience and knowledge from the non-analytical viewing became part of our 'data base', constituting a reflexive dimension to our work. Rather than yielding any final results, this procedure opened up some new dimensions for us, and I can recommend this approach heartily to those who are interested in the experience of TV news, whether or not they are researchers.

We found, for example, that after the first viewing, we had considerable difficulty with comprehension and recall if quizzed by a colleague (this despite our 'naiveté' being admittedly compromised by our research involvement). Much of the formal information was lost on us, not least, it seemed, because of the complexity of the sound-track and the visual track which competed for our attention. Yet, at the same time, during these initial viewings, we seldom *felt* very left out. Our failure in formal information absorption was apparently disguised by a strong experience of recognition of something familiar. Indeed, our spontaneous impressions were often a bit self-assured, and it was not until after repeated viewings of the videotapes and studies of the transcripts that we realised just how much we had missed.

Moreover, we found that the interpretation, the 'sense' of any given story, could vary considerably between us, even after repeated study. This had to do not only with the frames of reference we applied, our different stocks of knowledge, dispositions, chains of association, and so on, but also the 'mind sets' with which we approached the stories. For example, if one of us happened to be on the alert for the message dimensions while the other was more oriented towards experiencing the visuals, our respective 'readings' could be quite different. (If we were doing traditional content analysis, we would then have to put the whole research team through an intensive socialisation process so that we developed a unitary way of seeing – shared categories and so forth – to carry out 'reliable' coding).

It was also interesting to note that, in spontaneous encounters with the programmes, the sense we would make of stories many times exceeded the domain traditionally defined by the purposes of journalism. Our responses, reflections, associations and interpretations ranged across many themes and topics and emanated from reaches of the psyche not always linked to the process of becoming an informed citizen. Thus, the programmes could become a stimulus for trivial observations (for example, 'That minister looks just like my uncle'), global reflections on the state of the world, media-derived humour and impersonations of the figures on the screen, anxiety or anger not necessarily related to a specific story, reminders about one's own personal agenda (for instance, a story on new regulations about credit cards could prompt thoughts of an unpaid bill), among other things. The inventory is probably not infinite but it is important to emphasise the diversity of response which exists beside the traditional thought patterns oriented towards politics and current affairs.

I sketch some of these rather impressionistic observations not because they are in themselves so startling, but because they were central in compelling us to modify the direction and methodology of our research. Like others before us, we had begun our studies with sets of assumptions about the programme which excluded some of the central attributes of the experience of viewing. While we were concerned with how TV news contributes to the 'production of reality', we had exaggerated the extent to which it does so via the transmission of factual information which is received by viewers in a rational/ cognitive manner. (In passing, I can note that the persistence of the 'TV news as information' view is itself quite intriguing, given not least all the audience research which demonstrates the dismal level of comprehension and recall).

Thus, in coupling these observations with some theoretical

reflections, we found that our general perspective on TV news, as well as our research strategy, had to take into account some important features, a number of which would require further conceptual development.

First and most obviously, we had to remind ourselves of the limits of 'information transfer'. But we now wanted in addition to underscore the limits of formal cognitive processing as a way of describing the experience of viewing. Reception has also affective, intuitive dimensions which touch the depths of subjectivity.

Moreover, reception is active. The audience produces meaning out of viewing. This constructivist view should not lapse into idealism or psychological reductionism: we are, of course, aware of how social structure impinges on subjectivity.

The meanings produced by viewers, we further reasoned, may or may not have to do with the traditional sphere of current affairs. In fact, the 'knowledge' gained from a news story may not even have to do with the 'world out there' but may instead be of relevance as internal, private meaning. In other words, meaning may not necessarily reside wholly in the relationship between the message and the phenomena in the external world to which it refers. For the viewer, the reference to outer reality may appear weak, and meaning may be embodied more in the message's self-reference, fostering aesthetic involvement of some form. In Roman Jakobson's terms, the 'referential function' may at times be subordinate to the 'poetic function'.[3]

Yet, in contrast to the relative free play of sense-making suggested by such a constructivist perspective, we also have the experience of TV news providing a catalogue of meanings which appear given and determined; from the vantage point of everyday viewing they seem to offer little room for negotiation. The production conventions of the programme, with their repetitive narrative structures, limited repertoire of verbal and visual symbols, standardised dramatic motifs, and thematic contents, create an easily graspable and unambiguous 'image world'. In Sweden, as elsewhere, this image world of TV news is characterised by its relative stability: despite fresh facts each day, its essential, definitive ingredients recur from one day to the next.

We hypothesised that this tension between constructivist and determinist tendencies has a great deal to do with two inter-related force fields. One centres on the question of just which of the 'functions' (referential, poetic) a news story accentuates for the viewer; the other pivots on the reaches of the psyche – the mind set – with which the viewer attends to the story. As I shall develop below, there appears to be some correspondence between the two. For now, however, the lesson for us is to emphasise that the ideational process of TV news is both extra-informational and extra-rational. The constructivist/determinist issue required that we include some model of reception which stipulates not only its active component, but also that the process exceeds the boundaries of rational awareness, taking into account psychic forces which we associate with the *unconscious*.

Finally, and as a summary comment, it became apparent to us how little we had genuinely considered the *televisual* quality of TV news. We had overemphasised the *news* component (in the traditional sense) at the expense of paying heed to the medium's particular characteristics and biases.

For a Hermeneutic of TV News
While we could not hope to address all of these features thoroughly, the shift in our orientation seemed to account for them in a more satisfactory manner. At the risk of losing sight of some of the informational aspects of TV news which are undeniably pertinent, we reformulated our stance to emphasise the qualities of TV news as a televisual *cultural* phenomenon.

Television is a form of collective representation, a cultural form which, with its animated images, is unique. It touches its audiences both individually and collectively, both consciously and unconsciously. As Missika and Wolton put it, television programmes belong to a wholly particular class of perceived objects which are 'an intermediary between the visible world and the imaginary'.[4] The epistemic order of television, with its synchronic field of perception (to use Donald Lowe's[5] terms), is historically quite new. The bardic function, as Fiske and Hartley[6] put it, of this cultural arm of the industrial order (Gerbner's phrase) is by now conventional wisdom in many circles. But such discussions tend to be understood as referring to fiction or entertainment programmes. There seems to be a feeling that news and information broadcasts are still privileged, that they are really not what we mean when we talk about 'television'. This tendency derives from the understandable but questionable *a priori* distinction between 'information' and 'entertainment', which is still very current among both media professionals and researchers. I am not arguing for a necessary reversal of these categories, though at times it may seem tempting to make such a case. Rather, it is that such distinctions leave so much unsaid – or assume too much – in terms of our understanding of the cultural significance and viewer experience of television.

To treat TV news as a cultural phenomenon confronts us explicitly with the task of interpretation – of the programming and of the reception process, as well as the force-field between the two. In this light, TV news, like all programming, resists decoding by formalist linguistic models. What is 'really there' or what a particular segment 'is about' becomes more problematic as one's epistemological sensitivity increases. As Bernice Martin notes, 'Cultural phenomena, especially of a symbolic or mythic kind, are curiously resistant to being imprisoned in one unequivocal "meaning". They constantly escape from the boxes into which rational analysis tries to pack them: they have a Protean quality which seems to evade definitive translation into non-symbolic . . . terms. . . . Even verbal symbolism is very difficult to render *without remainder* in analytic language'.[7] This is all the more true of television, thanks to the very ambiguity and multivalence of its images.

For instance, the structuralist procedure behind many semiotic studies incorporates a view of meaning and consciousness (and even the unconscious) where the Subject is essentially dominated by the Object – the formal sign or code. This position is at base empiricist: the cultural text is reduced to an abstract grammar, with meaning residing wholly in its confines. The negotiation of meaning, and the historicity of consciousness is denied. Given our stance, it seems that an appropriate approach would have to be hermeneutic, at least in spirit if not in its formal techniques of analysis. In the interpretation of televisual discourse, claims for ultimate or final renderings smack of delusion and of hubris.

This, however, is not to give in to despair or methodological anarchy. Even if we cannot claim the traditional levels of exactitude when we are probing cultural phenomena, we should keep in mind that meaning is historically generated and socially situated. We can thus locate sense-making – its dynamics, forms, and products – in social contexts and examine the relationships thereby highlighted. Interpretation thus becomes 'socio-hermeneutics'. And even if objective finality remains elusive, such work falls well within the traditional tasks of social research.

Moreover, while the certitude of the findings is less than absolute, the very process of probing the phenomena, at different points in time and from different angles of vision, should be seen as edifying. This is not mere compensation, but an important consequence of research. Scrambling our traditional ways of seeing, challenging existing figure/ground relations, and exploring new possibilities of meaning, can contribute to our knowledge about the social world in ways not always attainable by the more traditionally scientific methods. And, not least, a socio-hermeneutic approach prompts a reflexive dimension to social research. One becomes more aware of how one is implicated in the reality under investigation and how one's own perceptions as researcher can shape how and what one sees.

In this regard, there is an important duality of valence in hermeneutics which is perhaps of particular relevance for media studies. Ricoeur[8] points out that, on the one hand, interpretation is a

240

reconstruction or restoration of meaning – a probe into the potential fullnes of its symbols and the power of its words. Facing in the other direction, hermeneutics also seeks to demystify. That is, it still treats its object as compelling, but for different reasons; it is suspect, seen as harbouring illusions which mask and distort, contributing to false consciousness. Ideology, here, is seen as meaning systems which serve to maintain social relations of domination. The task of hermeneutics is thus the critique of ideology, a project which has come to the fore in recent years in TV news studies.

Yet, if hermeneutics may at times align itself with critical theory, there is no fundamental reason that it must always and inevitably do so. There are different moments and concerns, as well as societal circumstances, which guide the direction of the hermeneutic endeavour; the researcher must choose. Fredric Jameson,[9] in discussing a similar theme, calls for an interplay between what he labels 'negative' and 'positive' hermeneutics: if the former approaches texts with the aim of demonstrating their ideological import, the latter tries to search out their utopian or anticipatory dimensions. By this Jameson means that cultural texts must be seen also as expressing human longing, in particular the drive for harmony, identification, unity and transcendence. Such cultural integration is expressed, evoked and embodied by symbols, rituals, and cultural products which convey shared meanings. It seems that in the recent critical climate of media demystification, this dimension has been somewhat neglected.

The point is that meaning must first be probed and elucidated before it can be deemed ideological, utopian, or whatever. And for our work, as I have suggested, the focus is still more elementary: we are less concerned with compiling meaning *per se* and more interested in the dynamics of meaning production. Yet the double valency of hermeneutics remains as a backdrop to our project, contextualising the mechanisms of TV news's ideational activity. Our purpose is not to defend or criticise TV news as such, but to deepen our understanding of how the programming and the audiences work together in the ideational process. To that end, for us, the analytic category of reception has become of central concern.

Reception and Epistemic Bias
The viewing of television, in fact attending to any media output, is perspectival, in the sense that it is always done from a social location. This, of course, has bearing on the patterns of meaning which people derive from the viewing. As David Morley[10] has indicated, the important categories for a social analysis of TV news viewing are not necessarily the traditional class lines, but rather more complex collectivities of subcultures, with their distinct frames of reference.

241

Further, viewing has its own particular social ecology; John Ellis[11] has recently written on the definitional impact of 'the home' and family life as the setting for reception.

But if we move to the level of cognitive activity, the dynamics of consciousness which come into play during the viewing of television, we need further to elaborate our understanding. Reception is not simply a trans-historical 'tuning in' of the viewers' consciousness to the programmes. Analysis of reception of TV, as well as of attention to any media form, must take into account the specific attributes of the medium. I am referring to those historically unique qualities – both of a cultural and technical nature – which constitute the medium's particular way of organising and structuring perception. Each medium fosters a somewhat different dispositional relationship between itself and its audiences; the audience must 'work' in different ways to attend to the output and make sense of it. I call this feature of a medium its 'epistemic bias'.

There is a growing body of literature contributing to our understanding of TV's epistemic bias; the works of Fiske and Hartley, Silverstone, Desaulniers, Missika and Wolton, Nevitt, Ong, Lowe and, of course, McLuhan, among others, have each made some contribution.[12] Such work draws upon a variety of intellectual traditions, and the views of the authors mentioned are by no means all compatible with each other. But some synthesis seems to be emerging, and it is just this growing consolidation of our understanding of TV's epistemic bias which can help inform our view of the reception process. In fact, a shuttling back and forth between studies of the reception process and the epistemic bias will help to clarify both, in a reciprocal fashion.

To summarise all the work on TV's epistemic bias is beyond my purposes here, but I can say that at present the outer reaches of the perspective are defined by, on the one hand, McLuhan's ruminations on 'hot' and 'cool' media, and, on the other, neurophysiological reflections on brain processes, especially on what is popularly referred to as left/right brain hemispheres and their respective functions, as applied to television watching. In between these poles, and more useful in my view, are Fiske's and Hartley's discussion on TV as a manifestation of a tension between oral and literate cultural traditions, Ong's concept of 'secondary orality' and Lowe's notion of 'multiperspectivity'. On the basis of this literature, TV's epistemic bias can be located in elastic polarities established by such couplets as synchronic/diachronic, mosaic/linear, evocative/analytical, with the resolution generally tending towards the former of each pair.

Another way to grasp some of the features of TV's epistemic bias is through Roman Jakobson's familiar model of the functions of communication. His use of the term 'function' may be a little misleading here; simply, he posits that meaning in communication is dependent on the relational balance between the various elements which comprise a communication. Thus, emitter, message, referent, medium, code and receiver can all be paired with each other in varying combinations, defining different functions. The resulting balance between these interfaces gives us strong clues as to *how* particular forms of communication transmit meaning. Space does not permit examination of the whole inventory, but three will be discussed here with regard to TV, which can help illuminate its epistemic order.

Jakobson begins with the referential function, which consists of the relationship between the message and its referent. This is the basis of information: the communication of accurate and verifiable messages about something, using symbols and grammar to signify external objects. Here we find the traditional purpose of journalism, for example, to inform. The analyses of television mentioned above, including studies of TV news, suggest that this function is comparatively subordinate to a number of the other functions, in particular the poetic and the phatic. Some authors have emphasised the distinctions between programme genres, arguing that within TV's general epistemic bias different programme forms each modify this bias in their own way. The discussion of the poetic and phatic functions here will be restricted to TV news.

The poetic function refers to the relationship between the message and itself. In other words, the referent becomes the message: the message is no longer an instrument of communication but is now the object of communication. For TV news, this has to do with the tendency whereby the world to which the programmes refer becomes partly supplanted by the world which it represents. The stylisations of the discourse, the familiar motifs and devices readily allow the viewer to become engaged in and experience TV news as an 'image world' with a minimum of involvement or knowledge about the external world to which it refers.

The phatic function is closely related to the poetic. In the phatic, the relationship is with the communication itself (while the poetic is with the message itself). The phatic function focuses on the maintenance of the communication – to keep it going and confirm the contact. It comes to the fore particularly in circumstances where the content of the communication is secondary to the fact that it is taking place. In this sense, it links emitter and receiver to something larger than both of them. Ritual, ceremony, routine occasions and religious or secular rites all emphasise phatic dimensions. Thus, the analysis of TV news discourse has revealed features which function essentially to hold the viewer's attention *or* to convey a sense of belonging or participation. The aura of being informed by fast-breaking news and getting reports 'as they happen' and so forth can be traced to rhetorical and dramaturgical elements in the TV news discourse.

The disposition towards the poetic and phatic functions away from the referential (again keeping in mind that this is a tension and tendency, not an absolute dichotomy) corresponds to my earlier comments about the limits of the transfer-of-information perspective regarding TV news. The extra-informational and extra-rational components can be brought more to centre stage by this framework. But I should add that the focus on functions is but one port of entry into the problematic of TV's epistemic bias; others are provided by the literature referred to above, as well as further themes such as the particular nature of visual animation and the implications of the cathode ray based technology of cerebral functions. Along these lines, Jerry Mander's book *Four Arguments for the Elimination of Television*, despite its lack of theoretical grounding and the diatribe quality of its presentation, offers some stimulating, if unnecessarily provocative perspectives.

Three Modes of Reception

Meaning in TV news broadcasts arises through the interface of audiences and programmes. In developing our theoretical scaffolding, the concept of epistemic bias in the television medium, further specified by the particular attributes of the news broadcasts, seeks to delineate and delimit the field of our hermeneutic inquiry and guide our interpretations. Yet the notion of epistemic bias requires, on the theoretical level, a complementary perspective on the process of reception. Only in this way can we genuinely model the production of meaning as an interface. Following and modifying the work of Northrop Frye and Fredric Jameson,[13] I develop a model of three modes of reception.

If information acquisition is one viable but limited conception of audience disposition to TV news, what are the other possibilities? In his *Anatomy of Criticism*, Frye develops a 'Theory of Symbols' in which he rewrites the traditional medieval four levels of meaning, calling them 'phases': the Literal and Descriptive, the Formal, the Mythical or Archetypal and the Anagogic. As Jameson points out, these are not so much different phases within the meaning of a text as much as they are labels for different modalities of the horizon of the audience's mind set – in short, modes of reception. In appropriating this logic, I am attempting to establish a typology of how viewers may attend to TV news programmes, through the scheme is intended to be of relevance for all genres of programming.

My basic line of reasoning is that television as a medium, via its epistemic bias, may favour one mode or a combination of modes over another, yet the specific programming (news) as well as particular

244

stories and their form of presentation can foster not only variations but also, more interestingly, tensions between the modes. In addition, modes of reception can vary with the social location of the viewers, the individual predilections of any single viewer, and so on. But the scheme is intended to be compelling in mapping possible interpretations of TV news output by situating it in relation to *how* the audiences may work on it. Also, it is to be of heuristic use in organising ethnographic studies of TV news viewing. The three modes are called *archival, associational* and *subliminal*.

In the *archival* mode of reception, viewer attention is directed towards the factual and informational, with the simple disposition of storing messages (or not) in the memory bank. The computer-based metaphor of 'man as a receiver of information' is applicable here, but only in terms of informational 'banking' – there is no real cognitive processing. The referential function prevails, with an emphasis on learning as simple cognitive memory. Successful archival reception can be gauged by the traditional recall tests and formal comprehension evaluation, for example, as to whether the terminology of a news story was understandable.

This mode captures the most rudimentary and familiar dimension of TV news viewing, minimising questions of viewers' subjectivity. It is fundamental, though limited both in daily practice and in theoretical import. However, it serves as a convenient 'baseline'.

Associational reception involves the viewer's pre-existing stocks of knowledge and frames of reference. Zones of relevance and schemes of typification are set in motion. Semantic and visual associations are activated; symbols and images play upon viewers' pre-existing thesaurus of factual knowledge as well as affective dispositions, prompting reinforcement and/or modification. The activist, constructivist perspective on meaning is clearly highlighted here, though of course modulated by factors of history and social structure. The vanguard of behavioural psychology, working with a different set of conceptual tools, seems to be approaching parallel formulations in their studies of TV news; the 'semantic network model'[14] of understanding bears considerable relation to the associational mode of reception, allowing for the differences in epistemological assumptions.

An important feature of the associational mode is that it is pivotal; it can encounter material obtained from the archival mode and process it, or it can veer off in the other direction, towards the subliminal.

The *subliminal* mode of reception is where the realm of the unconscious comes into play. The unconscious, as the region of psychic activity beyond rational awareness and conscious intentionality, is not just active, but creative. Thus, cultural phenomena such as TV

245

news are not only worked upon by this psychic domain in the act of reception but must be read as *expressing* the unconscious of those who produce the phenomena. To introduce the unconscious into a discussion of TV news is to launch ourselves into the realm of the mythic, of archetypes, of dream (both of nocturnal and daytime variety). I will return shortly to the question of the unconscious, but for now I wish to underscore that the concept of subliminal reception seeks to capture an important dimension of TV news viewing which is activist and non-determinist. It has nothing to do with the viewer being 'tricked' or deceived by messages bypassing his/her rational or critical faculties.

These three modes are, of course, classical 'ideal types', and I assume that all three are present to some extent in most TV news viewing. Further allowance has been made for the modes acting in a delayed manner, which is to say the analytic category of reception should not be taken to be limited to the time span during which the viewer is in front of the screen. Reception involves not just the impact of sense stimuli, but also the cognitive processing which follows. Particularly with associational and subliminal reception, this may not be achieved until later.

As indicated earlier, there are a number of features one can highlight in specifying the epistemic bias of TV; these are just some possibilities. More precision is required, and there is yet much to be done on this front. Nevertheless, as I have tried to suggest, the modes of reception constitute a continuum along which various dimensions of the epistemic bias can be mapped. Also, and of greater import, we can locate tensions between the differing modes, injecting a strong dynamic dimension to our view of the sense-making process. In particular, the lines of strain between associational and subliminal could be expected to be pronounced.

It must be kept in mind that this framework is not designed to categorise programme content or carry out other such empirical procedures. It has a more heuristic purpose, to help organise the interpretation of meaning within the broadcasts and the process of meaning production on the part of the audience.

The Cultural Unconscious

Though the concept of the unconscious dates from the early years of this century, it seems that our culture, with its rationalist commitments, still has difficulty accepting the idea and its implications. The non-rational side of the human psyche does not sit well in the instrumental logic and digital mind set of the post-industrial era. Mass-media research has manifested this unease as well. Particularly with the prevalence of Anglo-American traditions of behaviouristic social science, the 'dark side' of the human psyche was (perhaps unconsciously) neglected.

To introduce the concept of the unconscious here is not to identify with any particular faction within the warring camps of psychoanalytic theory. I take a rather general view here and wish to avoid loading the concept with unnecessary theoretical baggage.

In terms of the individual, the fact of the unconscious means that the Subject is divided and decentred, that psychic determination is cloven into forces within and beyond consciousness. But to posit that the psyche is not integrated and coincident with the consciousness of the Subject is not to deny the praxis of the Subject. In the heady wake of the structural reading of Freud, it seems that the only alternative to the infamous 'transcendental' Subject has been a view which treats the Subject not only as decentred by, but also created by, the grammatical structures of the unconscious. The unconscious becomes an abstract driveshaft of history, while the individual Subject is emptied of any conscious intentionality.

I find it more useful to see the Subject as something which exceeds grammatical formulations. That it is divided implies an inter-play between the conscious and the unconscious, with an inter-dependent and reciprocally constitutive mechanism mediating between the two. Neither is prior or more 'real' than the other, but we cannot understand one domain in the absence of the other. Neither can we understand the Subject, nor the sense-making process, without both.

For the purposes of the hermeneutic analysis of cultural phenomena, the unconscious is seen as being a creative and constitutive force for meaning not only for the Subject, but for collectivities as well. Jung, and Neumann after him, wrote of the 'collective unconscious' as a repository of trans-historical wisdom, which made use of a common, 'human' symbolism. This is a rather large ontology to swallow whole; while there are attractive elements to such a theory, I think there are more tenable foundations for a trans-individual unconscious to be found in sociological theory and cultural anthropology. If historical and cultural experience give rise to shared patterns of social consciousness and psychic organisation (i.e. character structure) it follows that the unconscious, and mediations to it, would also share common patterns. Hence, what I call the cultural unconscious: it is shaped by, responds to, and processes socio-historical experience at the collective level.

A strict structuralist approach is incompatible with the historicist dimensions of the hermeneutic horizon, and the Jungian model of eternal symbolic patterns and archetypes seems to assume too much of that which needs to be investigated. Yet I would argue for a modified trans-historical component to the cultural unconscious. A strong degree of consistency is witnessed, for example, by all the studies and inventories of myth from civilisations of the past as well as from disparate cultures existing today. (Here I weigh Eliade against Lévi-Strauss). But to the extent that TV and its news programmes can be said to manifest this continuity, I suggest it is still not a formal language or linguistic logic at work within, and expressed by, the cultural unconscious. That is, the cultural unconscious does not consist of a consequent grammar, permanent and specifiable units, firm rules for transformations and other manipulations. Rather than formal grammar, I think we have 'loose codes' at work. Rather than signs, we have symbols – not as standardised units of analysis within a grammar, but as cultural constructs which mediate between people and their lived experiences. A hermeneutic orientation would at best be a 'soft semiotics', which does not make unrealistic objectivist claims.

For the study of cultural phenomena, not least TV news, the notion of the cultural unconscious makes possible and necessitates a distinction between manifest and latent readings of meaning. Precisely because subliminal reception works within the unconscious, it must be 'recovered' by hermeneutic analysis. It should be recalled that psychoanalysis itself is *the* paradigmatic hermeneutic science of the 20th century. The subliminal mode, then, works on TV news in a manner parallel to the psychic operations involved in dream-work: condensation (metaphor), displacement (metonymy), inversion and dramatisation. (The strong similarities between TV and dream have been sketched in an introductory article by Peter Wood).[15] A hermeneutic of TV news, thus, must incorporate these dynamics of the unconscious, link them with meanings which arise from archival and associational modes, and situate this 'reception-work' in relation to the epistemic bias of television. From here, the *socio*-hermeneutic task involves contextualising these ideational processes in social, cultural and political terms.

References

1. Funded by the Humanities-Social Science Research Council, Stockholm. Project description submitted 1982.
2. 'Making Sense of TV News: An Ethnographic Perspective', *Working Papers in Communication* (Montreal: McGill University 1984). Also in *Rundfunk und Fernsehen*, vol. 31, no. 3–4, 1983 pp. 307–18.
3. Jakobson's model is neatly summarised in P. Guiraud, *Semiology* (London: Routledge & Kegan Paul 1975).
4. J-L. Missika and D. Wolton, *La folle du logis: La télévision dans les sociétés démocratiques* (Paris: Gallimard 1983) p. 174.
5. D. Lowe, *History of Bourgeois Perception* (Chicago: University of Chicago 1982).
6. J. Fiske and J. Hartley, *Reading Television* (London: Methuen 1978).
7. B. Martin, *A Sociology of Contemporary Cultural Change* (New York: St Martin's 1981) p. 28.

8. P. Ricoeur, *Freud and Philosophy: An Essay on Interpretation* (London: Yale University Press 1970) pp. 26ff. See also the collection of Ricoeur's articles edited and translated by John B. Thompson, *Hermeneutics and the Human Sciences* (London: Cambridge University Press 1981).
9. F. Jameson, *The Political Unconscious: Narrative as a Socially Symbolic Act* (Ithaca: Cornell University Press 1981) pp. 66–9.
10. D. Morley, 'Cultural Transformation: the Politics of Resistance', in H. Davis and P. Walton (eds.), *Language, Image, Media* (London: Blackwell 1983).
11. J. Ellis, *Visible Fictions* (London: Routledge & Kegan Paul 1982).
12. See Fiske and Hartley, op. cit.; R. Silverstone, *The Message of Television* (London: Heinemann 1982); J-P. Desaulniers, *La télévision en vrac: Essai sur le triste spectacle* (Montreal: Editions Albert Saint-Martin 1982); Missika and Wolton, op. cit.; B. Nevitt, *The Communication Ecology* (Toronto: Butterworth 1982); W. J. Ong, *Interfaces of the World* (Ithaca: Cornell University Press 1977); Lowe, op. cit.; M. McLuhan, *Understanding Media* (London: Routledge & Kegan Paul 1964).
13. Northrop Frye, *Anatomy of Criticism* (Princeton: Princeton University Press 1957); Jameson, op. cit. pp. 69–74.
14. For a summary of this work, see W.C. Woodall et al., 'From Boob Tube to the Black Box: Television News Comprehension from an Information Processing Perspective', *Journal of Broadcasting*, vol. 27 no. 1, winter 1983 pp 1–23.
15. P. Wood, 'Television as Dream' in H. Newcomb (ed.), *Television: the Critical View* (New York: Oxford University Press 1979).

IEN ANG

The Battle Between Television and its Audiences: The Politics of Watching Television

Recently, television studies has been confronted with the difficulty of reconciling two theoretical approaches, the histories of which have largely been unfolding independently from or in opposition to each other: the 'sociological' and the 'semiological' approach. Whereas the sociological approach (embodied in such diverse research trends as the political economy of the media and the uses and gratifications paradigm) has traditionally been dominant in mass communications theory, a semiological point of view has gained popularity during the last two decades or so, as a result of the limitations felt in the preoccupations of the 'sociologists'. In summary, these limitations concern the neglect of the *specificity* of television as a system of representation, and an over-simplistic idea of communication as the transmission of transparent messages from and to fully autonomous subjects.

Instead, semiological approaches have put forward the conception of media products as texts. The analysis of the construction of meanings in and through televisual discourses is stressed, as are questions relating to the modes of address presented in televisual texts, influencing the way the receiver ('reader') is positioned in relation to those texts. Thus, the semiological approach has attempted to overcome any idea of conscious institutional or commercial manipulation on the one hand, and of free audience choice on the other.

However, discontent with this relatively new theoretical point of view has already been voiced for several years. The nearly exclusive attention to textual structures is seen to have created new blind spots: the established semiological approach tends to ignore the social, political and ideological conditions under which meaning production and consumption take place. As a way out, more and more researchers insist nowadays on the necessity of combining sociological and semiological insights. As Carl Gardner and Julie Sheppard have recently put it:

> ... analysis of any mass medium has to recognise its complex *dual* nature – both an economic and industrial system, a means of

production, increasingly turning out standardised commodities, *and* at the same time a system of representation, producing meanings with a certain autonomy which are necessarily multivalent and unpredictable.[1]

This new credo in television studies has usually been translated into a formulation of the so-called text/context problematic. It is stressed that an analysis of a text must be combined with an analysis of its social conditions of existence. In empirical research, this text/context problematic has been elaborated in relation to the delicate relationship of texts and viewers, based on the so-called encoding/decoding model.[2] One of the goals of this model was to undermine the implicit assumptions of many sophisticated, semiologically based analyses, according to which the subject/viewer of a text coincides with the subject position constructed in the text. For instance, David Morley has attempted to develop an 'ethnography of viewing', by sorting out the different readings or decodings made by different groups of viewers (defined according to socio-cultural criteria) in relation to a specific set of texts.[3] Working within a similar theoretical model, Charlotte Brunsdon has adopted a different strategy to tackle the same problematic: her concern is how female viewers are capable of reading and enjoying soap operas, a capability which she locates in the specific cultural competences women have, i.e., their familiarity with the narrative structure of the soap opera genre, their knowledge of soap opera characters and their sensibility to codes of conduct of personal life and interpersonal relationships. In other words, instead of emphasising the differences between readings or decodings, Brunsdon has tried to account for the specificity of the confrontation between one type of texts (soap operas) and one category of viewers (women).[4]

Both theoretically and politically, this new problematic constructs a more dynamic conception of the relation between texts and viewers. It acknowledges the fact that characteristics other than textual ones play a part in the way viewers make sense of a text. Thus it places the text/viewer encounter within a firm socio-cultural context. It conceives of viewers as more than just passive receivers of already fixed 'messages' or mere textual constructions, opening up the possibility of thinking about television viewing as an area of cultural *struggle*.

However, the model has limitations. Apart from various problems having to do with, for example, an adequate theorisation of the concept of decoding,[5] the encoding/decoding model can be said to have a quite narrow view of the role of the audience: its effectivity is limited to negotiations open to viewers within the given range of significations made possible by a text or genre of texts. Moreover, this model's very conception of the audience tends to be a limited one. For this research model, the sole problem is the way in which texts are received/decoded in specific socio-cultural contexts, failing to take into account that decodings are embedded in a general practice of television viewing. It then becomes possible to question the relevance of the concept of decoding, with its connotations of analytical reasoning, for describing the viewer's activity of making sense of a text, as watching television is usually experienced as a 'natural' practice, firmly set within the routines of everyday life.[6] It goes without saying that a practice which is *felt* to be 'natural' structurally is not natural at all. However, it seems reasonable to assume that the 'naturalness' of the experience of watching television has an effect on the ways in which individual texts are received and dealt with.

What is at stake here is the way in which television audiences relate to watching television as a cultural practice. What does that practice mean and how are those meanings produced? One cannot deal with this question without an analysis of the way in which televisual discourse as a complex whole of representations is organised and structured, as it is through this discourse that a relationship between television and its audiences is mediated and constructed. In other words, here too an articulation of the 'semiological' and the 'sociological' perspectives will be necessary.

In this essay I would like to propose that different conceptions of the social meaning of watching television as a cultural practice are at play, and that these differences are related to the structuring of televisual discourse, with its heterogeneity of representations and modes of address. In doing this, I would like to stress the specific position of popular audiences as an effective category. First, I shall try to show that televisual discourse constructs a variety of types of involvement for viewers; in the second part, I shall illustrate how this heterogeneity of positionings has functioned socially and culturally in the history of Dutch television. However, much of what I am to say will not be more than (theoretically informed) speculation, which will need further refinement.

The Television Institution and Heterogeneity of Address
An institutional approach will serve as a starting point. I use the term 'institutional' in its comprehensive meaning, as applied, for example, by Christian Metz in relation to cinema: 'The cinematic institution is not just the cinema industry . . . it is also the mental machinery . . . which spectators "accustomed to cinema" have internalised historically and which has adapted them to the consumption of films.'[7] Although this formulation remains caught within the well-known semiological framework in so far as the

252

position of the spectator/audience is only dealt with as a discursive/ institutional effect, such a starting point has the advantage that it analyses cinema-as-such as a distinctive system of representation, and to which people relate in a specific way. An analogous argument may be applied to television. It enables us to move away from the isolated text towards an analysis of the ways in which television, as a discursive system, addresses people as potential viewers.

More precisely, an institutional approach opens up the possibility of reflecting on how the contextual is already structurally implied in the textual. That is to say, the structures within which televisual discourse is produced necessarily create an environment within which a certain type of consumer activity is assumed and 'propagated'. Thus, the production of texts and the organisation of a general context of consumption are closely inter-linked. Again, Christian Metz has given an imaginative description of the problem concerned (although I will not follow his psychoanalytic colouring of the picture here). Thus he writes about the task set to the cinematic institution:

> In a social system in which the spectator is not forced physically to go to the cinema but in which it is still important that he should go so that the money he pays for his admission makes it possible to shoot other films and thus ensures the auto-reproduction of the institution – and it is the specific characteristic of every true institution that it takes charge of the mechanisms of its own perpetuation – there is no other solution than to set up arrangements whose aim and effect is to give the spectator the 'spontaneous' desire to visit the cinema and pay for his ticket.[8]

Applied to television, then, the question can be formulated as follows: how does television as an institution succeed in making people buy TV sets and in making the idea of watching television seem attractive? Which strategies has it developed to persuade people to become members of the TV audience? It might be useful here to bear in mind that television has tended to be very successful in completing this 'mission', in making its existence and presence as a cultural form so taken for granted. Television, after all, has in all industrial societies become an institution which is central to both the public and private spheres. From an institutional point of view, analogous to that outlined by Metz, it is the 'arrangements' (both 'outside' and 'inside' the viewer) set up by the television institution through which a desire to watch television is roused and sustained, which must have been essential to this success. If the arrangements constructed by the cinematic institution are based on legitimised voyeurism, as Metz and many other film theorists have put forward, can we find an analogous construction in relation to television?

However, to avoid a determinist stance, we can only accept Metz's formulation of the problem in a qualified form. The setting-up of specific arrangements, the social channelling of desire, do not take place within a cultural void. They only get rooted when these arrangements can be fitted into existing cultural patterns and ways of life. These arrangements cannot be imposed authoritatively, as the above quotation of Metz might wrongly suggest. In other words, it is not enough that the cinematic or televisual institutions set up arrangements which construct and offer a position of involvement for the spectator/viewer, it is also necessary that the spectator/viewer, given her or his cultural dispositions, considers that position to be not only a sensible one, but also an attractive and pleasurable one. The question to be asked is then twofold. First, which are the arrangements constructed by the television institution for attracting viewers? and second, in which ways do the position(s) of involvement inscribed in televisual discourse relate to the audience's cultural orientations towards watching television?

In his book *Visible Fictions* John Ellis has developed a consistent view of the specificity of televisual address. In a certain sense, Ellis has relied on the institutional approach outlined above as a guideline for his book, which he presents as 'an attempt to sketch out cinema and broadcast TV as social forms, particular forms of organisation of meaning for particular forms of spectator attention'.[9] He argues that 'broadcast TV has developed distinctive aesthetic forms to suit the circumstances within which it is used'.[10] Central to his argument is the idea that television adapts the material it presents to the situation within which television viewing is normally assumed to take place: in the private homes of isolated nuclear families. This everyday domestic setting makes it very difficult for television to make its presence more than merely casually noticed and to hold the audience's attention – as a matter of fact, the private home does not seem to be a very favourable context for a concentrated spectatorial activity, as the cinema is. It is to ensure that the viewer will keep on watching, says Ellis, that television has developed distinctive discursive forms:

> TV draws the interest of its viewers through its own operations of broadcasting. The viewer is cast as someone who has the TV switched on, but is giving it very little attention: a casual viewer relaxing at home in the midst of the family group. Attention has to be solicited and grasped segment by segment. Hence both the amount of self-promotion that each broadcast TV channel does for itself, the amount of direct address that occurs, and the centrality given to sound in TV broadcasting. Sound draws the attention of the look when it has wandered away.[11]

Ellis's position is interesting here as he treats the aesthetic modes developed by television not as neutral or arbitrary forms, but as

254

rhetorical strategies to attract viewers. One could say that every rhetorical strategy is based upon assumptions about the best way to reach the target group. Thus, Ellis suggests that television recruits the interest of its viewers by creating a complicity of viewing: through its discursive organisation television is able to pose itself as an institutional eye which looks to the world *on behalf of* the viewers. It is especially through the device of direct address (i.e., presenters, newscasters, talk-show hosts, and so on, apparently speaking directly to the viewer at home, thereby creating an illusion of immediate presence) that television explicitly invites viewers to join it in its looking at the world. According to Ellis, television not only assumes that it has certain kinds of viewers, it also attempts to bind these viewers by pretending to speak for them and look for them. (In this respect, one of the favourite promotion slogans used by TROS, Holland's most popular/populist broadcasting organisation, is instructive: 'TROS is there for you!' The other side of the coin, namely that 'you are there for TROS!', is very sensibly suppressed.)

It is on the basis of this generalised view of the rhetoric of television that Ellis puts forward his thesis about the place of the TV viewer in relation to televisual discourse. He stresses that the position offered to the TV viewer is not the voyeuristic position, as is the case with the cinema spectator. Instead, the TV viewer is invited/summoned to delegate her/his look to TV itself: to trust in television 'as a safe means of scanning the world outside'.[12] And, by presenting 'the world' in a specific way, i.e., as an endless flow of events and things which have no connection to one another (just as every news item is separate from the next one; each one of them is written down on a separate sheet of paper), the TV viewer is placed in a very specific ideological relation to that world: according to Ellis, the formal strategies of televisual discourse give rise to the ideological positioning of the TV viewer as a 'normal citizen'. Ellis typifies this position as follows:

The viewer-as-citizen is uninvolved in the events portrayed. . . . Citizenship recognises problems outside the self, outside the immediate realm of responsibility and power of the individual citizen. . . . Citizenship therefore constitutes the viewer as someone powerless to do anything about the events portrayed other than sympathise or become angry. The whole domestic arrangement of broadcast TV and the aesthetic forms it has evolved to come to terms with this domestic arrangement provides broadcast TV with the capability to do this and no more. The citizenship that it provides as the position for its viewers is a position of impotence: TV viewers are able to see 'life's parade at their fingertips', but at the cost of exempting themselves from that parade for the duration of their TV viewing.[13]

It is doubtful whether this account of the subject position implied in the practice of watching television is a satisfactory one. This doubt becomes stronger when we take into consideration that, in so far as Ellis is concerned with the rhetorical strategies of televisual discourse, it will be necessary to explain that the position proposed to the viewer must somehow be attractive to her/him. In this sense, it seems to be a particular weakness in Ellis's account that the position of 'normal citizenship' as he defines it tends to be so contradictory. On the one hand, it is a position of entering the world, a position of knowledge (of being informed), but on the other hand it is at the same time a position of withdrawal from the world, a position of 'sceptical non-involvement'. It seems hard to imagine how and for whom such a contradictory position can be a position of pleasure, and thus a positioning which can explain why people like watching television so much. It will be more adequate, then, to state that the position of 'normal citizen' only exists in a formal sense, abstracted from concrete encounters between viewers and televisual discourse. Real viewers will never take up the position of 'normal citizen': if they find it pleasurable to be informed, they will be involved somehow in the representations offered (for both feelings of sympathy and anger *are* forms of involvement); if they really are uninvolved they won't be interested in being informed in the first place and probably won't watch at all, or won't watch attentively. However, as Ellis's theoretical framework remains within the problematic of semiologically informed discourse theory, in which viewer practices only appear from the point of view of textual effectivity, he doesn't pay attention to the readability or rather acceptability of televisual discourse from the point of view of the viewers themselves.

But there is another, related problem which is relevant here. Ellis continually speaks about broadcast TV in general and tends to give a generalised account of televisual discourse which is consciously abstracted from the specificities of different programme categories, modes of representation and types of (direct) address (indeed, his preoccupation seems to be with what *unifies* televisual discourse into one 'specific signifying practice').[14] As a result, it becomes difficult to theorise the possibility that television constructs more than one position for the viewer. For example, it is characteristic that Ellis's elaboration of the formal and ideological structuring of televisual discourse is mainly based on a more or less implicit reference to news and current affairs programmes. That these parts of television programming are indeed built on the discursive elements stressed by Ellis seems convincing enough: not only is there the familiar, though 'objective' direct address of the newscaster, but there is also the mosaic-like, ever-continuing compilation of relatively autonomous, short segments about the world's events – a structure based on an implicit appeal to a viewer's self-conception as someone who is interested in finding out 'what's happening in the world', from the position of a disengaged onlooker. The pleasure of this position does not have anything to do with the impotence of the 'normal citizen', as Ellis would have it. It has rather to do with the (imaginary) mastery of the world. In this case, then, the rhetoric of televisual discourse is based on the call: 'Watch, so that you will keep yourself posted!' It is a rhetoric which tends to be inscribed in a journalistic ideology, with its values of interest in public affairs, topicality and mediated responsibility.

However, many other programme categories do not seem to make the same appeal. In family quiz programmes, for instance, the direct address of the quiz master tends to be used to create an atmosphere of cosy togetherness, by literally inviting the viewers to join the club, as it were, thereby placing the viewer in a position of (imaginary) participation. (Some quiz formulas even create the possibility for viewers to play their own game at home.) Here, the rhetoric of televisual discourse is based upon the call: 'Watch, so that you will be one of us!' – an appeal which is part and parcel of a more popular ideology, in which values of communality, emotional involvement and humour predominate.

It seems, then, that different types of involvement, based upon different ideological positions, can be constructed by televisual discourse. It does not make sense, therefore, to see televisual discourse as a basically unified text without essential internal contradictions, despite its apparent diversity. An analysis of televisual discourse as a whole might prove to be more fruitful if we look for the real tensions in it, for the contradictions in the appeals it attempts to create for the viewers. In other words, we should analyse the *different* positions offered to viewers in relation to televisual discourse, and the ways in which these positions are inscribed within different parts of levels of TV programming. From here, we can then go on to ask how viewers relate to those positions. Or to put it in a slightly different way: how do socially defined audience preferences correspond to the variety of televisual address?

It is an empirical fact, for instance, that different sections of the social audience relate differently to specific programme categories. To avoid a wholly sociological explanation of this we should attempt to relate the alternation of acceptance and rejection of what TV offers its viewers to the heterogeneous structure of televisual discourse itself, and to the fact that the types of involvement suggested by televisual discourse don't all have the same rhetorical power. In this way, the socio-cultural effectivity of television, which is merely stated in Ellis's work, can be returned to the analysis, for it is the connection of rhetorical strategies (or the failure to achieve such a connection) to the audience's perspective of viewing which is at issue here.

The Politics of 'Trossified' Television

To make this theoretical argument rather less abstract, I shall now use a re-interpretation of the history of Dutch television. More precisely, I would like to say something about one particular moment in this history, which has come to be known as the moment of 'trossification' ('vertrossing'). This neologism stands for the increase of commercialised programming within Dutch broadcast television from the early 70s onwards – a development which has led to a lot of worried debates among media specialists, journalists, politicians and other intellectuals. I would like to take issue with their gloomy reflections here and will try to show that 'trossified television' can be seen as a consequence of the failure of Dutch broadcasting politics to take into account the audience's perspective of viewing and to make the viewers feel involved with its programming policies. First, however, it is necessary briefly to outline the Dutch broadcasting system.

It is relevant here to note that heterogeneity of televisual discourse is a legal requirement laid down in the 1967 Broadcasting Act. This Act contains a clause which decrees that every broadcasting organisation entitled to transmission time should present a 'comprehensive' programme schedule, consisting of 'cultural, informative, educative and entertainment' programmes.[15] Although this formalised heterogeneity does not necessarily coincide with a heterogeneity of modes of address, as the formal categories refer primarily to a prescribed heterogeneity of social functions of televisual discourse, it should be clear that, ideologically speaking, this formal distinction of programme categories reveals an official aversion to one-sidedness. It reflects the wish that televisual discourse *should* address the viewers in different ways. More precisely, it reflects the wish that television should not only be producing what is popular among the viewers (usually located in the category of 'entertainment'), but should also offer them 'serious' stuff (i.e. 'culture', 'information' and 'education').

What is noteworthy is not so much the existence of this opposition between the 'serious' and the 'popular' (after all, a distinction is also made between a 'serious' press and a 'popular' press), but that both modes are intermingled within televisual discourse. Although serious television and popular television can be seen as two ideologically contradictory projects which seek to address viewers in contradictory ways and whose ideals are aimed at creating very different types of involvement,[16] they are not expected to be watched by different categories of viewers. On the contrary, it is one of the ideals of the television institution as it is organised in Holland to present serious

258

television and popular television as parts of a unity: an evening of television programming usually consists of an amalgam of serious and popular programmes, and of serious and popular modes of address within programmes. Thus the two modes are considered as parts of a whole, and not as independent entities which have no relation to each other. Clearly, this reflects a definition of how television *should* be watched: viewers are invited to take up 'serious' and 'popular' positions in turn; a varied 'viewing diet' should be composed.

This seems to be the politics of 'comprehensive programming': ideally, it should be mirrored in 'comprehensive viewing'. Unfortunately, it is obvious that this is not how audiences *actually* watch television. It cannot be denied that an uncontrollable and 'spontaneous' split between 'serious' and 'popular' audiences exists, which is reflected in the well-known fact that the various programme categories have different rates of popularity (in terms of audience figures). In other words, the 'comprehensive viewer' (the 'normal citizen'?) turns out to be non-existent. Surprisingly enough, then, despite its success in transforming so many people into TV viewers, television doesn't seem to have a hold on the way television watching has developed into a cultural practice of consumption, or on the meanings given to television viewing by the audiences themselves. Television has largely become an 'entertainment machine', whether you like it or not.

However, the Dutch broadcasting system has yet another important strategy for securing and regulating heterogeneity in televisual discourse. The Dutch broadcasting system is based upon a unique 'subcultural approach': broadcasting time on the (at present) two TV channels is filled for the most part by organisations which 'represent a specific social, cultural or religious current within the population', as the Broadcasting Act formulates it. They are then assumed to satisfy the cultural needs of a specific, socially relevant 'subculture'. From the beginning of broadcasting in the Netherlands (radio started in the 20s, television in the early 50s), five broadcasting organisations have monopolised the system: the Roman Catholic KRO, the Protestant NCRV, the socialist VARA, the Liberal-Protestant VPRO, and the 'neutral' AVRO. The whole system then was organised around the conception of plurality of ideologically defined, pre-existent cultural or religious indentities among the Dutch people/nation, reflecting the myth of Dutch tolerance and of Holland as a country of 'unity in diversity'. It is assumed that the programming policies of each organisation should comprehensively reflect both its founding ideology and the needs and concerns of the 'subculture' it represents, although it is clear that there cannot be a direct translation of an overarching ideology or world view into all concrete programmes.

259

Nevertheless, for a long time Dutch television was generally assumed to be a fair reflection of the plurality of existing ideologies structuring Holland's national life. The Dutch broadcasting system has been celebrated for its perfect incorporation of principles of democracy and freedom. In other words, the system has been regarded as the best model within which television can be used as a medium which justly places people as citizens of a pluralist society. Implicitly inscribed in the system is a definition of television viewing as a very respectable practice: your television viewing activity should be in accordance with your pre-existent ideological world view. In other words, the ideal viewer is not only a 'comprehensive' viewer, but also an ideologically motivated one. For instance, if you are a socialist, you are supposed to be a member of VARA and your favourite programmes must be VARA's programmes. Thus, your television viewing is determined by the fact that you are part of the subculture of the 'Red Family'.

But basically, however, the system represents a *paternalistic* relationship between television and its audiences: audience preferences only become explicit and legitimised in so far as they fit into the organisation's definition of the subculture and the place of that subculture within the larger national community. It is a system in which the élites governing the broadcasting organisations claim to know what is good for the people and what they like to see, because they pretend to share their audience's needs and concerns: it is assumed that production and consumption stem from the same ideological community. In this system, the 'serious' and the 'popular' are not conceived of as opposite to each other, but as parts of an organic, communal whole, with the 'serious' occupying the position of a vanguard.[17]

This represents only the ideal functioning of the system, however. It does not say anything about how the audiences actually watch television. The lack of fit between ideal and reality became apparent in the late 60s with the foundation of a new broadcasting organisation, TROS. The philosophy on which TROS's programming is based is essentially populist and devoid of any explicit ideology: its aim is 'to give people the programmes they want to see'. TROS doesn't pretend to represent an ideologically defined 'subculture', but the people in general. The success of this strategy was overwhelming: according to an inquiry held in 1975, 36 per cent of the Dutch population preferred TROS above all other broadcasting organisations (followed by AVRO with 13 per cent and VARA with 10 per cent), whereas 47 per cent held that TROS's programmes (mainly entertainment, American series and very light information) were the best.[18] As a consequence, panic resulted. Except for VPRO, which developed a non-conformist, artistic style of programming to construct its distinctive identity (which had little to do with its original religious background), the traditional broadcasting organisations felt obliged to react to TROS's success by copying its programming policy and modes of address. For example, current affairs programmes, in which broadcasting organisations could express their respective ideological backgrounds most explicitly, were scheduled at prime time during the 60s, then adopted more popular modes of address and were moved to a later hour in the evening. Instead, prime time became filled with popular entertainment programmes (TV series, shows, quizzes, and so on). While still trying to maintain their ideological identity as the basis of their existence, the broadcasting organisations now wanted to address a general mass audience.

In Dutch intellectual circles, the advent of TROS was blamed for introducing an 'Americanised' commercial logic into the system of Dutch broadcasting. Even the word 'trossification' was invented to denote the process of decay – a word which dominated all Dutch debates about television in the 70s. In these debates, the 60s were constructed as 'the Golden Age of Dutch television', during which the broadcasting organisations accepted their cultural responsibility, whereas the 70s have been deplored as a period of decline, in which television became the repository of irresponsible and debased mass culture. According to Herman Wigbold, a leading Dutch journalist with socialist affiliations, TROS has been a major cause of this decline because the broadcasting system

> could not hold its own against a new broadcasting organisation that was the very negation of [that] system based as it was upon a conception of giving broadcasting time to groups that had something to say. It did not know how to react to an organisation that had nothing to say but nevertheless became a great success.[19]

Yet is it not possible to interpret this history in another way? What is painfully absent in Wigbold's account is the active role of the audiences in the whole process of 'trossification'; their position is reduced to that of passive target or even victim of developments in which they have no effectivity of their own. In short, what has been suppressed is that large numbers of the audiences actively welcomed TROS when it came into existence. Thus it is not true to assert, as Wigbold does, that TROS had 'nothing to say', for it is its 'great success' which speaks for itself. At the very least, TROS's success (and later that of Veronica)[20] can be read as an indication of the fact that many people were not involved in the existing broadcasting politics, that they didn't feel represented by the traditional organisations, and that they were not satisfied with the television offered them. It may be said that TROS's success is based on a discontent with the

261

moralising surveillance or denial of popular tastes and preferences by the traditional organisations. In other words, through TROS the 'silent majority' spoke. More specifically, it signified a refusal by the popular audiences to be put into a position from which they were incited to be watching television: a position from which 'serious information' is recognised as the most valuable part of televisual discourse and 'entertainment' is tolerated as a diversion as long as it gives 'enjoyment' and not 'fun'.[21]

The success of TROS, then, can be interpreted as an articulation of a contradiction between the way large parts of the television audience define watching television as a cultural practice, and the ideas about the use of television inscribed within the institution. Of course, it would be wrong to assert that, with the advent of TROS, the people finally got what they wanted, as TROS officials would have it. 'Trossified television' could only become so popular because it filled a space left unfilled by the traditional broadcasting organisations, and because it brought a distinctive mode of address into televisual discourse which had until then been absent and which could be experienced as something new and different: a popular mode of address which is presented as independent from ideological world views and fixed cultural identities. Instead, this address is constructed around another type of involvement: one which is characterised by *instant pleasure*. It is an address in which pleasure is equated with 'entertainment'; in which fun is not only presented as perfectly legitimate but also as being in opposition to 'boring information' or 'education'.

Most explanations of 'trossification' usually refer to changes in the ideological make-up of Dutch society during the late 60s, in which the influence of solid ideological subcultures as the basis for constructing identities and as guidelines for living was waning and was being replaced by valueless pragmatism and superficial and senseless consumerism. For instance, an often-heard ironical remark in this respect points to the observed paradox that so many working-class people who vote for the Labour Party do not become members of the socialist broadcasting organisation (which they supposedly should have done had they been conscious of their social position), but of TROS, thereby proving to be too weak to resist the seductions of commercialism! What is overlooked in this explanation is the relative autonomy of watching television as a cultural practice, and the distinctive politics inscribed in it. What is at stake here is a struggle for pleasure: or more precisely, a struggle about the definition of watching television *with pleasure*, and not about the definition of watching television in a socialist way (or as a Roman Catholic, or as 'normal citizen', and so on). In other words, what matters from the audience's point of view is whether television discourse constructs positions of pleasure in its representations, and not whether these positions are ideologically OK.

Of course, this doesn't mean that audience preferences are only directed at programmes which fall into the category of 'entertainment'. Indeed, the institutional categorisation of televisual discourse, which constructs an opposition between the serious (= what really matters) and the popular (= easy pleasure), obscures the fact that, from the point of view of the audiences, 'information' can also be pleasurable. The problem is that in televisual discourse 'informative' programmes, especially when they are about 'serious' politics and culture, are too often constructed as the important – and thus unpleasurable – which the viewers are supposed to watch because it is 'good for them'. As a result of such an address these parts of televisual discourse will often be rejected as 'useless knowledge' and as attempts to put something over on you.

Of course, it is not true that the traditional organisations don't make use of the pleasurable as a working principle for creating audience involvement. However, from *their* point of view, pleasure in itself is not enough. It even seems to be something dirty to them. They mostly seem to pretend to give *more* than simple pleasure, thereby marginalising the pleasurable itself and making it instrumental to the overall 'pedagogic' framework of their programming. It is this ambivalent attitude towards pleasure and the pleasurable, which has given the explicitly commercially oriented organisations the space to monopolise the work of constructing and defining the pleasurable in an active and positive way. Ideologically, watching television with pleasure is the only thing they pretend to offer.

At the very least, then, this should lead us to another ironical remark. It seems that it is the very logic of commercialism, because it is a wholly opportunistic logic without any explicit missionary impulses, which, to quote Ian Connell, 'led the way in making connection with and expressing popular structures of feeling'.[22] What has made debates about commercial television (or about public service television using the methods of commercial thinking, as is increasingly the case in Holland) so obscure is the conflation of commercialism as an economic principle of production, which is utterly capitalist, with commercialism as a cultural principle of producing goods for consumption, which certainly has connections with the popular. The success of the commercial logic lies in the fact that it takes the pleasure of consumption and consumption for pleasure seriously, in the fact that it actively engages in the construction of what is pleasurable, and the fact that it has used the pleasurable as a structuring principle for addressing viewers.

Conclusion

Ellis's basic proposition that television's aesthetic forms can be explained from the necessity to come to terms with the familial, domestic conditions within which television is watched should now be given some nuance. After all, that domestic setting itself is not given. When it comes to constructing the meaning of watching television, it is part of the problem. It is this very domestic setting which was seen by some as an excellent opportunity to integrate people's personal lives into the official life of the nation, in short, to continue to educate them even when they are at home. As one Dutch scholar wrote: 'Exactly because television reaches man when he is on his own or is to be found in the smallest social unit, the family, it is worth the trouble . . . to use the medium to drive a wedge between the often collective prejudices which impede a healthy development of the (national) community.'[23] However, because in our culture the home is often felt to be a 'haven in a heartless world', watching television is mostly experienced and cherished as one of those activities in which one is one's own master or mistress,[24] and it is thus perfectly understandable why so many viewers resist being made to use television as an extension of the classroom.

Thus, in a formal sense, it is correct to say that television's rhetoric is aimed at holding the viewer's attention by modes of direct address, by dividing programmes into short segments, by using sound to catch the look, and so on. But underlying these formal discursive strategies are ideological principles which can be traced back to a continuing struggle over the meaning of watching television as a cultural practice, a struggle which, at least in the case of Dutch television, is constructed as a struggle between television-as-education and television-as-pleasure. In televisual discourse, this struggle is expressed in a continual attempt to secure heterogeneity by combining the two constructed options. Thus, almost every news and current affairs programme is structured in such a way as to find a compromise between the 'educative' and the 'pleasurable': the light popular tone, the magazine format with 'difficult' items sandwiched between more 'frivolous' ones, the populist stance from which events are represented, etc. However, these developments can merely be seen as attempts to make a pedagogic ideology work in front of an 'unwilling' popular audience; they don't represent a positive intervention in the definition of the 'pleasurable' itself.

Ultimately, then, it is the impossibility of controlling television consumption and the will to watch television for pleasure which accounts for the contradictions in television's rhetoric and the heterogeneity of its address. And as long as popular desires and preferences are merely seen as negatives which have to be overcome or as an alibi for placing the audiences in a paternalist framework, and as long as the pleasurable itself is not taken seriously as something to be actively constructed, the agents of commercialism will be, to use a Dutch expression, the laughing third.

References

1. C. Gardner and J. Sheppard, 'Transforming Television: Part I, The Limits of Left Policy', *Screen*, vol. 25, no. 2, 1984, p. 38.
2. S. Hall, 'Encoding/Decoding', in S. Hall et al. (eds.), *Culture, Media, Language*, (London: Hutchinson 1980).
3. D. Morley, *The 'Nationwide' Audience* (London: BFI 1980); see also D. Morley, '"The 'Nationwide' Audience" – A Critical Postscript', *Screen Education*, no. 39, Summer 1981, pp. 3–14.
4. C. Brunsdon, 'Crossroads: Notes on Soap Opera', *Screen*, vol. 22, no. 4, 1981, pp. 32–7.
5. See J. Wren-Lewis, 'The Encoding/Decoding Model: Criticisms and Redevelopments for Research on Decoding', *Media, Culture and Society*, vol. 5, no. 2, 1983, pp. 179–97.
6. For example, see Peter Dahlgren, 'Die Bedeutung von Fernsehnachrichten', *Rundfunk und Fernsehen*, vol. 31, no. 3/4, 1983, pp. 307–18.
7. C. Metz, 'The Imaginary Signifier', *Screen*, vol. 16, no. 2, 1975, pp. 18–19.
8. Ibid. p. 19.
9. J. Ellis, *Visible Fictions* (London: Routledge & Kegan Paul 1982), p. 20.
10. Ibid. p. 111.
11. Ibid. p. 162.
12. Ibid. p. 170.
13. Ibid. p. 169–70.
14. The problematic of television as a specific signifying practice has been outlined in S. Heath and G. Skirrow, 'Television: A World in Action', *Screen*, vol. 18, no. 2, 1977, pp. 7–61.
15. It is impossible to describe in detail the complex structure and development of Dutch television here. For an established but adequate overview in English see H. Wigbold, 'Holland: The Shaky Pillars of Hilversum', in A. Smith (ed.), *Television and Political Life: Studies in Six European Countries* (London: Macmillan 1979).
16. The distinction between serious television and popular television has been used in a theoretical sense by, among others, P. Corrigan and P. Willis, 'Cultural Forms and Class Mediations', *Media, Culture and Society*, vol. 2, no. 3, 1980, pp. 297–312.
17. In other words, what predominates here is a very *folkish* idea of the audiences, which contradicts the conception of the audience as an anonymous mass as usually implied in mass-media systems.
18. W. Jungman, 'TROS wint op alle fronten', *Het Parool*, 16 December 1975.
19. Wigbold, op. cit. p. 225.
20. Veronica is a new broadcasting organisation which stemmed from a pirate radio transmitter. In 1976 this organisation applied for transmission time and finally was allowed into the legal system, although it was not clear which religious or cultural current was represented by Veronica. Being more aggressive and noisy than either TROS or AVRO (which has been the most successful in copying TROS's populist style), Veronica has developed a very distinctive popular mode of address, which is based on the slogan: 'You are young and you want things!' and which is often deliberately truculent

('Veronica fears nothing!'). In terms of programming, this means a lot of pop music, spectacular films and 'sex-'n-violence'.

21. See J. Smiers, *Cultuurpolitiek in Nederland, 1945–1955* (Nijmegen: SUN 1977), p. 57.
22. I. Connell, 'Commercial Broadcasting and the British Left', *Screen*, vol. 24, no. 6, 1983, p. 76.
23. H. Schaafsma, *Beeldperspectieven* (Amsterdam: Het Wereldvensder 1965) pp. 19–20.
24. Of course, we should not overlook the conflicts and the unequal relations of power within the family here, in which the father or husband is mostly in the dominant position. An analysis of popular television and of constructions of the pleasurable in televisual discourse should take into account the ways in which representations and modes of address assume positions which are specific to gender, race, age, etc.

I should like to thank Chris Iles for her help in preparing the English text.

APPENDIX

ITSC 1984

ACKNOWLEDGMENTS

The success of the first International Television Studies Conference was due in no small way to the resourcefulness and dedication of the Conference Organiser, Caroline Merz. She was ably assisted by Lucy Douch, Georgiana Garwood and Lilie Ferrari (BFI) and Susan Gibbons (Institute of Education) in co-ordinating the considerable administrative detail of such a large international gathering.

Invaluable technical assistance was supplied by the Institute of Education's Department of Educational Media together with Erich Sargeant, Jim Adams and Peter Flower of the BFI. We are grateful to Roma Gibson and Diana Watt who ran the bookstall, and Patience Coster who acted as Press Officer for the event. Special thanks are due to Shirley Hobart of the BFI print room and Bruce Howell, Head of Marketing and Membership at the BFI, in making available copies of the papers presented.

The Conference was ably stewarded by the following postgraduate Media students of the University of London Institute of Education: Jane Arthurs, Mike Conway, Pauline Crossan, Helen Doherty, Mary Eyton, Bob Fox, Chris Hibbs, Liz Hill, Jenny Lazenby, Bill Lewis, Tony Mitchell, Sui Yiu Ng, Derek Reid, Sandra Sinfield. (*Eds.*)

Organising Committee

DAVID BUCKINGHAM	Institute of Education, University of London
ED BUSCOMBE	British Film Institute
RICHARD COLLINS	Polytechnic of Central London
JIM COOK	British Film Institute
PHILLIP DRUMMOND	Institute of Education, University of London
ROBERT FERGUSON	Institute of Education, University of London
CAROLINE MERZ	Conference Organiser
RICHARD PATERSON	British Film Institute

Strand 1: New Technologies – The State – Political Economy and Institutions
Co-ordinator: Ed Buscombe

Session 1
Chair: Richard Collins
Discussant: Michael Tracey
Papers: Herbert I. Schiller, 'Electronic Information Flows:
New Basis for Global Domination?'
Eileen Mahoney, 'Changing Patterns of Information
Flows: Multilateral, Bilateral, Unilateral'

Session 2
Chair: Gill Branston
Discussant: Richard Collins
Papers: William Bonney and Helen Wilson, 'Networking and
Control in Australian Commercial Television'
Colin Hoskins and Stuart McFadyen, 'National Policy
Towards Television in Canada'
Marc Raboy, 'Public Television, the National Question and
the Preservation of the Canadian State'
Giuseppe Richeri, 'Television from Service to Business:
European Tendencies and the Italian Case'

Session 3
Chair: Ed Buscombe
Discussant: Sylvia Harvey
Papers: Ian Connell and Lidia Curti, 'Popular Broadcasting in Italy
and Britain: Some Issues and Problems'
Jean-Pierre Desaulniers, 'Television and Nationalism:
From Culture to Communication'
Martin McLoone, 'Television in Ireland: Ideology in Flux'
Taruna Tanwar, 'Foreign Serials and the Indian Television
Audience'

Session 4
Chair: Graham Murdock
Discussant: Jill Forbes
Papers: J.J. Smolicz and M.J. Secombe, 'Multicultural Television
for All Australians'
Linda Fuller, 'Television of the People, by the People, for
the People: Public Access'
Joe Foote, 'British and American Opposition Access to
Network TV'

Session 5
Chair: Len Masterman
Discussant: Herbert Schiller
Papers: Christopher Dornan, 'Fear and Longing in the United
Kingdom: Cultural Custody and the Expansion of
Cable Television'

Sean Cubitt, 'How to Watch TV 1984'
John Downing, 'The Soviet Intersputnik System'
Slavko Splichal, 'Social Functions of Television
Advertising in Socialism'

Session 6
Chair: David Buckingham
Discussant: Cary Bazalgette
Papers: Kezban Tamer, 'Television and Cultural Differences'
               Erhard U. Heidt, 'Cultural Tradition and National
               Identity: The Case of Singapore'

Strand 2: Programme Categories – Representation – Education
Co-ordinator: Bob Ferguson

Session 1
Chair: Anne Karpf
Discussant: David Buckingham
Papers: David Berry, 'Science and Technology on Television:
               Why So Little Research?'
               Roger Silverstone, 'Narrative Strategies in Television
               Science: A Case Study'

Session 2
Chair: David Lusted
Discussant: Jim Cook
Papers: Paul Attalah, 'Television and Situation Comedy'
               Robert C. Allen, 'Studying Soap Operas: The Legacy of
               Empiricism'
               Ellen Seiter, 'The Hegemony of Leisure: Aaron Spelling
               Presents *Hotel*'
               E. Ann Kaplan, 'A Postmodern Play of the Signifier?
               Advertising, Pastiche and Schizophrenia'

Session 3
Chair: Bob Ferguson
Discussant: David Lusted
Papers: Susan Boyd-Bowman, '*The Day After:* Representations of
               the Nuclear Holocaust'
               Gillian Dyer, 'Unravelling the Threads'
               Shekhar Deshpande, 'The Viewer in Television History:
               One Body Too Many?'
               Kathryn Montgomery, 'The Political Struggle for
               Prime-Time'
               Bruce Carson, '*The Cheviot, The Stag and the Black, Black
               Oil:* Investigation of a Television Drama'

269

Session 4
Chair: Paul Kerr
Discussant: Charlotte Brunsdon
Papers: Max Robinson, 'Television as Storytelling'
                     James Donald, 'Teaching Television on a Popular Culture
                        Course: The Crime Series'
                     Caren Deming, 'Control Over Chaos: *Hill Street Blues* as
                        Narrative'
                     Sandy Flitterman, 'Thighs and Whiskers: The Fascination
                        of *Magnum P.I.*'

Session 5
Chair: Ruth Baumgarten
Discussant: Noel King
Papers: Alan Jenkins, 'Looking at Contemporary China'
                     Michèle Mattelart, 'Education, Television and Mass
                        Culture: Reflections on Research into Innovation'
                     Maurice Mouillaud, 'Trois Emissions sur le Livre'
                     Mike Phillips and Keith Yeomans, 'Ethnic Minority
                        Broadcasting: The Policy of Failure'

Session 6
Chair: Charles Barr
Discussant: Christine Gledhill
Papers: John Bird, 'Historical Drama Serials: British TV at its
                        Best? A Case Study of *Edward and Mrs Simpson*'
                     Alison Beale, 'Duplessis'

Strand 3: History – Theory – Methodology – Audience
Co-ordinator: Phillip Drummond

Session 1
Chair: Susan Boyd-Bowman
Discussant: Gillian Skirrow
Papers: John Hartley, 'Encouraging Signs: Television and the
                        Power of Dirt, Speech and Scandalous Categories'
                     Harry Bouwman, Uta Meier and Folke Glastra, 'The
                        Meaning of Semiotics for Content Analysis of
                        Television Programmes: Some Examples of Dutch
                        Research'

Session 2
Chair: Richard Paterson
Discussant: Richard Dyer
Papers: Nick Browne, 'The Political Economy of the Television
                        (Super) Text'
                     Beverle Houston, 'Viewing Television:
                        The Metapsychology of Endless Consumption'

Kevin Robins and Frank Webster, 'The Revolution of
the Fixed Wheel: Television and Social Taylorism'
Claus-Dieter Rath, 'The Invisible Network – Television as
an Institution in Everyday Life'

Session 3
Chair: Anthony Smith
Discussant: David Morley
Papers: Tamar Liebes and Elihu Katz, 'Cross-Cultural Readings of
                Dallas: Poetic and Referential Statements'
                Ien Ang, 'The Battle between Television and its Audiences:
                The Politics of Watching Television'
                Leonard Henny, 'Soap Operas and Cultural Identity'

Session 4
Chair: Phillip Drummond
Discussant: Anthony Smith
Papers: Jane Feuer, 'Producer/Industry/Text: Writing the History
                of MTM Enterprises'
                Jeanne Thomas Allen, 'The Democratic Potential of the
                Walkie Talkie: World War II and After'
                William Boddy, '"The Shining Centre of the Home":
                Ontologies of Television in the "Golden Age"'
                Suzanne Regan, 'Female-Centred Programming in 1950s
                Television'

Session 5
Chair: Susan Boyd-Bowman
Discussant: Jane Root
Papers: Virginia Wright-Wexman, 'The Television Love Goddess:
                Defining Female Beauty Within the Family'
                Nan MacLeod-Engel, 'A Cross-Cultural Analysis of the
                Images of Women in the Mass Media of 12 Countries:
                A Longitudinal Approach'
                Cynthia Scheibe, Ronald E. Ostman and John C. Condry,
                'Character Portrayals and Social Values in US
                Network TV Commercials'
                Chris Berry, 'Commodity Genres: Towards a Theory of
                Television Commercials'

Session 6
Chair: Andy Medhurst
Discussant: Philip Simpson
Papers: William Lewis, 'Not Winning But Drowning: the
                Positioning of Spectator/Participant in the
                Game Show Discourse'
                Margaret Morse, 'Talk, Talk, Talk: The Space of Discourse
                in Television News, Sportscasts, Talk-Shows, and
                Advertising'

Strand 4: News
Co-ordinator: Richard Paterson

Session 1
Chair: Richard Paterson
Discussant: Philip Schlesinger
Papers: Miguel de Aguilera Moyano, 'A Sociological Analysis of
                    Spanish Television News'
                    Mordechay Ayalon, 'A Comparative Study of British and
                    Israeli Television News'
                    Anna Celsing 'Seeing is Believing: On the Function of the
                    Image in TV News' Production of Reality'
                    Jean Gouazé, 'L'Appareil Enonciatif du Journal Télévisé'

Session 2
Chair: Richard Paterson
Discussant: Peter Golding
Papers: Justin Lewis, 'Decoding Television News'
                    Peter Dahlgren, 'The Modes of Reception: For a
                    Hermeneutics of TV News'
                    Anthony Easthope, 'Trade Unions in British
                    Television News'
                    Rosalind Brunt and Martin Jordin, 'The Controversial
                    Candidate: British Television's Coverage of the
                    Chesterfield By-Election'

(Translations for papers in French, German and Spanish were provided by
Ginette Vincendeau, Ruth Baumgarten and Philip Schlesinger)

CONTRIBUTORS TO THIS VOLUME:

IEN ANG lectures in political science and cultural studies at the University of
Amsterdam. She has been a member of the editorial board of *Skrien*, and is
author of *Watching Dallas* (London: Methuen, 1985).

WILLIAM BODDY is an Assistant Professor in Communication Arts at Saint
Francis College, New York. He has published articles on film and television
in *Cinetracts, Millennium Film Journal* and *Screen*.

IAN CONNELL is Senior Lecturer in Communication Studies at Coventry
Polytechnic and he has written extensively on the media.

LIDIA CURTI is a Lecturer in the Department of English Language and
Literature at the University of Naples. She has written widely on the theatre,
television and contemporary cultural issues and is presently preparing a book
on the avant-garde in Britain.

PETER DAHLGREN is Universitetslektor at the School of Journalism,
Stockholm University. His research on TV news and other media has
emphasised questions of social theory and cultural perception.

JEAN-PIERRE DESAULNIERS is a Lecturer in the Department of
Communications at the University of Quebec at Montreal. He is author of *La
Télévision en vrac: essai sur le spectacle*, and *Mine de rien, notes sur la violence
symbolique* (with P. Sohet), both Editions St. Martin: Montreal, 1982.

E. ANN KAPLAN teaches film and literature at Rutgers University. She is author of *Women and Film: Both Sides of the Camera* (London: Methuen, 1983) and edited *Women in Film Noir* (London: BFI, 1978) and *Regarding Television* (Frederick MD: AFI/University Publications of America, 1983).

ELIHU KATZ is Professor of Sociology and Communications at the Hebrew University of Jerusalem and at the Annenberg School of Communications, University of Southern California. His books include *Broadcasting in the Third World* (with George Wedell) (London: Macmillan, 1978) and *Mass Media and Social Change* (co-edited with Tamás Szecskö) (London: Sage, 1981).

JUSTIN LEWIS teaches and researches media studies and broadcasting policy. He has published a number of articles on the mass media in *Screen Education* and *Media, Culture and Society*.

TAMAR LIEBES lectures in the Department of Cinema and Television at the University of Tel Aviv, and is a senior radio producer at the Israel Broadcasting Authority. She is completing her doctoral dissertation at the Communications Institute of the Hebrew University of Jerusalem.

MICHÈLE MATTELART is presently director of a research project on television at the CNRS in Paris. She has published a number of books and articles on the mass media, women, culture and politics including *La cultura de la opresion femenina* (Mexico: Ediciones Era, 1977), *De l'usage des medias en temps de crise* (with Armand Mattelart, Paris: Editions Alain Moreau, 1979), and *International Image Markets* (with Armand Mattelart and Xavier Delcourt, London: Comedia, 1984).

MARC RABOY is a journalist and media researcher in Montreal. He is the author of *Movements and Messages: Media and Radical Politics in Quebec* (Toronto: Between The Lines, 1984), and currently teaches journalism at Concordia University. Research for his article was partially supported by a grant from McGill University.

CLAUS-DIETER RATH works at the Institute for Semiotics and Communication Theory at the Freie Universität, Berlin. He edited *Rituale der Medienkommunikation* with H. Pross (Guttandin and Hoppe, 1983).

GIUSEPPE RICHERI has written books and essays on communications problems including *Le televisioni in Europa* (Milan: Feltrinelli, 1976), *La radio, origini, storia, modelli* (Milan: Mondadori, 1980), and *L'universo telematico* (Bari: De Donato, 1982).

KEVIN ROBINS lectures in Communication Studies at Sunderland Polytechnic. He is co-author, with Frank Webster, of *Information Technology: a Luddite Analysis* (New Jersey: Ablex, 1985).

HERBERT I. SCHILLER is Professor of Communication at the University of California, San Diego. Among his most recent books are: *Information and the Crisis Economy* (New Jersey: Ablex, 1984) and *Who Knows: Information in the Age of the Fortune 500* (New Jersey: Ablex, 1981).

ELLEN SEITER is Assistant Professor of Telecommunications and Film Studies at the University of Oregon. Her articles on soap opera have appeared in *Film Reader, Journal of the University Film and Video Association* and *Tabloid*.

FRANK WEBSTER is currently Lecturer in the Department of Social Studies at Oxford Polytechnic. He is the author of *The New Photography* (London: Calder, 1980) as well as numerous articles on information technology with Kevin Robins.

OTHER SPEAKERS

MIGUEL DE AGUILERA MOYANO Adjunct Professor in Faculty of Information Sciences, Department of Audiovisual Media, University of Madrid.

ROBERT C. ALLEN Associate Professor, Department of Radio, Television and Motion Pictures, University of North Carolina at Chapel Hill.

JEANNE THOMAS ALLEN Assistant Professor, School of Communications and Theatre, Temple University, Philadelphia.

PAUL ATTALAH McConnell Fellow in Graduate Programme in Communications, McGill University.

MORDECHAY AYALON Community Video Maker and lecturer, London.

ALISON BEALE Lecturer, Department of Communications, University of Quebec at Montreal.

CHRIS BERRY Department of Theatre Arts, University of California, Los Angeles.

DAVID BERRY Lecturer in Film and Television and Director of Futures Research Associates (UK) Ltd.

JOHN BIRD Lecturer in Film Studies, Dacorum College, Hemel Hempstead.

WILLIAM BONNEY Associate Head, School of Humanities and Social Sciences, New South Wales Institute of Technology.

SUSAN BOYD-BOWMAN Producer, The Open University.

HARRY BOUWMAN Institute for Mass Communications, Catholic University, Nijmegen.

NICHOLAS BROWNE Associate Professor of Film and TV Study, Department of Theatre Arts, University of California, Los Angeles.

ROSALIND BRUNT Senior Lecturer in Communication Studies, Sheffield City Polytechnic.

BRUCE CARSON Lecturer in Sociology, Film and TV Studies, London.

ANNA CELSING Member of Swedish research team working on the international project 'TV News and the Production of Reality' for the International Sociological Association.

SEAN CUBITT National Organiser, Society for Education in Film and Television, London.

CAREN J. DEMING Associate Professor and Chair, Broadcast Communication Arts Department, San Francisco State University.

SHEKHAR DESHPANDE Doctoral Student in Speech Communications, Southern Illinois University at Carbondale.

JAMES DONALD Lecturer in Education, The Open University.

274

CHRISTOPHER T. DORNAN Lecturer in Department of Communication Arts, Cornell University.

JOHN DOWNING Professor and Chair, Communications Department, Hunter College, City University of New York.

GILLIAN DYER Senior Lecturer in Communication Studies, Sheffield City Polytechnic.

ANTHONY EASTHOPE Senior Lecturer in English and Cultural Studies, Manchester Polytechnic.

JANE FEUER Assistant Professor of Film Studies, University of Pittsburg.

SANDY FLITTERMAN Lecturer in Film, Rutgers University.

JOE S. FOOTE Visiting Assistant Professor, Department of Communication Arts, New York State College of Agriculture and Life Science.

LINDA FULLER Lecturer in the Marketing Department, School of Business, Western New England College.

JEAN GOUAZÉ Lecturer in Information and Communication, University of Lyon II.

JOHN HARTLEY Lecturer in Mass Communication and Cultural Studies, Polytechnic of Wales.

ERHARD U. HEIDT Reader in Education and Mass Communication, University of Bielefeld.

LEONARD HENNY Lecturer, Centre for International Media Research, State University of Utrecht.

COLIN HOSKINS Professor, Department of Marketing and Economic Analysis, University of Alberta.

BEVERLE HOUSTON Division of Cinema-Television, University of Southern California.

ALAN JENKINS Senior Lecturer in Geography, Oxford Polytechnic.

MARTIN JORDIN Senior Lecturer, Communication Studies Department, Sheffield City Polytechnic.

WILLIAM LEWIS Lecturer in Communication and Media Studies, Exeter College.

STUART MCFADYEN Professor, Department of Marketing and Economic Analysis, University of Alberta.

NAN MACLEOD-ENGEL Associate Director, International Television Research and Information Cooperative, University of Alberta.

MARTIN MCLOONE Education Officer, The Irish Film Institute.

EILEEN MAHONEY Department of Radio-Television-Film, Temple University, Philadelphia.

UTA MEIER Institute for Mass Communications, Catholic University, Nijmegen.

KATHRYN MONTGOMERY Assistant Professor of Film and Television Studies, Department of Theatre Arts, University of California, Los Angeles.

275

MARGARET MORSE Adjunct Professor, Academy of Art Co-operative Programme, University of San Francisco.

MAURICE MOUILLAUD Lecturer in Information and Communication, University of Lyon II.

MIKE PHILLIPS Senior Lecturer, School of Communication, Polytechnic of Central London.

SUZANNE REGAN Director of Broadcasting, Department of Communication Studies, California State University.

MAX ROBINSON Head of Media Studies, Victoria College, Australia.

CYNTHIA L. SCHEIBE Co-Director, HDTV Archive, Department of Human Development and Family Studies, Cornell University.

ROGER SILVERSTONE Senior Tutor, Department of Sociology, Brunel University.

J. J. SMOLICZ Reader in Education, University of Adelaide.

SLAVKO SPLICHAL Head of Department of Journalism, Faculty for Sociology, Political Science and Journalism, University of Ljubljana.

KEZBAN TAMER Lecturer in Television Production and Communication, Mimar Sinan University, Istanbul.

TARUNA TANWAR Reader in Development Communication, Indian Institute of Mass Communication, New Delhi.

HELEN WILSON Lecturer in Communication, New South Wales Institute of Technology.

VIRGINIA WRIGHT WEXMAN Department of English, University of Illinois at Chicago.

KEITH YEOMANS Consultant Producer, London.

INDEX

279